# The Biss Tribe:

## Where You Activate Your Goddess Power

Book 1 in The Biss Tribe Series

# Elizabeth Ann Atkins

Copyrighted Material
*The Biss Tribe: Where You Activate Your GoddessPower*
By Elizabeth Ann Atkins
Copyright © 2024 Elizabeth Ann Atkins. All Rights Reserved.

No part of this publication may be reproduced, stored in a retrieval system or transmitted, in any form or by any means—electronic, mechanical, photocopy, recording, or otherwise—without prior written permission from the publisher, except for the inclusion of brief quotations in a review.

*Disclaimer: If you have a serious mental or physical medical condition, please continue with your doctor's prescribed medical regimen and seek clearance before beginning the practices herein that include and are not limited to meditation, exercise and dietary changes.*

*The women attending the retreat are fictional characters.
Any similarity to actual people, living or dead, is purely coincidental.*

For information about this title or to order other books
and/or electronic media, contact the publisher:

Two Sisters Writing and Publishing
18530 Mack Avenue, Suite 166
Grosse Pointe Farms, MI 48236
www.TwoSistersWriting.com

ISBN  978-1-945875-74-8 (Hardcover)
ISBN  978-1-945875-75-5 (Paperback)
ISBN  978-1-945875-7-2 (eBook)

Printed in the United States of America

Cover and Interior design: Van-garde Imagery, Inc.

Back cover author photo: Clarence Tabb, Jr. In My Eye Photography

Artwork and graphics created by Two Sisters Writing & Publishing®
on Adobe Firefly and Canva.

# Goddess

You! A woman who fearlessly ignites the infinite power of your mind, body & spirit —and learns to use supernatural energy to transform your pain into power, live your dream life and build your empire on the foundations of

Power, Pleasure, Prosperity, Protection and Peace.

You rule your life from a throne of power, wearing a crown of confidence.

© Elizabeth Ann Atkins 2024

# Welcome to The Biss Tribe: Where You Activate Your Goddess Power

### *Goddess is your Supernatural Self*

She is infinite. She is limitless.

She defies reality.

She simultaneously radiates love and joy and peace while magnetizing all that, plus immeasurably abundant blessings for herself and her loved ones.

She is **you,** waiting to escape the confines of your past and current reality, so you can build your personal and professional empire that you rule with a crown of confidence from a throne of power.

But if the word Goddess makes you think of rainbows, butterflies and candlelit bubble baths while sipping champagne... or being a diva with people bowing at your feet, fanning you with palm fronds while feeding you grapes and chocolates, think again.

Goddess means being a bad ass woman.

A boss.

A bold, brave bitch.

It means you boss up to yourself and your life, to partake of all the best that life has to offer in a realm of prosperity and pleasure that is divinely protected.

## Welcome to The Biss Tribe

It means you serve yourself, your loved ones and the world with an important mission that helps people everywhere.

It means you're activating your female superpowers to transform from the inside out, to ignite the fire of your spirit to shine brightly and illuminate the shadows where struggle, suffering and sadness may lurk.

Join me on this extraordinary quest to find her—your Supernatural Self—when you activate your GoddessPower here in The Biss Tribe.

With this book, you are stepping into a portal where profound transformation awaits.

## How to Use This Book to Change Your Life

This book invites you to immerse in your imagination and embark on a week-long retreat among the 22 women who join The Biss Tribe on the mind- and life-shifting journey up Infinity Mountain.

Along the way, you will engage in meditations and writing exercises that help you activate your GoddessPower.

To make this process simple for you, you'll find QR codes throughout the book, which will connect you with audio and video recordings for guided meditations, The GoddessPower Promise, and other helpful recitations.

You can also use the accompanying workbook, *PowerJournal to Activate Your GoddessPower,* available here:

*Order Here*

## Where You Activate Your Biss Power

And you can take this experience to the next level by joining The Goddess RoundTable online community and by attending virtual and in-person GoddessPower Retreats led by me. Please learn more at TheGoddessPowerShow.com.

The secret to your success in The Biss Tribe is that you get out what you put in.

Remember, how you do anything is how you do everything. When you give it your all, you reap exponential rewards beyond your wildest dreams. On the contrary, mediocrity and half-assed efforts keep you stuck.

So, now it's time to invest your mind, body and spirit into this experience, and you will hardly recognize the woman you become, living the life that—until now—you've only dreamed about.

You can do it, Goddess, because *you* have the power!

I believe in you with infinite love,
Biss
Elizabeth Ann Atkins
Author & Creator of The Biss Tribe
Creator & Host of The GoddessPower Show
with Elizabeth Ann Atkins®
Co-Founder of
Two Sisters Writing & Publishing®

# Contents

Welcome to The Biss Tribe:
Where You Activate Your Goddess Power. . . . . . . . . . . . . . v

How to Use This Book to Change Your Life . . . . . . . . . . vi

Dedication & Acknowledgement . . . . . . . . . . . . . . . . . xiii

A Message from the Ancestors . . . . . . . . . . . . . . . . . .xv

## Your Itinerary for The Biss Tribe Retreat

### Sunday Day 1: Your GoddessPower Activation Begins

Goddess, It's Time to Fly! . . . . . . . . . . . . . . . . . . . 3
Welcome to The Biss Tribe Inn—Charting Your Ascent. . . .13
Time to Change . . . . . . . . . . . . . . . . . . . . . . . .19
A Nature Walk with Esmerelda . . . . . . . . . . . . . . . .21
Time to Change . . . . . . . . . . . . . . . . . . . . . . . .22
Take Your Throne and Meet Biss in the Ballroom . . . . . . .22
Your Favorite Lunch is Served. . . . . . . . . . . . . . . . . 30
Touring Valley Village . . . . . . . . . . . . . . . . . . . . 48
Fly up to SeaGoddess Castle . . . . . . . . . . . . . . . . . 53

## Welcome to The Biss Tribe

Introductions & Intentions: Baring Your Soul in
The Biss Tribe Class #88 . . . . . . . . . . . . . . . . 59

GoddessAwakening: The Biss Tribe's Origin Story . . . . . . .79

Step into Your GoddessLife . . . . . . . . . . . . . . . . 89

Write Your GoddessLife Script . . . . . . . . . . . . . .97

Find Your POWER by Identifying
How You Feel POWERLESS . . . . . . . . . . . . . . . . 119

Take a Break to Belly Dance. . . . . . . . . . . . . . . .120

A Preview of Your Personal Podcast in
The GoddessPower Studios . . . . . . . . . . . . . . . 132

The GoddessFeast: On Being a Goddess Bad Ass . . . . . 137

Quiet Time in Your Room . . . . . . . . . . . . . . . .146

## Monday Day 2:
## GoddessPower Activation Station #1

## The GoddessPower Pyramid

Welcome to The GoddessPower Pyramid . . . . . . . . . .153

The Meditarium. . . . . . . . . . . . . . . . . . . . . .154

Your GoddessPower Activation Begins . . . . . . . . . . .156

The Four GoddessPower Activation Tools
That Awaken Your Supernatural Self . . . . . . . . . . . . 159

A Goddess Practices Daily Spiritual Hygiene . . . . . . . .164

    GoddessPower Activation Tool #1: Pranayama. . . . .164

Let's Cleanse Our Energy in a Shower of
Light and a Sound Bath . . . . . . . . . . . . . . . . .166

    GoddessPower Activation Tool #2:
    Chakra Clearing . . . . . . . . . . . . . . . . . .166

## Where You Activate Your Biss Power

Connect with Spirit and Your Supernatural Self . . . . . . . 170

    GoddessPower Activation Tool #3: Meditation. . . . . 170

Finding Your GoddessPower in the Divine Dimensions . . . 177

Lunchtime: Food is Fuel for Your GoddessMission . . . . . 196

Rev Your Body with GoddessPower Fitness! . . . . . . . . . 206

A Simple GoddessPower Activation: Sitting with Om . . . . 211

Getting Guidance from Your GoddessVoice . . . . . . . . . 216

    GoddessPower Activation Tool #4: Journaling . . . . 220

Get Into Your GoddessGenius Zone . . . . . . . . . . . . . 230

Sounding the Alarms in Your GoddessPower
Mission Control Center . . . . . . . . . . . . . . . . . . . . 234

Dinner in the Vortex—
The GoddessFeast in the Pyramid . . . . . . . . . . . . . . 238

GoddessFeast Speaker: The Sasha Maxwell Story. . . . . . 242

A Dance Party Celebration . . . . . . . . . . . . . . . . . 256

Continue Your Transformation on Infinity Mountain . . . . 257

Stay Connected and Inspired in the
Goddess RoundTable Community. . . . . . . . . . . . . . . 259

Roster . . . . . . . . . . . . . . . . . . . . . . . . . . . . . 261

About the Author . . . . . . . . . . . . . . . . . . . . . . 269

# Dedication & Acknowledgement

*The Biss Tribe: Where You Activate Your GoddessPower* is dedicated to every woman who ever lived, is living, or will ever live—and all humans who are created by us.

Thank you, Goddess Seshat, for inventing writing and serving as the Egyptian Goddess of writing, wisdom and knowledge, and for your work as the Mistress of the House of Books.

# Foreword
# A Message from the Ancestors

Dear Modern Woman:

We are your ancestors—women who lived long ago in a society that robbed us of any opportunity to do what you can so freely do in your lifetime—whenever, wherever and however you desire.

In contrast, we were not allowed to read, write, own property, make decisions or even own our bodies.

Those of us who dared to speak out, speak up and celebrate our powers as healers, storytellers, sexual beings and spiritual leaders were persecuted as witches—and often burned at the stake.

You don't know our names, because we lived in a world where we blended into the gray-beige background of life—cooking, cleaning, tilling farms and tending to children and husbands. We longed for the opportunities that you have, though we had no idea what they might be.

But we did know what we lacked.

Freedom.

And power.

Today, you as a modern woman have so much power.

Infinite, immeasurable, limitless power!

## Welcome to The Biss Tribe

Power that is a golden, glittering starburst inside you, waiting to be ignited and freed in a world that has tried so hard to snuff it out... dim it... extinguish it.

No! This power is yours, beautiful, brilliant Goddess!

Activate it, own it and flex it!

Find the courage and the means here in The Biss Tribe to activate the GoddessPower that we are all born with. Then use it to evolve into the best you, committed to a mission that shines light on the collective of all humanity. Starting here and now, right where you are.

You must do this, because sadly, even modern women are often too oppressed, brainwashed and depleted to know that we have this infinite Source of creation within us.

So, ignite this power!

Explode it big and bright.

Be bold and bodacious.

Blaze!

Fly!

Do it on behalf of us and your female ancestors who are cheering you on to represent the dreams and desires of countless women who suffered, struggled and survived—so that our spirits may now live through you as extraordinary leaders for humanity.

Let nothing and no one stop you. Immerse in this experience with all the gusto you can muster. Savor every second. Learn. Take action. And remember that we are here, in the ethers, conspiring to help you activate your GoddessPower, and do for all, what we were never able to do.

Carry on, woman warriors.

Write. Speak. Act. Lead. Change. Represent.

Feel our presence in the sparkling stars, the blazing sunshine, the chirping birds, the blooming flowers and the flowing waters.

### A Message from the Ancestors

Our energy nurtures Mother Earth and you, along with the current generations of humanity.

We are working on a higher plane for your success. So go, make your magic to do great things, so that we may live vicariously through your victories, your celebrations and your achievements.

We have been encouraging Elizabeth to follow her Goddess path for many years. Now she's learned enough lessons and cultivated the courage to guide you into a higher dimension where you activate your GoddessPower and rule your realm for the betterment of all.

We see you.

We hear you.

We celebrate you.

We love you.

Remember us and be bold on our behalf.

Be the Goddess you are born to be.

— The Council of Women Writers

# Your Itinerary for
# The Biss Tribe Retreat

# Sunday Day 1

## Your Goddess Power Activation Begins

# Goddess, It's Time to Fly!

You're at the airport, standing at crowded Gate B8 to board your flight for this trip to an oceanside mountain town that you've never heard of. You're holding a brochure that shows a castle surrounded by purple mist and sparkly cheetah print. It says:

"Be the star of your life and light up the world as you write a new script on this transformational experience with The Biss Tribe to activate your GoddessPower, and soar into your most limitless life. We'll provide the tools to build your unique empire where you rule with a crown of confidence from your throne of power."

Excitement, then doubt and dread, seep through you. This whole deal is a huge commitment. You had to fill out that *looooong* application, wait for approval, answer all those detailed questions during a virtual interview, pay the registration fees and clear your schedule for a week.

Plus, you're not allowed to use phones, laptops, cameras or tablets the entire time. No devices! You'll be totally unplugged!

But you signed up for this experience—trekking up a mountain to reach a castle and find your power along the way, really?—because it sounds fun and adventurous. And you've committed to the intensive immersion in each level of the experience.

The bustle of travelers all around you becomes a peripheral blur as you wonder if you'll ever reach a space of inner peace, total confidence, and ultimate success, however you define that.

## Welcome to The Biss Tribe

Will you find the answers and action steps at this retreat? Will you figure out what's been blocking you, and finally blast past it to become that dream version of yourself who right now is just a fantasy in your head?

Meanwhile, you're hoping this won't just be an extended girls weekend with lots of *ra-ra* speakers who sound good in the moment, but as soon as you come home, it's back to the frustration, even misery, of the same unresolved problems that sent you there.

You just want to change the dreadful realization that haunts you every day as the years—and decades!—tick past:

*This isn't how I thought my life would be!*

*I can't just keep trudging along, year after year, knowing I can be better and do better.*

*I want to live on my terms, as my most authentic self, experiencing the life that I dreamed about—before reality took me elsewhere.*

You glance at The Biss Tribe's brochure, which promises that this trip will help you find your Power, Pleasure, Prosperity, Protection and Peace.

What more could you ask?

Excitement and hope tingle through you—until another hot wave of cynicism sinks your optimism. If it were that easy, you would already be, have and do all that you're dreaming about.

If only it weren't so drowned out by the torturous noise in your head with your vicious inner critic saying, *You can't... you don't deserve it... get real... get your head out of the fucking clouds... true happiness and power are for other people... it'll never happen.*

That inner critic is so loud right now, making your mind whirl with reasons that you shouldn't take this trip. The time. The energy. The inevitable disappointment of *one more thing that didn't work.*

Another failed attempt to find what's missing in your life, to let your wildest side be free to fly, and to live with adventure and excitement. Not the daily drudgery that seems to cloud everything.

## Sunday, Day 1

"Now boarding Flight 211," a flight attendant announces, as you focus on the crowd of passengers around you.

They include several women who, like you, are decked out in The Biss Tribe swag that arrived at your front door with instructions to wear it on the trip.

Your heartbeat quickens as you scan the women in baseball caps and tank tops emblazoned with The Biss Tribe logo that has sparkly leopard print and smoky purple behind the words.

"Girlfriends, it's now or never," exclaims a woman beside you. "I hope this Biss Tribe thing is for real. I'm about to turn 55, and if I don't figure things out now, I never will."

The woman's close-cropped, peroxide-blonde waves create a striking contrast to her bronze complexion, which glows like sunshine beaming through a jar of molasses. Her light brown eyes sparkle despite puffy under-eye bags that aren't-so-concealed by her concealer.

Snug jeans hug her curves and taper down to sparkly designer gym shoes. A big diamond wedding ring glimmers as she holds the leather strap of her expensive shoulder bag.

This woman looks like she has it all. What could she possibly be seeking at this retreat? In fact, she looks familiar. Is she a celebrity?

The woman shakes her head, glancing at the other retreat-goers as she says, "I've done too many conferences where you get all pumped up, meet new people, learn new things, promise to change, then come home to stay stuck in the same ol' rut. Girlfriend, not this time, okay?"

"I hear you, sis," says a younger woman with pink hair as she gives the woman a fist-bump. Tattoos of green vines sprouting blue flowers and Greek goddess busts adorn her milky-white arms. She presses a hand to her thick waistline and says:

## Welcome to The Biss Tribe

"I'm literally so tempted to just go back home and make love to that ice cream in my freezer while I watch a movie about all the romance and hook-ups that I'm not having. By choice!" Blue eyeliner accentuates her hazel eyes and round, slightly plump face. "I'll keep it one hundred. I'm doing celibacy while I figure myself out. Adulting sucks. It would be so easy to just give up."

"Never!" says another woman whose long, black ponytail swishes from the back of her Biss Tribe baseball cap. As she shifts on long legs, she fingers the sterling silver hummingbird pendant on her turquoise-beaded, choker-style necklace that compliments her caramel-hued complexion

"Hey everybody, I'm Sunshine Bylilly." Her large, dark eyes simultaneously radiate pain and power, accentuated by perfect black-winged liner and thick, natural lashes. Her full lips glisten with pearlescent gloss as she says, "Grateful to meet you all. I've already been through so much in my life. Now I'm on a healing journey, hoping this trip helps me personally and professionally. I am sooooo tired of struggling!"

"Ditto!" A fourth woman raises a power fist to the group. "Hey all, I'm Andi. Andrea Sullivan, actually. But Andi is the real me," she says with a Boston accent. "In a massive shift right now. Massive! No more hiding the real me! Gotta stop feeling stuck, scared and mad as hell!"

The woman with pink hair high-fives her and says, "Go, sis!"

Andi, who's tall with a thick, masculine build, wears belted gray cargo pants with her Biss Tribe T-shirt. She has an oval, cosmetic-free face distinguished by thick brows, gray eyes and freckled beige skin with tiny lines extending from the outer corners of her eyes as she smiles.

She removes her hat and runs her hand through chestnut-brown hair that's shaved bald on one side and falls in a straight chop toward her chin on the other. Multiple silver hoops

## Sunday, Day 1

in each ear match the rings on her fingers and thumbs, including one adorned with a rainbow flag.

"So pumped to meet you all," she says.

"Yeah, girl, I'm Celeste Williams," says the glamorous woman, whose diamond ring sparkles as she waves to everyone.

"Jade Rogers," announces the woman with pink hair and tattoos. "Was hoping to connect with a new sisterhood, and here we are, already. Like it says, The Biss Tribe. Every time I see Biss, I think, *bliss*. I need that!"

The women turn to you. Celeste glances at your T-shirt, then smiles, looking in your eyes. "Hey, girlfriend, you're joining the Tribe, too. What's your name?"

You introduce yourself.

*Ching!* Your cell phone alerts you of a text message. Chimes ring around you, and the other women hold up their phones.

"Hey, listen!" Andi says, looking at her device. "Did we all get the same text? Mine says, 'Goddess, it's time to fly! In just a few short hours, you'll arrive at The Biss Tribe Inn to start your ascent up Infinity Mountain. You'll be greeted at the airport by Esmerelda, who will escort you and the others to the Inn for Orientation with Biss.' Yeah?"

"That's it," Sunshine says as several 20-something women rush toward the group, laughing about how their connecting flight from Miami was late.

One of the women has almond-shaped eyes, brown sugar-hued skin and a mane of straight black hair. A taller woman who seems joined at her hip has loose blonde curls, blue eyes, a vanilla complexion and glossy pink Betty Boop lips. They both have hourglass curves and wear black leggings with their Biss Tribe T-shirts knotted at the waist to expose peeks of toned abs.

"Wow, you're all so stunning," Andi says. "I guess this shatters the myth that beautiful women have it all figured out, yeah?"

"Uh, *yeah!*" dark-haired woman exclaims with a laugh. "Hi, I'm Marla Santos." She puts her arm around the blonde woman. "And this is Sammie Smithville. I have a million followers on three platforms and she has more. We're launching the best skincare line ever—it's called Samla Marmie, a combination of our names—and we need to learn some wisdom from older women—"

"—before we thousand-X our businesses and our brands to become billionaires," Sammie says with a slight Southern accent. "We need to stay smart and sexy AF, and we want to hit the *Forbes* 30 Under 30 List."

Andi stares at them in awe.

"New levels, new devils," Sunshine adds. "My grandmother always warned me and my cousins that beauty is more of a curse than a blessing, because you get so much unwanted attention. It can be so toxic and distracting and even deadly, like it was for my mom."

*Ching!* Sunshine glances at her phone, then lights up. "Oh, here's another one. It says, 'Goddess, it's time to fly!'"

The newcomers raise their arms and dance. Marla exclaims, "Time to fly, bitches!"

You watch them as they laugh and pose for their cell phone cameras. Sammie twists her face and sticks out her tongue for the camera, then says: "Yo' boss bitches! Me and my girl Marla are officially on the way to Goddess paradise with The Biss Tribe! I don't know how we're gonna make it with no pics or vids this whole trip, but that's the rule and we gotta be good!"

"Or maybe not!" Marla says, popping into Sammie's video. "Who has more fun, a good girl or a *baaaaad* girl?"

They exclaim in unison: "A *baaaaad* girl!"

One of their friends tosses her platinum-tipped brunette hair over a shoulder and joins the selfie, saying, "I say a bad girl who's very good at it!" Her almond skin is so smooth that it looks plastic,

## Sunday, Day 1

and she purses her plump lips to blow a kiss to the camera phone. Then she turns to you and the women. "Hey ladies, I'm Kiki Khalil."

As you and the group greet her, another woman, who has corkscrew-curly silver hair and is wearing a denim jacket with a Biss Tribe T-shirt, steps into line. She catches your eyes and winks.

"It's quite fascinating," she says with a deep, buttery voice as she tucks her shoulder-length curls behind an ear, "that despite our different ages and appearances, we're all seeking the same thing. Whether you're young like them or celebrating 75 like me, it's all about finding ourselves. I'm Delaney Cohen."

Andi stares at her and says, "You remind me of Meryl Streep, my favorite actress. You look like her and you have her elegant poise and grace."

"Thank you," Delaney says, shaking Andi's hand.

You introduce yourself, then watch each woman with wonder; they all look so unique and great, yet they're all missing something that they're hoping to find during this retreat. Celeste turns to you and asks, "So, what brings you on this trip?"

As you respond, you half-hear the chatter of women around you expressing nervousness about sharing their personal vulnerabilities to strangers on this retreat.

You glance at them, then back at Celeste, and say, "I'm feeling some of that, too."

"We got you, girl," Celeste says as the other women reach out to high-five or fist-bump you.

Another woman rolls up in a powered wheelchair. Rhinestones adorn the brim of her Biss Tribe cap, as well as the scoop neck of her matching tank top. Orange crystal bracelets circle her wrists, a tiny Mexican flag pendant sparkles at her neck, and a silver butterfly ring glimmers as she works a knob to stop her chair.

"Look at all of you!" she exclaims. Her tumbles of turquoise hair frame her peaches-and-cream skin and match the birds and flowers in the large tattoo on her upper arm of Frida Kahlo, the Mexican artist. "I'm Bianca Hernandez."

"Welcome to the Tribe, girlfriend," Celeste says amidst the other women's greetings.

Marla admires Bianca's tattoo. "Frida was the first selfie queen, ever, with paint! Fun facts!"

"I love her self-portaits," Sammie says. "She was a girl boss before that was even a thing. Can you imagine, every time you want to take a selfie, spending hours or even weeks *painting* yourself?!?"

"A goddess for sure," Kiki says.

"Frida inspires me," Bianca says. Her angular face—which has a silvery scar on her left cheek—and large brown eyes glow with excitement as she smiles up at Celeste, Marla and Sammie, then at you and the other women. "I feel like her spirit is with me all the time. I have every book about her and pictures of her all over my condo in San Diego."

Marla marvels at the rhinestones adorning Bianca's hat and shirt, then asks, "Did you bling out your hat and tee? I love that!"

Sammie adds, "We shoulda done that! Bianca, you sparkle, mama!"

Bianca flashes a smile, revealing turquoise braces. "I feel sad if I don't sparkle and wear bright colors! That's my thing. Makes me happy."

"Hey!" Jade exclaims, then reads from her phone: "Now it says, 'Get ready to activate your GoddessPower.'" She looks up at you and the group. "At first I thought that sounded really sus, like airy-fairy, but this program actually sounds like—"

"A real ass-kicker," Andi says with a laugh.

"Well, I'm in a better mood already, meeting all of you," Celeste says. "I drank half a bottle of wine last night, just so I wouldn't scream at my husband or cuss out my kids for having the *nerve* to ask me to cook a big steak dinner after they trashed the house

# Sunday, Day 1

with their friends—other dads and kids, mind you!—and left the mess for *me* to clean up."

She exhales loudly. "This, after I chaired a board meeting where everybody's in hysterics over our company's merger that's all over the news. I'm tellin' *you!* Where is the damn escape hatch on my life?"

"This might be it," Andi says. "Listen, I did my whole life for everybody else. Went to the same college as my parents. Found a good husband. Took over the family business. Had kids. And all I did was live the same life as my parents. Except I wanted to be an artist. Now I'm 61. Got more time behind me than ahead of me. So it's time to finally live as the real me."

"Yes, that's kinda like my story, even though I'm 35," Jade exclaims. "I'm in a girl band! The Star Chix."

"Cool," Andi says.

A flight attendant announces, "Now boarding main cabin section two."

You and the women inch toward the gate.

"So, listen," Andi tells Jade, loudly enough for you and the group to hear. "My husband was in the closet our whole marriage. Ran away with a dude 20 years younger than me. Now I'm like a rebel with a good cause. Wanna sell the family business, open an art studio on the beach, and come out as the authentic Andi—"

"Yessss!" Sunshine says. "I want to self-actualize, finally. Get over my trust issues and lack mindset. But this trip? I'm anxious. We don't know where we're going. They're taking us to some mountain retreat near the ocean."

"It's bizarre," Jade says. "But adventurous. Feels kinda mystical."

Delaney leans in and says: "I was attracted to the word 'tribe.' A sisterhood, to help us rise up together."

"Tribe," echoes Andi. "Never had that. Need it. Want it."

## Welcome to The Biss Tribe

Sunshine nods. "Suddenly I don't feel so alone. Or scared or skeptical."

You board the plane, and a very tall, athletic woman takes the seat beside you. Long, skinny dreadlocks spray from the back of her Biss Tribe cap.

"Hey," she says. "My connecting flight was late. Had to run through the airport to make it. Looks like you're goin' on the retreat, too. I'm Zeusse. Like the Greek god, but with two 'esses' and an 'e.'"

She smiles, flashing perfect white teeth that contrast with her cosmetic-free skin that's as rich and smooth as coffee beans. Something about her wide-set eyes conveys wisdom and an old soul energy.

You introduce yourself and chat.

"I'm in a big life transition," Zeusse says. Her voice is velvety, and she speaks with the Queen's English softened by swag. "Ready for change and seeking guidance. I've been playin' ball all my life, just retired. Want to start a girls basketball academy to create the next superstars. But I need an infusion of courage and confidence to push me up to where I need to be. So, I'm diggin' those text messages we just got from The Biss Tribe." She glances at her cell phone and holds it up to show you.

"Ascend or stay stuck," Zeusse reads. "One hundred percent. That's what's up."

Your stomach flips as the plane lifts off. You close your eyes.

*I've been stuck long enough. I'm ready to fly.*

# Sunday, Day 1

*Dear Goddess Reader:*

*Now that you've met some of the other women on the retreat, you can refer to The Biss Tribe Class #88 Roster at the back of this book, in case you need clarity on who's who. It's on page 261.*

*They've just shared snippets of why they're here.*

*Briefly, if you were introducing yourself and sharing what issues brought you to The Biss Tribe, what would you say?*

_____

_____

_____

_____

## Welcome to The Biss Tribe Inn-Charting Your Ascent

After the plane lands, you descend the airport's escalator to baggage claim, where a tall, clean-cut person wearing a dark chauffeur's uniform—black pantsuit, crisp white shirt, purple bowtie—is holding a sign with your name emblazoned under the logo: a castle scrolled with The Biss Tribe.

"Hi, that's me," you say, overwhelmed with comfort by the glow on this person's face. They seem familiar, but—

"I'm your personal Concierge," they say. On their breast pocket is a nametag that simply says "Jami, Concierge for" above your name.

You glance at the nametag, then the person's face.

They say, "My name is Jami and I'll be with you for the duration of your trip. You can simply call me 'Concierge.' At your service."

## Welcome to The Biss Tribe

Incredulous, you ask, "Personal Concierge?" You notice that someone is greeting each of the other women, including a dozen ladies who were not on your flight.

You glance back at your Concierge, and a panicky feeling seeps through you, as if you've been tricked. "Is there an extra charge for that?"

The person's eyes sparkle. "My service is complimentary. Consider me your personal assistant, catering to needs you didn't know you had."

You let that sink in, wondering what other surprises await, and you say, "Well, Biss sent me a note saying that she's my Muse for the trip."

The person nods. "True, so now you have two guides on your team. Simply call me Concierge or Jami."

They retrieve your small suitcase that contains only a few personal items, because the retreat's instructions said all your clothing, shoes and needs would be provided upon arrival at each GoddessPower Activation Station. Concierge guides you outside to a sleek black bus, where other people dressed like them are loading bags into the cargo hold.

The women you met at the airport are also looking with awe at the Concierges who are handling the luggage. Some are male, some are female, and some are androgynous. Their complexions range from milky white to licorice black.

Nearby, at least eight tall women are standing around the group, looking around. They wear dark bodysuits with The Biss Tribe logo over the left breast. Discreet coils extend up from their shirt collars into earpieces. Each one has a black leather bag whose strap is over the left shoulder, with the bag hanging close to their torso on the right side.

Celeste stares in awe and asks, "Who are the Amazon warrior ninja chicks?"

## Sunday, Day 1

"They are *hawt!*" Zeusse says with a smile. "My kinda females."

Jade's eyes grow wide. "Are we like, in danger, though? They act like the president is about to get on this bus."

"They also look like they're packin'," Andi adds. "What do you think is in those bags?"

You wave for your Concierge to come close and you ask, "Why the security? Are we at risk?"

Concierge nods toward you and the women and says, "Why do you think you have to take a trip off the grid to a remote place for a week to activate the GoddessPower that you were born with? Because we live in a world where not everyone wants you to know the secrets you're about to learn."

Celeste exclaims, "Damn, I never thought about it like that. I guess if all of us become warrior bitches busting out of here to conquer the world, we'll be a force to be reckoned with."

Andi quips, "And the powers that be in this man's world, will get pissed!"

"Let's do it, bitches!" Marla exclaims. "Sammie and I get so many weirdos on our social media pages and channels. We have to block them all the time. Now I know we're safe here."

"Safety is rule number one," Bianca says as a Concierge activates a lift that elevates her in her chair onto the bus.

Before you can board, you line up with retreat-goers at the door of the bus. Everyone is getting checked in by a woman with long, jet-black hair, ice-blue eyes, and a sparkling nose ring. She's holding a tablet and wearing a short black skirt, a form-fitting purple-and-cheetah-print shirt splashed with The Biss Tribe logo, and black athletic shoes. Her name tag says "Panther."

"Hi," she says, calling you by name. "Welcome to The Biss Tribe. Here's your name badge to help the other women get to know you."

## Welcome to The Biss Tribe

As you step on, the bus driver, a petite woman with fluffy emerald-green hair and colorful mermaid tattoos covering her arms, says to you and each woman, "Hi, I'm Vee. Cool to meet you."

After you board, you look out the window, watching the Concierges board another bus, while The Biss Tribe security team gets into several black SUVs with dark windows.

Except for two. They board the bus, and collect each woman's cell phone and other devices, slipping them into velvet bags marked with each person's name. You reluctantly forfeit your phone and watch it disappear into the purple velvet bag. Other women groan and say, "Bye, bye, world," as they do the same.

"As you know," The Biss Tribe security officer announces, "cell phones, tablets, laptops, cameras and recording devices of all kinds are strictly prohibited on this retreat. To protect the confidentiality of each guest and to ensure your focus on transformation, we strictly enforce this rule to create a safe environment for each of you to feel comfortable sharing and being vulnerable, so that what you reveal about yourself on Infinity Mountain, stays on Infinity Mountain."

Tears well in Marla's eyes as she hands over her phone.

"I'm in withdrawal already," Sammie says, surrendering her device.

"As you know," The Biss Tribe security officer says, "should any emergency back home require your attention, your loved ones can contact us directly through the number we provided for you to share with them, and we'll alert you immediately and make arrangements if necessary."

Celeste dramatically drops her phone into the bag and exclaims, "Hallelujah! I'm free! I am so happy to get rid of this damn phone for a whole week!"

# Sunday, Day 1

The Biss Tribe security officers leave the bus, which is full. A woman steps on board and the doors close. She stands near the driver, facing you and the passengers.

Wearing a sleeveless purple sheath dress that reveals trim, toned muscles, she has skin that's so dewy and smooth, it reminds you of melted milk chocolate. Her blue eyes glow brightly from the luminescent contours of her face. Snow-white swirls of hair cascade down her back. It's impossible to tell her age or her ethnicity, and she radiates mesmerizing authority and warmth.

"Ladies, I'm Esmerelda," she says as the bus begins to move. "Welcome to the most transformative experience of your life! We're heading to The Biss Tribe Inn, where we'll enjoy a meal with Biss, take a virtual tour of Valley Village, then enjoy a surprise excursion. Tomorrow, we'll head up to the GoddessPower Pyramid."

You listen and watch in awe, feeling a million miles away from the reality of your life. You're anxious and excited. And desperate for change.

Zeusse, who's sitting across the aisle from you, looks awestruck. "Aw snap! That's the most beautiful older woman I've ever seen. She glows. I wanna come out of this retreat and glow like *her!*"

Sunshine, who's seated in front of you, says, "My Native American grandmother Nani is like that. It's spiritual power. It glows inside them like the sun."

Esmerelda continues: "I'd be happy to answer any questions. Let me warn, this is literally an uphill battle. You'll be working your way up Infinity Mountain. If it were easy, everyone would do it. Your success depends on the work you invest in your ascent. This program requires your imagination and your grit, your heart and your soul, your physical and mental strength, your belief in yourself and higher powers as never before. Are you ready?"

The women shout out affirmations.

## Welcome to The Biss Tribe

"Right now, there are 22 of you," Esmerelda says. "When you board the bus to return to the airport at the end of this journey, we may have a smaller group. If you choose to drop out during the journey, know that you can return at any time to repeat the program and keep pushing until you finally arrive at your personal SeaGoddess Castle where you rule your realm as part of The Biss Tribe."

You spend most of the short ride looking out the window, wondering if anyone on this bus will drop out. When the bus pulls into the curved driveway to The Biss Tribe Inn at the foot of a huge mountain, you take in as much of the opulent view as you can, but realize the peak is obscured by clouds. As you step off the bus, the air smells salty like the ocean, but you can't see water anywhere.

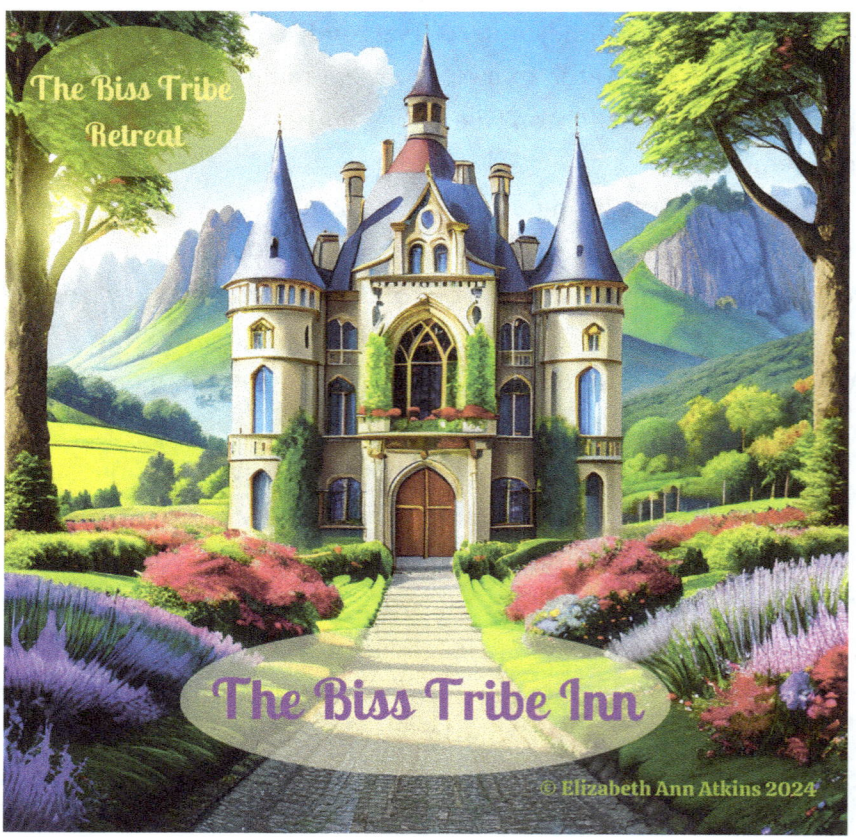

## Sunday, Day 1

The bus parks and you and the others step down and begin walking toward The Biss Tribe Inn, which resembles a mini chateau with huge, carved, double wooden doors. The security team flanks you and the women as you proceed into a white marble foyer. Sweeping double staircases and glistening chandeliers evoke gasps from the women around you.

"Holy shit!" Marla exclaims. "I'm like fiending to shoot video right now! I'm in phone withdrawal. How can I not even take a selfie here?"

A Concierge steps toward her, whispers in her ear, and she blanches.

Flowers and green vines burst from the banisters, vases and archways leading into rooms whose measurements feel otherworldly.

"Ladies," Esmerelda says, "your Concierges will escort you to your rooms to freshen up, change clothes, enjoy a snack, then reconvene in the courtyard for an energizing walk with me in 15 minutes."

## Time to Change

Concierge Jami escorts you to a luxurious private room and bathroom whose furniture, fixtures, colors, textures and style seem custom-designed for you. It's so silent and still, you can hear yourself breathe.

"As you can see," Concierge says, pointing to a closet containing a selection of your favorite leisurewear and accompanying footwear, "your room and your attire are customized to your tastes."

Then Concierge points to a basket and ice bucket, both brimming with your favorite snacks and beverages. They say, "This should tide you over until your first GoddessFeast with Biss."

You change, marveling at the perfect fit of the clothing. Then you enjoy the food and drink. No wonder The Biss Tribe application had asked all those personal questions; everything so far feels perfectly tailored to your preferences. And why does everything taste better here? True, you feel far away from your regular life. But will this pampered-retreat feeling last?

*Dear Goddess Reader:*

*Your GoddessPower activates best when you're living and loving yourself with the royal treatment that you desire and deserve, personally and professionally.*

*When you pamper yourself with the utmost care, respect and honor, you show others how to treat you, and you set a new standard to accept that or better.*

*This activates powerful energy in and around you, even when you're alone, or running errands, or going to the gym. Goddesses don't schlep. Goddesses don't grunge. Goddesses present ourselves in ways that reflect the inner joy, peace and power of our Supernatural Selves. We are divine royalty—here in this lifetime for a powerful purpose that requires us to work to become our best in every way.*

*So, regarding clothing, Goddesses dress in comfortable, flattering clothing that we love—not necessarily what's trendy. We also adorn our bodies with jewelry, accessories, hairstyles, makeup, piercings and artwork (such as tattoos and henna) that express our personalities.*

*Sometimes it takes time to discover our personal style by unraveling it from how we "should" dress and appear, according to what other people, trends, cultural beliefs, religious doctrine and patriarchal rules have deeply imposed on our psyches.*

# Sunday, Day 1

*Activating your GoddessPower here in The Biss Tribe will help you find yourself and step into your future with your own personal style.*

*How you present yourself can lower or raise your vibrational frequency and your GoddessPower—because your favorite comfortable clothes, hairstyle, makeup and body art will boost your confidence. So donate any clothes, shoes, boots, coats, jewelry and accessories that don't fit or make you feel anything but elevated when you wear them.*

*Now, describe your personal style that reflects your Supernatural Self, as part of a divine royal sisterhood, coming together to create your dream life as you do powerful things in the world.*

_____

_____

_____

_____

# A Nature Walk with Esmerelda

As you walk with Esmerelda and the group through the beautiful garden and forest trails around the Inn, you're super comfortable in the clothing and shoes provided by The Biss Tribe.

"Getting your daily dose of Mother Nature," Esmerelda says, "detoxes your mind, body and spirit while raising your vibrational frequency, which increases your GoddessPower."

As you walk, the scent of earth and pine trees and flowers, plus the warm sunshine and cooling breeze, seem to suck the stress out of your body.

"When you go home and apply what you learn here," Esmerelda says, "you should spend time in nature every day as part of your high-vibe GoddessPower Lifestyle that enables you to create the new you and the empire that follows."

## Time to Change

A short time later, after returning to your suite to shower and change into a dressier but comfortable outfit that fits you perfectly, Concierge Jami escorts you to the lobby, where each woman wears some variation of your outfit, all styled according to her personality, with The Biss Tribe colors of purple, black, gold and pink accented by cheetah print.

Delaney wears a flowy linen dress. Zeusse and Andi sport pants and collared shirts. Marla, Sammie, Kiki and their group look photo-shoot ready in minidresses. Celeste and Sunshine wear curvy sundresses, while Bianca and Jade look comfortable in leggings and sleeveless, flowy tops that show off the tattoo art on their arms.

## Take Your Throne and Meet Biss in the Ballroom

Two Concierges open tall double doors to reveal a ballroom that looks royal. Lining the ruby-red carpet are four rows of gilded tables with ornate gold throne-style chairs, 22 in all, one for each woman. Concierge Jami guides you to the one where your name is scrolled on a card that's displayed within an artful bouquet of your favorite flowers in a crystal vase. You sit in the giant chair, sinking into the velvet seat cushion, loving this fantastical experience. It's only a short time into the retreat and you're realizing that it's far more opulent than what you expected. Yes, this trip was expensive, but they are over-delivering on your best expectations.

On the table is a treasure chest that's the size of a large boot box. It looks like something that pirates would bury on a tropical

## Sunday, Day 1

island to hide their gold coins and jewels. You run your fingertips over the plush velvet fabric covering its sides and showcasing The Biss Tribe's trademark leopard print and smokey shades of purple. On the top, your name is inscribed in a small gold oval plate above The Biss Tribe logo. Gold hardware adorns your GoddessTreasure Chest, and includes a latch secured with a purple metal padlock. You glance around the table for a key to open it, but finding none, you pull on the padlock.

Concierge Jami appears out of nowhere and says with a warning tone: "You may not open your GoddessTreasure Chest until instructed to do so. It's a ceremonial experience."

You stiffen, feeling like maybe you're in trouble. So, you sit still, taking it all in. Tall French doors along the far wall open to a terrace dripping with purple flowers amidst green ivy. Crystal chandeliers glow with lavender light, sparkling above the tables. They face a small stage framed by huge bursts of yellow and white flowers—sunflowers, roses, Gerber daisies, daffodils, lilies, and gardenias amidst ivy. Electric purple light glows from behind the flowers, and the scent is luscious.

Nestled in the flowers and greenery are life-size statues of a cheetah, a lion, a black panther and a white tiger, all with sparkling, bejeweled eyes.

Sexy global fusion chill music booms through the ballroom as Esmerelda steps onto the stage. Her silvery sheath dress reminds you of a 1920s flapper.

"Ladies!" she exclaims, her long hair cascading around her shoulders. "Are you ready for a power surge that transforms you into the Goddess that you're meant to be as a modern woman doing positive and influential things in the world?"

"Yes!" the women cheer.

"Are you ready to do the work to ascend to your personal SeaGoddess Castle, the empire that you create and rule to experience your greatest dreams and desires?"

A chorus of yesses fills the room.

"Are you ready to shift into a new mindset and know with every ounce of your being that you are limitless, infinite, and fully capable of making anything happen?"

"Yes!"

"Then get ready to step through the GoddessGateway," Esmerelda says. "Starting here, now, with your guide, Biss."

The sultry music blasts louder.

Biss steps onto the stage in curve-hugging leather pants that are the same French vanilla color as her sleeveless, waist-cinching lace blouse that exposes her toned shoulders. Her gold sneakers glimmer.

An aura of peace and power glows around her sunburst of curls, while her eyes sparkle with excitement toward you and all the women.

"My beautiful Goddesses!" she exclaims with a commanding voice that's amplified through an invisible microphone over the speakers. "Welcome to The Biss Tribe!"

The music blasts.

"Stand up and dance!" Biss shouts, jumping down from the stage and dancing with the women as they shoot up and boogie between the tables.

"This is a celebration of you!" Biss points to Zeusse, then Sammie, then Bianca, then you, and every one of the women in the ballroom. "And you! And all of you beautiful sisters. This is a transformation of you! A reinvention! A reconnection of self! A love affair with your own heart and soul, your mind and body, that will make you bliss out on your life! Every day!"

## Sunday, Day 1

Biss dances her way to each woman, and when she reaches you, she gently embraces you in a soft cloud of rose-gardenia perfume, then pulls back to stare lovingly into your eyes. She welcomes you by name and says:

"I see you. I hear you. And you belong here in The Biss Tribe. Together we're going to make magic happen to create your GoddessLife!"

Peace and confidence surge through you as you look into her eyes. In this moment, you actually believe this can work. You dance among the women as their energy electrifies the air and they exude a collective release of tension and anxiety.

Biss continues her way through the women, embracing and speaking to each person.

"I have chills from head to toe!" exclaims Jade as she dances past you. A few women remain seated, some snapping their fingers and swaying to the music. Others look shy and anxious.

With her eyes closed and a serene expression, Kiki is vibing solo in the moment, dancing and tossing her hair around.

Biss hops back onto the stage, gazing down with adoration toward everyone. "You're about to step into your GoddessLife that elevates you into becoming such an extraordinary version of who you're meant to be, that you wake up so happy and grateful every day, feeling like you want to give your life a good morning kiss! Then you go through the day feeling like life is making love to you! Who's ready for *that?*"

The dancing women explode with cheers and clapping. Biss steps to the edge of the stage and raises her arms up and out to the crowd.

"So, are you ready to get unstuck, stop being scared, and stop playing small, so you can speak up and soar into the life you truly desire and deserve?"

"Yessss!" the women scream.

## Welcome to The Biss Tribe

"Are you ready for more Power, Pleasure—" she pauses with a playful expression. "I said, Pleasure!"

"Oh, hell yeah!" Celeste and Sunshine shout in unison amidst a chorus of "Yes!" while women dance to the sultry beat.

Biss yells: "Along with Prosperity, Protection and Peace?"

The ballroom is a frenzy of dancing women, shrieking with joy. More women stand and dance. Tears stream down Andi's cheeks. Bianca is dancing in her chair and waving her rhinestone hat like a tambourine. The 20-somethings who include Marla and Sammie dance in a cluster of tossing hair and blissed-out faces that mirror Delaney's smile. Though a half-century older, she moves in unison to the beat alongside them.

"Alright!" Biss shouts. "Now tell me, are you ready to activate your GoddessPower?"

Arms shoot into the air.

"It's your superpower," Biss says. "We need to stoke it, and make it blaze!"

"Let's do it!" Sunshine shouts. "Light me up, baby!"

She and Zeusse and several women dance toward the stage and high-five Biss. She hops down and dances among them.

"Ladies, are you ready to fly?"

The women roar so fiercely, the chandeliers sway.

"All of you!" Biss shouts. "It's your time! And your time is NOW!"

The women explode, arms upstretched, dancing in a way that's like flower petals blooming.

The volume lowers on the music and Esmerelda announces, "Ladies, please take your seats. It's time to make the magic happen."

As you sit on your throne, six, black-suited Amazonesque security women enter the ballroom and stand at equal distances around the entrance, the French doors leading to the terrace, and the stage. Their faces are expressionless except to announce

## Sunday, Day 1

that they will pounce on anything or anyone who disrupts this experience.

A silent chill falls over the room.

"Are we safe?" Celeste asks. "Why are they here?"

Biss nods. "There's a conservative organization called BRUTE—it's an acronym for Brothers Reversing Ur Total Empowerment—that espouses patriarchal dominance over women like us. They want to destroy us and stop us from liberating women from the brainwashing and societal constructs that oppress us. We are BRUTE's worst nightmare and number-one threat."

Marla stands up. "It's scary as fuck that we need bodyguards here. Your brochure didn't say anything about us being targets—"

"Every empowered woman is a target," Celeste says.

"We get that shit online," Sammie quips. "From trolls and weirdos who harass us or try to shame us in our DMs."

"Online trolls are the foot soldiers of BRUTE," Biss says. "They're perpetuating the philosophies of BRUTE that are inflicted on us and instilled in us, starting at birth, as girls and women. Our job here is to undo that submissive programming by activating our GoddessPower, Pleasure, Prosperity, Protection and Peace."

Delaney raises a hand. "Isn't this group related to the one that protested Husbands, Incorporated?"

"Men for Traditional Marriage—MFTM," Celeste says. "I followed that whole shitshow. They tried to shut the place down because Venus Roman and Raye Johnson created a company to give women the power and pleasure in relationships in a radical new way. Then Sasha Maxwell wrote *hot* books about it."

Andi runs a hand through her hair. "So how much of a threat is this to us right now?"

Biss glances at the guards. "Our goal is to provide a safe space for you to focus and do the work. So, let's do it."

Several women cast anxious looks at the guards.

## Welcome to The Biss Tribe

"This is freaking me out," Bianca says. "I'm not trying to get killed here."

"And we don't have our phones to call for help," Sammie adds.

"They're here so you won't have to," Biss says.

She glances at the security guards, then the women. "They'll be with us for the entirety of your stay here on Infinity Mountain. Rest assured, you're safe. You may know that women who transform here in The Biss Tribe go out into the world to disrupt the patriarchy on every level, wherever there's imbalance, inequality and injustice."

Biss paces the stage. "Our graduates leave unjust marriages and disrupt oppressive family dynamics. They instigate change for equal pay in corporations. They advocate for women's reproductive rights, better health care and childcare, as well as opportunities to help single mothers rise out of poverty. They organize protests in Washington, D.C. and state capitols. They lead global movements for peace, justice, women's rights and the environment."

Andi stands and cheers, shooting her fists in the air. Jade does the same as other women applaud.

"So, GoddessLife is not all rainbows and butterflies," Biss says. "It's a mission. And it can be a dangerous one."

Esmerelda steps forward. "Relax and focus. This is an excellent exercise to practice dealing with reality out in the world. Because as you build your empire, forces *will* try to stop you. You'll need to implement safety measures to protect yourself, so you can invest your brainpower into creating your GoddessLife."

Several women look worried as the Concierges appear and hand each of you a leather-bound *PowerJournal* emblazoned with The Biss Tribe logo, and a matching pen; your name is inscribed on each. The *PowerJournal* matches the treasure chest. You finger its butter-soft texture and the satin ribbon tied around it.

## Sunday, Day 1

"This process is intense," Biss says, walking between the tables, looking you and each woman in the eyes. "You'll lose all sense of time and space. Because you're going on a journey of self-discovery while experiencing the sensory extravaganza of this unique program. A program that helps you solve whatever problem that brought you here. Then you'll go home and build your empire."

She stops at your table. Suddenly you feel overwhelmed with peace. You're also consumed by intense curiosity to learn what she knows. Because she radiates a vibe of someone who has sacred secrets, and draws confidence from them, and you want to know them all, so you can have that kind of fire blazing in your eyes, too.

"Here you'll experience a fusion of mind, body and spirit," she tells you, "and everything you've learned over the years will finally come together in moments of epiphany, revelation and change. You are the very auspicious class number 88 of The Biss Tribe. The number eight is the infinity symbol pointing toward the sky, and you have it double, so let's *goooooo!*"

A heart-shaped diamond solitaire sparkles on her left ring finger, and she wears two necklaces. The shorter one has yellow crystal beads and a shimmering gold *Om* symbol pendant. The longer one has round opalescent crystal beads and a gold ankh pendant.

"So," Biss says, "poise those pens over your paper. During the next week, you'll be writing your GoddessVision, and the script to manifest your wildest dreams."

The fiery sparkle in her eyes infuses you with optimism and confidence that you *can* do this! You smile, and she beams back at you.

"Then you go home to design your unique realm," Biss says, "and fly into your heart's greatest desires while doing something powerful to improve our world."

## Your Favorite Lunch is Served

Concierge Jami approaches with a silver tray, then places your favorite meal and beverage in front of you.

"Ladies, before you take a bite," Biss says, "let's close our eyes and give thanks to the infinite, divine powers for gifting us with this experience and this nourishment that fuels our minds, bodies and souls to activate our GoddessPower here at The Biss Tribe Inn, so we can create luscious lives that illuminate the world. And so it is spoken, and so it is done. Please repeat that with me."

You join the women in repeating a deep chorus of: "And so it is spoken, and so it is done."

You savor the delicious meal prepared exactly to your tastes. It's so exceptionally good, you're lost in the tastes and textures as the room fills with excited chatter and the clink of silverware on gold china plates.

"Man!" Zeusse declares from a nearby table, "this food is straight-up orgasmic. Exactly how I like my Chilean sea bass: pan-seared, crispy on the outside but tender inside, with capers and olive oil, a sweet potato and mixed greens with champagne vinaigrette." She takes another bite and closes her eyes as other women exclaim delight over their favorite meals.

"Ladies," Esmerelda announces, "the food is prepared precisely to your tastes because we want you to go home and demand the best for yourself, all day, every day, including the foods you love. We tailor your experience here, to set the stage for you to create a GoddessPower Lifestyle that affirms and celebrates who *you* are, uniquely, every day."

# Sunday, Day 1

*Dear Goddess Reader:*

*Your GoddessPower activates best when you're nourishing yourself with healthy foods and beverages that honor our bodies. Food and drink can lower or raise your vibrational frequency—you'll learn more about this at the GoddessPower Pyramid—so we need to include our favorite high-vibe foods in our daily meals.*

*List your favorite foods, how you like them prepared, and how you can enjoy them every day.*

_____

_____

_____

_____

Bianca uses chopsticks to raise a shrimp from her colorful vegetable stir-fry. "I feel so spoiled right now. I don't want to leave this place."

Andi smiles. "I feel like a king."

Biss steps onto the stage and shouts, "So let's get to it, my beautiful Goddesses! I'm big on definitions and making up my own to ensure that you have crystal clarity on what we're doing here. So, let's start with The Biss Tribe definition of Goddess."

The hip-hop music has transitioned into a soft, sultry beat with a female voice singing wordless songs that create a soothing vibe through the ballroom.

"You are Goddess!" Biss exclaims. "A woman who embodies the infinite, supernatural power of the universe. You're going to learn how to use the four GoddessPower Activation Tools to access and activate this energy, which awakens your **Supernatural Self.**"

## Welcome to The Biss Tribe

A screen drops in the archway of flowers behind Biss and shows this:

"Your Supernatural Self is the Goddess version of you who's led by your Spirit, and is fueled and informed by the currents of power pulsing in and around you from the universal field of knowledge. This supernatural energy amplifies your truth, guides your every thought and action, and synchronizes your manifestations and life mission."

Jade raises her hand. "What do you mean by mission?"

"That's your life purpose," Biss says. "Your calling. Your divine life assignment."

## Sunday, Day 1

"What if we don't know what it is?" Kiki asks.

Biss smiles. "Stay tuned, because your Supernatural Self will tell you."

Kiki looks confused as you and the women savor your meals and listen with rapt attention as Biss points to the screen.

"Does everyone understand how Goddess is your Supernatural Self?" Biss pauses to make eye contact with you and several women. "She's limitless and free to fly, charting a course navigated by her unique purpose and passion. Her GoddessMission."

Sunshine lets out a sigh, closes her eyes, tilts her head back and shoots her arms up. "Yes, oh my goodness, thank you! I am so blissing out on this. I need this so bad."

Andi shakes her head. "Wait, stop. Biss, I'm confused. What does that mean? It sounds woo-woo."

"Your Supernatural Self is powered by Spirit," Biss says. "She learns how to access this divine energy and allows it to activate her infinite power within, and she allows this internal guidance to direct her every step."

Kiki raises a hand. "What if you're atheist and don't believe in God or Spirit?"

"Then replace Spirit with your Higher Self," Biss says, "so the power is coming from within you. This is not a religious concept. It's spiritual and all about energy that's available to every human being."

Kiki nods.

Biss continues, "When your Supernatural Self guides you, you stop living from the outside in, doing what others have programmed you to think, be and do, and you start thinking, speaking, behaving, living and loving from within yourself. You operate *from the inside out* to be and do what's best for *you*, as opposed to thinking and living *from the outside in*, which means shaping yourself to conform to what your family, religion and society may dictate for how you should live, love, work and play."

"That's what's up," Zeusse says.

"Oh shit," Andi says. "That's me. Outside in all my life. Makes me so mad, man."

Biss nods. "When you awaken to what's really going on, it's infuriating! Your Supernatural Self has been powerless to guide you, because she's been silenced and suppressed by how we're programmed, starting as baby girls, on how we should be."

"Hate that!" Jade exclaims. "Ten thousand percent, I despise that reality."

Biss points to the screen, which shows the definition of GoddessPower.

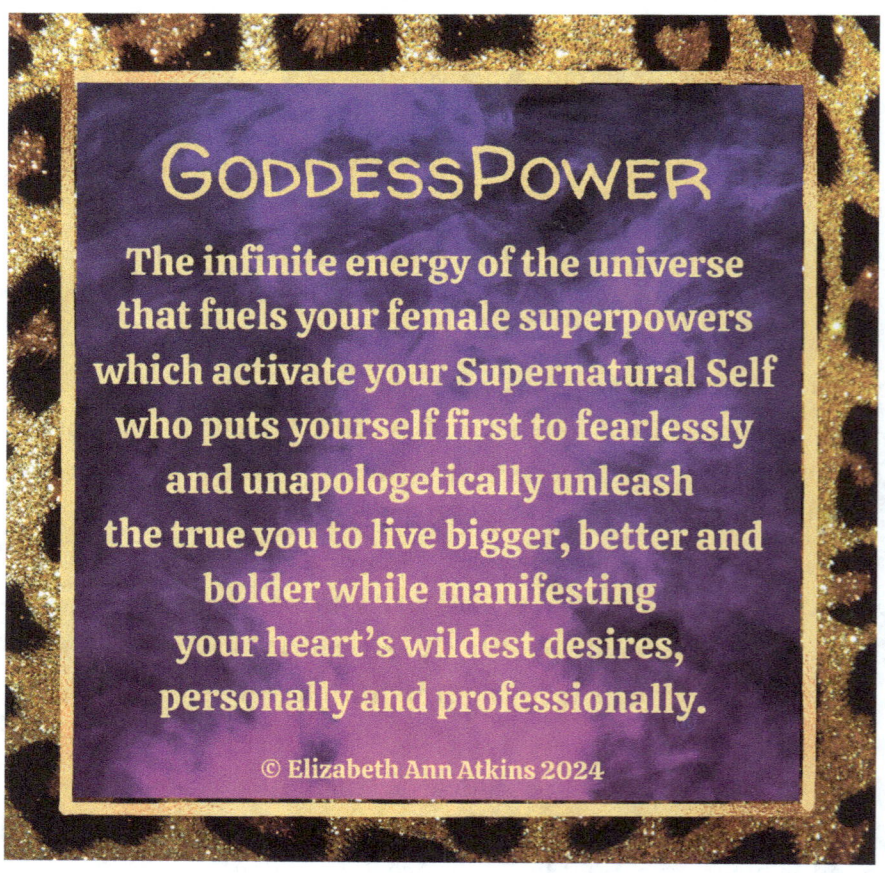

## Sunday, Day 1

"That's why you're all here at Infinity Mountain with me," Biss says, "to connect with your Supernatural Self and activate your GoddessPower, which is your ability to heal, blast past whatever's been holding you back, and do *you* unapologetically on every level. It makes you fearless and confident that you have the talent and ability to set a new standard with yourself, in relationships, at work as a professional, and in the world. You become a bad ass boss bitch who loves herself first and creates a life that prospers, delights and fulfills you while helping the world be a better place. Who's ready for *that!?*"

Zeusse whistles.

"Long overdue!" Andi exclaims as women cheer.

"Rebel Goddess bitches in the house!" Marla cheers as Sammie, Kiki and their friends join her in fists pumping into the air.

"It's time to fly, my Goddesses!" Biss points to the screen with a clicker that casts a purple dot on The Biss Tribe Inn at the base of Infinity Mountain.

"This is an experience unlike any other," Biss says, "as you take a mind- and life-shifting trip up a mountainside, where you immerse in intensive training at five GoddessPower Activation Stations, where you learn the five foundations of GoddessLife. They lead to the peak of Infinity Mountain, where—if you make it through the program—we celebrate at SeaGoddess Castle."

On the screen appears a black glass pyramid nestled in trees on the mountainside.

"Tomorrow, we'll head to The GoddessPower Pyramid," Biss says, "where you'll learn how to activate your power in mind, body and spirit."

Just above the Power Pyramid on the mountain, a Moroccan tent with drapes, lanterns and tassels pops onto the screen. "Next is the Goddess Pleasure Tent. It's a lush, plush, delicious

# Welcome to The Biss Tribe

experience where you learn to embrace and cultivate Pleasure as you've never known. Who wants more pleasure in your life?"

## Sunday, Day 1

The women cheer so loudly that the chandeliers seem to sway.

"That sounds dreamy," Sunshine says, shifting in her chair.

But Marla and Sammie, who are sitting in front of you, share an anxious glance. Marla covers her face in her hands and shakes her head.

The screen shows a cave with a golden glow. "A Goddess needs to handle her money to build her fortune," Biss says. "So, our next stop up the mountain is The GoddessTreasure Cave. Here you'll begin to release all the issues that have stopped you from making money and living in abundance, so you can understand how wealth and abundance are your birthright. It's time to get your riches!"

Biss turns to the screen as images of a woman with a bow and arrow, alongside a woman meditating, pop up with a medieval-looking fortress on the mountain.

"So, you've got your Power, your Pleasure and your Prosperity," Biss says. "Now you need Protection. The GoddessWarrior Fortress are where you learn how to protect and shield your mind, body and spirit at all times."

Next, the image of a waterfall surrounded by lush greenery and flowers appears near the top of Infinity Mountain.

"Finally," Biss says, "after we master those four foundations, we arrive at The GoddessPeace Garden. And after we explore some lessons on how to cultivate forgiveness and peace in ourselves and the world, you'll receive your key to SeaGoddess Castle where the Coronation takes place."

The beautiful castle that you saw on the brochure and in the private online community for The Biss Tribe appears on the screen. Excitement wells in you.

Welcome to The Biss Tribe

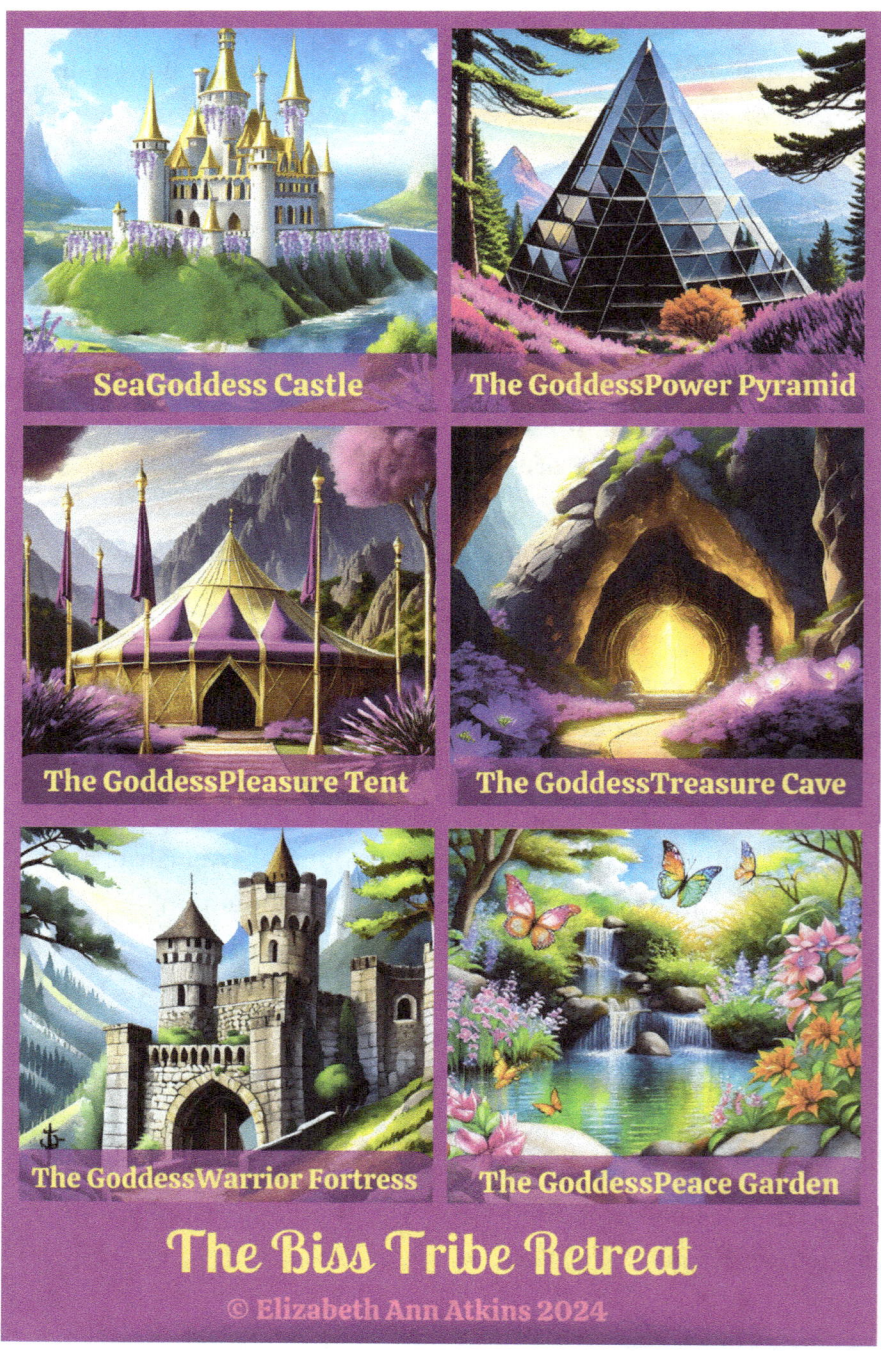

## Sunday, Day 1

"SeaGoddess Castle," Biss says, "looks out over an infinite sea—S-E-A—where you can see—S-E-E—everything necessary to create and sustain the magnificent life that you've been dreaming about, but so far, failing to experience. This is so exciting, because what you'll see at SeaGoddess Castle will be your inner vision, which we call your GoddessVision, because it comes from a supernatural source that I'm going to teach you how to access and use to make magic happen in your life."

"I'm all in!" Andi says amidst a chorus of "Me!" and "I am!"

The screen shows close-ups of the towers, and wide shots of the sea.

"We'll spend the weekend in the castle," Biss says, "while you finalize your script to create your new life. Then I'll invite you into The GoddessPower Studios where I do my podcast, The GoddessPower Show with Elizabeth Ann Atkins®. There you'll record the audio, which will be your own personal podcast that reprograms your mind, and you'll take that home to continue your transformation."

Biss smiles. "You ready for all this?"

"Never been more ready!" Andi shouts.

"Let's do it!" Zeusse says as the women cheer.

"Yessssss!" Biss exclaims, beaming. "So, to conclude, you'll experience The Biss Tribe Coronation. We celebrate during the formal GoddessFeast with music and dancing, then you're free to return home to rock your realm, and we'll see you back in the near future for your GoddessPower Intensives."

The image of SeaGoddess Castle glows on the screen as Biss says, "Give this experience your all, and you'll get exponential results. Sound good?"

"I am all in!" Celeste cheers along with the other women.

You're hoping this isn't too good to be true, and a few women behind you whisper the same fear.

# Welcome to The Biss Tribe

"Here in The Biss Tribe," Biss says, we strengthen our sisterhood and individual power with rituals, symbols and ceremonies. However, the essence of this experience is not in a thing or an action. It's in activating the fire of your spirit to burn away what's blocking you, so you can illuminate yourself and the world. It's time to be seen, be heard and belong. Because *you* are infinite GoddessPower."

Celeste raises her glass. "Preach it, girl!"

Biss smiles. "Please repeat after me: My GoddessMission in The Biss Tribe is to activate the fire in my spirit to activate my Supernatural Self, the Goddess in me, to know my purpose and to burn away what's blocking me, so I can illuminate myself and the world. It's time to be seen, be heard and belong. Because I am infinite and unstoppable in my GoddessPower."

The words appear on the screen behind Biss, so you and the women can read along. As everyone's voices vibrate through the ballroom, Concierge Jami appears, presenting a purple velvet pillow that holds a tiny gold key; the same happens for each woman.

Esmerelda, standing beside Biss, says, "Now please open your GoddessTreasure Chests."

You insert the key and turn it. The padlock opens, and popping-open-lock sounds ripple through the ballroom.

"This is so fun!" Marla exclaims.

As you lift the lid, a soft light inside the chest casts a golden glow over its purple velvet-lined compartments, including six that are covered with lids, each labeled with gold letters: Power, Pleasure, Prosperity, Protection, Peace and SeaGoddess Castle.

"Please," Esmerelda orders, "do not open any compartments until instructed here and at each Goddess Activation Station up the mountain."

## Sunday, Day 1

One open compartment holds a satin eye-covering, the kind used for sleeping. And on the velvet-covered top interior of the box, two hooks hold a beautiful charm bracelet.

"Please place the bracelet on your left wrist," Esmerelda says. "With every stop up the mountain, you'll receive a charm symbolizing your power in that area. For now, notice the charms for The Biss Tribe, along with crystals that help attune you to a vibrational frequency that activates your GoddessPower."

Jingles echo through the room as the Concierges place bracelets on each woman's left wrist.

"Wear this bracelet with pride," Biss says. "It symbolizes your commitment to this life mission that is bigger and bolder than most people dare to attempt. You're here because you've finally chosen to do *you*, Goddess!"

Claps and cheers rock the room.

"Why is this experience so powerful?" Biss asks. "Because Infinity Mountain sits on a spiritual vortex. Under the earth are massive deposits of iron and crystal, which charge the energy here with a supernatural forcefield of healing and transformation. Do you feel it?"

"Really strong," says Bianca, sitting on her throne with her wheelchair parked by a back wall, "as soon as the bus pulled up to the Inn. Gives me chills."

"Me, too," Delaney adds, "like the earth is pulling the negative energy from my body. I feel extremely mellow, and I'm usually quite high-strung."

Several women nod.

"Now that you have your *PowerJournals*," Biss says, "you'll be chronicling your experiences here—including vivid and possibly prophetic dreams—along with the exercises we'll be doing every step of the way. So, write how you're feeling."

## Welcome to The Biss Tribe

Biss holds up a *PowerJournal*. "In this, you'll be writing the guidebook for the new you. Our *PowerJournal* method here in The Biss Tribe promises to make the rest of your life... the best of your life. It's the blueprint for the realm you're going to create. It will also serve as a guiding light to illuminate your hope and determination when the shadows inevitably try to pull you back into **the way you were—and will never be again** after this."

"I receive *that!*" Zeusse exclaims.

Marla raises a hand. "*Ugh*, do I have to write by hand?"

"Yeah," Sammie says. "Don't you have laptops so we can type?"

"Yuck, handwriting is so much work!" Jade gripes.

Biss shakes her head. "I get it. I type 90 words a minute, like lightning. However, when it comes to manifesting and activating your GoddessPower, the physical act of handwriting is far more powerful, because it synchronizes energy between your brain, body and spirit, all beginning the physical manifestation of your GoddessVision as words on paper. Trust me. It works!"

A few women groan.

Biss looks annoyed. "I *said*, it works! And that takes *work.*" She points to the window. "Everybody out there in the world is looking for a magic pill, a quick fix, a shortcut! I'm here to testify, the magic pill might make you sick. The quick fix might cause even bigger problems later on. And the shortcut might get you lost."

The room is silent as Biss casts a piercing stare at you and each woman. "If becoming the supernatural superstar version of yourself were easy, you'd already be her. But you're not. Yet! So, buckle your seatbelts and let's make it happen! Are you with me?"

Celeste looks around. "Sister-girls, Biss couldn't be more right! Let's do this work!"

"True that," Zeusse says.

"I'm in," Bianca adds.

## Sunday, Day 1

Biss points to the door, where three Amazonesque security guards are standing. "Anybody who's *not* willing to do the work can leave now. Our security team can take you to the airport."

The women are silent and still.

"The key word here is activation," Biss says. "And our voices have the power to activate our GoddessPower. That's why every morning and every night, we recite The GoddessPower Promise."

Sammie whispers to Marla: "I like sitting here on my throne, eating and receiving gifts. Reciting a double daily monologue sounds like too much work—"

Biss casts a piercing stare at Sammie. "I'll say it again. Anyone who is unwilling to do the work to change, needs to board the bus back to the airport, right now. And no, you don't get a refund, honey. You came here because you're ready to stop fucking around and letting your dreams die inside you, while you suffer from your own self-sabotage."

Biss points toward the doors leading to the lobby. "So please leave now if you'd like to return to the drudgery of your daily reality—even if it's glamorous on the surface—that prompted you to join The Biss Tribe in the first place."

Everyone is quiet. Sammie stays put.

"Now, in your GoddessTreasure Chest," Biss says, "you'll find six mini scrolls, each secured with a purple satin ribbon. Please take out the first one and open it."

The rippling and unrolling of thick parchment paper punctuates the still-tense silence.

"Now," Biss says, walking from table to table while looking directly at each woman, "the work begins. You're holding a scroll with The GoddessPower Promise. This is the daily commitment that we live by. We recite it morning and night. To make it more impactful, we'll go into the recording studio at SeaGoddess Castle at the conclusion of this experience for those who make it, to record with your own voice, The GoddessPower Promise, as well as your GoddessLife Script that you'll compose in your *PowerJournal*."

Esmerelda, who's also walking around, leaving a gentle waft of jasmine in her wake, adds, "Ladies, The GoddessPower Promise contains some wording that may seem unfamiliar, but over the coming days, you'll understand it."

Biss nods. "It's the first step to reprogram your mind with your own voice. Let's start by reciting The GoddessPower Promise in unison. This is the overview. You'll learn a new section at each stop up Infinity Mountain."

She raises her arms and smiles. "In other words, my beautiful Goddesses, get ready to make some magic happen!" Without reading from a scroll, she leads the group in reciting the Promise, which also appears on the screen behind her:

# The GoddessPower Promise

*Your Name*

---

I am Goddess: a woman who has ignited the infinite power of my mind, body and spirit—and uses it for the betterment of myself, my family, all living beings and Mother Earth.

I take aggressive, strategic action each day to fortify the solid foundation of my GoddessLife to build my personal and professional realm upon the five foundations of Power, Pleasure, Prosperity, Protection and Peace.

## Sunday, Day 1

I understand that the essence of GoddessPower is pure energy, and that I have the ability to use the energy of my thoughts, my words, my actions and my spiritual practices to transmute this energy and manifest the best possible outcomes for myself and people everywhere.

I know that the key to unlocking my ultimate Goddess potential requires that I slay the most vexing and vicious demons of my mind, body and spirit which have blocked my ability to soar into my limitless potential.

Once I slay these demons—by using my GoddessPower tools to hunt and heal these demons within—I can then fully unveil my greatest gifts, talents and abilities that are unique to me, so I can use them and present them to the world in ways that enrich all of humanity.

I am worthy of living and loving with limitlessness in every area of my existence, as created by a mindset, a code of conduct, a lifestyle and a spiritual practice that launch me above and beyond barriers to creating my personal empire built on the pillars of Power, Pleasure, Prosperity, Protection and Peace.

Each morning and night, I recite my GoddessPower Promise to remind myself that every moment of every day, I am thinking, speaking and behaving in ways that create the life that I desire and deserve.

This activates my female superpowers to transform me from the inside out, to ignite the fire of my spirit—that starburst of GoddessPower within me—and that helps me blast past any barriers. That enables me to partake of all the best life has to offer in a realm of prosperity and pleasure that is divinely protected. It means I serve myself, my loved ones and the world with an important mission that helps people everywhere.

I know that Goddess means being a bad ass woman. A boss. A bold, brave bitch when necessary. It means I boss up to myself and my life, to create the empire that I rule with a crown of confidence from a throne of power.

This is my divine birthright. I claim it. I believe it. I know it. I live it. Because I am infinite and unstoppable in my GoddessPower.

*Dear Goddess Reader:*

*Please record The GoddessPower Promise by reading it with your own voice into the video or audio app on your phone, then listen to it privately when you first wake up in the morning, during the day and at night as you fall asleep.*

*If you'd rather hear Biss reading it to you, just scan this QR code:*

GoddessPower Tools

## Sunday, Day 1

When you and the 21 women finish reciting The GoddessPower Promise, you sip water and pause.

"Did you feel that?" Biss asks. "The explosive energy that each of you exudes into a collective magic that's booming through this ballroom! It's the perfect segue for tomorrow at the GoddessPower Pyramid."

The room feels infused with mellow energy as Biss looks directly at you.

"You're going to walk away from this experience transformed like never before," she says. "And it all starts in the mind, with words like those we just spoke. Before you know it, especially after you start listening to The GoddessPower Promise recorded in your own voice, you'll commit this to memory, and when a situation occurs, the right words will pop into your mind to provide the courage to stay on your metaphoric throne to stay in your power as you resolve whatever situation may arise."

Delaney sighs. "I want to take a shower in these words every day until they saturate me down to the bone."

Andi looks disturbed. "I can recite all this 'til I'm blue in the face. But it feels lofty and unrealistic, and I know I'm gonna catch hell from people who want me to keep conforming to the meek, mild doormat I've been all my life." She balls a fist. "That makes me feel so damn mad, man."

Biss strides quickly toward Andi, casting an empathetic gaze into her eyes. "I hear you! I see you. I know how you feel. I'm here to testify that you *can* become everything we just recited. I used to be that furious people-pleaser who had no boundaries. I was miserable. Even *sick* from it! But here's how you start to change. With the tools you're about to learn. Then people will start to respect you and treat you better. Trust that."

Andi rakes a hand through her hair and squeezes her eyes shut; tears roll down her cheeks as her fists remain balled tightly in her lap.

## Touring Valley Village

As Concierge serves your favorite desert and accompanying beverage, and you indulge unapologetically, the lights dim and the screen lights up.

"My Goddesses, let's go on a virtual tour of Valley Village," Biss says, while video whizzes you along the dusty, dirty streets of a medieval town whose gray-beige buildings create a somber feeling. "This is not a real place, but the symbolism and metaphors are a good way to explain where too many women see themselves when they come here."

The screen shows a glimmering ballroom. "This is SeaGoddess Castle, and we're going to help you catapult from your metaphoric Valley Village up to the grandeur of this—" Biss says as the screen flashes video of castle towers, then a terrace offering spectacular views of the sea and sky "—by providing the tools to rise from struggles to success."

You savor the dessert, one of the best you've ever had.

Video of the somber town reappears on the screen as Biss says, "This is the proverbial village of despair in the shadow of a mountain where the peak holds all the promises of your happiest life. Though the peak is attainable, many of us have felt like poor peasants, trapped and oppressed in a system run by other people—or worse, by our own thoughts and behaviors."

The screen flashes to a creepy-looking medieval metal helmet over a woman's head and face.

# Sunday, Day 1

"Sometimes," Biss says, "we wear a heavy, restrictive helmet of fear, shame, guilt and worthlessness. It blocks our vision, holds us down, causes headaches and amplifies our negative self-talk."

On the screen, hands remove the helmet and place a gold crown sparkling with jewels on the woman's head. She smiles.

"Ladies," Biss says, "I want to replace that restrictive helmet with your rightful crown of power. That will happen at SeaGoddess Castle at the end of this experience."

Next, the screen shows a woman wearing dull clothing. She's sitting on a splintered, wobbly chair in a dim, candle-lit room as she gazes sadly out through a half-shuttered window at a garbage-strewn alley.

"It's time to glow up and leave lack and discomfort in the past," Biss says as a large, velvet-lined throne—like the one you're sitting on now—appears on the screen. "And sit in your power, literally and figuratively."

Next, video shows haggard, despondent women scrubbing floors, cooking over bubbling pots on open fires, tending to large families and toiling in fields on farms. Close-ups show their scarred hands, some with fresh blood and wounds.

"Often we as women miserably work ourselves to the bone with little reward," Biss says. "These images are symbolic of the endless work we do, taking care of everyone and everything, neglecting the most important person in your life. You."

"I'm here to testify!" Celeste whispers. "That is my story!"

The women are rapt. The room is silent and still.

"Here, now," Biss says, "is where all of the above will change. Let your transformation begin! Here's proof."

Video shows a woman with a bruised eye and bloody lips.

"This was Laila, shortly before she came here," Biss says as a photo of Laila at The Biss Tribe Inn leads into video of her as a well-dressed woman in a sleek office, leading a board meeting, looking online at a seven-figure bank account, driving a luxury convertible, traveling in an exotic place, exercising, meditating, and laughing with people over a decadent meal at an opulent restaurant.

"Laila built a multi-million-dollar business by training survivors of domestic abuse as her staff," Biss says. "Her pain became her power, just like Sarah."

The next video clip shows a woman in a hospital bed attached to a heart monitor, as a doctor says, "You had a heart attack from stress."

A photo of Sarah at The Biss Tribe Inn fades into video of her—happy and healthy, leading a yoga class under palm trees on a beach, in front of a resort called Sarah's Sanctuary.

"She transformed her trauma to create a yoga retreat center that specializes in helping stressed-out women," Biss says.

After that, video shows an exhausted, unhappy woman. "Janelle was a burned-out schoolteacher," Biss says, "whose big ideas for improving education were ignored by bureaucrats." Then a photo of Janelle at The Biss Tribe Inn leads into video of her cheering with happy children in front of The Janelle School.

"So she got a loan and opened a school of her own," Biss says. "These women excelled here in The Biss Tribe. Like hundreds of women initiated into The Biss Tribe through this program, they catapulted up and out of the hell of their own Valley Village to launch a personal and professional Goddess empire. This destiny is yours, living in joy and fulfillment while handling all your responsibilities and experiencing your wildest dreams, on *your* terms."

Next, video shows a beautiful woman and man on a palace balcony that's overflowing with flowers. The woman's stunning evening gown looks very uncomfortable, and she's gazing into the distance with a sad expression as the man stares in the opposite direction.

## Sunday, Day 1

"And even those who appear to have it all," Biss says, "money, marriage, kids, a beautiful home, career success—can still feel that something is missing. They're trapped in a gilded cage, aching to express their authentic selves and be free."

The video screen shows Sasha Maxwell in her *QueenPower Show* studio. Its white brick walls are backlit with pink light as Sasha—who has radiant butterscotch skin framed by an afro-esque burst of gold-bronze-brown-platinum corkscrew curls—speaks into a microphone, interviewing an attractive man and woman, while her tattooed engineer works the sound board.

"For those of you who watch and or listen to my podcast," Biss says, "then you *must* know Sasha Maxwell, creator and host of *The QueenPower Show with Sasha Maxwell*."

"We love her!" Marla shouts as most of the women's hands shoot up. "We've learned so much about dating and relationships from her show."

Biss beams. "Sasha is one of our greatest success stories here in The Biss Tribe. Shortly after her horrible divorce, one of our benefactors sponsored her tuition here, where she wrote her GoddessVision to launch her show and write her best-selling books."

The women are rapt as Biss continues: "And within 11 months, Sasha landed a $50 million deal with Meteor Multimedia, the world's most influential video podcast streaming platform. She also liberated her sexuality, as you may have read in her book, *Eleven Men*. It was published by my company, Two Sisters Writing & Publishing®, and it's about her quest to enjoy 11 lovers after suffering that many years of sexual deprivation in her bad marriage."

Jade raises her hand. "I read it, and now I'm reading her next book, *Eleven Women*. It's pure fire! Like she says, you need gloves to hold the book, so you don't burn your fingers."

Celeste fans herself. "She has a way of describing the act! And her First Love story in *Eleven Men*—whew! I wore my husband out after I read that one. I don't know if I'm having a hot flash or if I'm just hot thinking about that book."

Biss holds up a *PowerJournal*. "My Goddesses, I can't emphasize enough the importance of writing your life story. You'll actually compose major passages right now as you journal here, so record as many thoughts, feelings and ideas as you can while you're in the vortex of Infinity Mountain. Every Goddess needs a book, especially after you build your empire and people keep asking how you did it. You can share your blueprint in your book."

Delaney's face flashes angst and excitement all at once. "I've been trying to write my memoirs for decades. But I gave up, because something has been telling me it could never be good enough and that no one would read it."

Biss shakes her head. "Write that book! Every Goddess needs a book! Tell your story. Share your knowledge!" Biss flashes a smile. "Esmerelda, should I share the surprise now?"

"Yes!" Sammie shouts.

Esmerelda smiles and nods.

"Tomorrow at the Power Pyramid, our guest speaker at the GoddessPower Feast will be—" Biss cups her hand behind her ear and raises her eyebrows.

"Sasha Maxwell!?!?" Marla shrieks as the women explode with cheers and clapping.

"Yes, Sasha Maxwell, our superstar graduate who was just named one of the 100 most influential women in the world, will tell you first-hand how she did it, and how you can, too. Who's ready for *that?*"

You join the women's voices thundering through the ballroom.

"You can make that happen here!" Biss shouts. "Repeat after me: Power! Pleasure! Prosperity! Protection! Peace!"

The women repeat each word like a roar that seems to make the walls shake.

"Yes, let's do this!" Biss cheers. "So, let's get started! Follow me." She jumps off the stage and dashes toward the terrace doors. "Bring your *PowerJournal*, your pen and all your heart's desires."

# Fly up to SeaGoddess Castle

As you join the women gathering around Biss at the doors, she says, "Ladies, the word 'intention' gets tossed around a lot these days. But we have to set our intention for our mission. We have to focus on a very clear vision of our destination. We have to see it with crystal clarity, before we can reach it."

She steps through the doors and leads you onto the terrace. And there you see, at the top of the mountain—a spectacular castle in the sunshine.

"That," Biss exclaims proudly, "is SeaGoddess Castle. Our destination. Come!"

"Oh, hell *yeah!*" Zeusse exclaims.

"Wow," Celeste sighs. "That's so beautiful I could cry."

"I am!" Bianca says. "I can't believe it. I feel like Cinderella."

"It's real," Andi says, "and it looks like we're goin' up there!"

"I feel like Alice in Wonderland," Jade exclaims. "But I don't want to go home and feel like after you visit Disney World, where it was all a fantasy, an escape, and you're back to the reality that you hate."

"I'm with you on that, mama," Sammie says.

Biss and Esmerelda lead you down a staircase across an emerald lawn to a small tarmac where four jumbo helicopters await. The security guards follow. But several women stop in their tracks when they realize you're supposed to board the aircraft as Biss is doing.

"Whoah!" Sammie shrieks. "I didn't sign up to get on a helicopter up a mountain! That shit was not in the brochure!"

"That's freaking terrifying," Marla says. "I am literally shaking!"

Concierges appear out of nowhere and say, "Come, you will be fine. You are safe. Fear not."

They take your hands to help you and everyone on board. They lift Bianca in her wheelchair and secure it in a designated space.

Marla looks nervous. "Oh my God, my stomach is flipping," she says over the noise as you ascend.

In a very short time, you land in a forest-lined field that doesn't feel like a mountaintop, except that your ears have popped and as you disembark, the air is cooler and smells like fresh forest.

"Ladies, follow me," Biss says, leading you along a stone-lined path that feels like a tunnel of trees because the woods are so thick, they form a canopy overhead. Afternoon sunshine filters through them to create an emerald-green haze.

"This is so enchanting," Delaney sighs. "I feel an even stronger magnetic pull in my body, like the earth in this higher elevation is detoxing the tension from my cells."

"Not me!" Sunshine quips, glancing around nervously. "My nerves are jumping. Some animals could be lurking in those woods!"

Finally, you reach a clearing. Biss turns around to face you and says, "Ladies, welcome to SeaGoddess Castle!"

Several women gasp as you all behold the castle.

"This feels surreal," Celeste says, "like we've stepped into another dimension. And I *love* it!"

"I'm definitely dreaming," Jade says. "Somebody pinch me."

Zeusse gently pinches Jade's arm and says, "You ain't dreamin', sweetheart."

## Sunday, Day 1

"Come," Biss says as you follow her and Esmerelda across the grass, up a grand stone staircase, to a terrace. You and the women line the stone banister, staring out at the deep blue ocean that's glistening under the bright blue sky. Pink and gold clouds shroud the horizon.

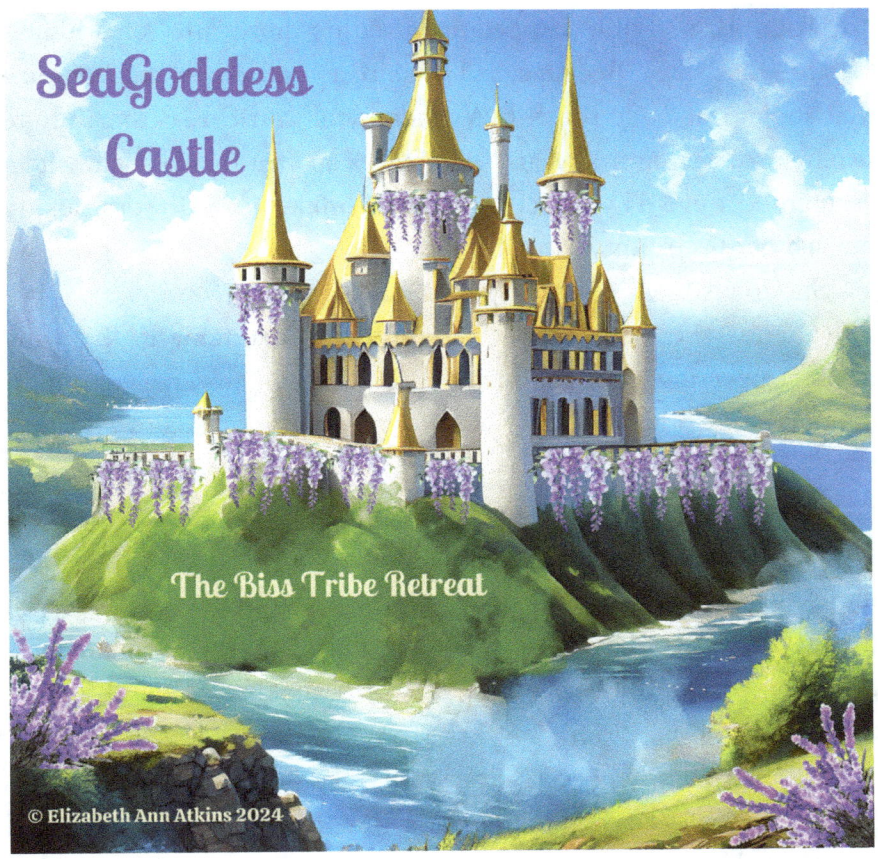

"This is why we call it SeaGoddess Castle," Biss says. "It has double meaning. When you look out at the sea and sky, you can see into infinity. Endless water. Endless sky. It's symbolic of the Goddess energy inside you. Imagine that your entire being is shimmering the same way the sunshine is sparkling like tiny diamonds on the water."

You and the women stare silently out at the water.

"My beautiful Goddesses," Biss says, "this is where the magic happens." She steps to the banister, facing you and the women, with the endless blue water and ocean behind her.

"Your Biss Tribe experience begins here in SeaGoddess Castle," Biss says, "because, as I've said, it symbolizes your empire that looks out over the S-E-A where you can S-E-E the infinite expanse of sea and sky just as clearly as you can envision it in your mind's eye as you activate your female superpowers during our ascent up Infinity Mountain."

She turns toward giant open doors.

"Come," she says, almost skipping with excitement. "It's time to start creating your blueprint to build your empire, your metaphoric SeaGoddess Castle where you rule your realm and love your life."

As you step through huge doorways into a long hallway that seems ancient and modern all at once, you marvel at the enormous dimensions that feel otherworldly. Sunbeams shoot down through stained-glass windows, each patterned in the form of a goddess from cultures around the world, making colorful formations on the stone floor.

"I feel so happy here," Bianca marvels. "I want to live here!"

You follow Biss and Esmerelda into a white marble-floored ballroom. Huge crystal chandeliers sparkle from the high, gilded ceiling. Golden sunshine beams through tall windows over enormous fireplaces whose mantles are carved with goddesses, flowers, ivy, lions and cherubs.

Centering the room is a giant, round, gold table surrounded by 24 gilded throne chairs, with high backs made of wood carved with goddesses, cherubs, ivy vines and lions. Cushions of jewel-toned

## Sunday, Day 1

velvet—red, purple, emerald, cobalt blue and gold—cover the high back and seat of each throne. On the table, a velvet pillow displays a gold crown in front of each chair.

The Concierges guide you to a throne marked by a sign scrolled with your name. They place your GoddessTreasure Chest in front of you and each woman. As everyone sits on her throne, and Bianca is lifted into hers, you get comfortable on the plush seat that's large enough to sit with your legs crossed.

The six security guards stand near the doors and by the fireplace with a view of the doors and entire room. Biss and Esmerelda stand behind their thrones, facing each of you.

"Ladies," Esmerelda says, "please get comfortable, but don't touch the crown. That's your reward if you survive the journey back up here. You have to earn it."

Zeusse lets out a cynical, "Uh-huh. Always a catch. They're talking a good game. But what if it doesn't work?"

"Hey, sis," Jade says, "I'm game to try anything to escape my miserably mediocre life back home."

"Escape!" Celeste exclaims. "That's the key word here. You know it's bad when you're thinking, *Where is the escape hatch from my own life?*"

Delaney groans. "Been there, despised it."

You stare at the crown, imagining it on your head, even for a moment.

"I feel super disconnected from reality," Jade says.

"Yeah," Sunshine says sadly, "like we're in an impossible dream."

"I gave up on the fairy tale a looooong time ago," another woman says.

"A fantasy world," Andi moans.

Biss looks directly at you and several women. "I know what you're thinking. Too many of us women suffer with insecurities and lack of self-worth that make the idea of wearing a crown seem like a little girl's fantasy—not a grown woman's reality."

Groans of agreement rumble from the women around the table.

"That's exactly how I feel," Sunshine says.

"Me, too," Delaney says.

"I feel massive resistance right now," Andi adds. "Like, royalty? That's not me. I don't deserve it."

"Yes!" Biss exclaims, "Yes, you *do* deserve it!"

She makes eye contact with each woman.

"Guess what, my Goddesses! Wearing this crown—literally and symbolically—is your divine birthright! So if you're having any doubt about being worthy of the regal power implied by a crown, you're about to have a massive mind-shift, and your life will follow. It's not decided by what you were born into, or where your life is now. It's decided by your decision to tap into the supernatural power of God, Goddess, Universe, Spirit... and live as the supernatural being that you can become!"

Esmerelda, standing beside Biss, adds, "As you succeed at each Goddess Activation Station, you'll receive a powerful crystal. Then, if you make it back to SeaGoddess Castle for The Biss Tribe Initiation, your five stones will be fixed to your crown. If you continue your Goddess journey with our Intensives, you have the chance to earn a diamond."

Jade says, "My family is gonna think I lost my mind, walking around with a crown on my head."

"Do it, girlfriend!" Marla cheers. "Our families already know we're cray-cray."

Sunshine stares longingly at the crown and tells the group, "I am so struggling with the idea of wearing a crown."

Andi nods. "You're not alone on that one, lady."

Esmerelda casts a tender stare at Sunshine. "I thought exactly that when I first came here. I was so beaten down and defeated. I'd lost my family in an earthquake, escaped an abusive husband, and recovered from an eating disorder that almost killed me. I was so lost when I came to The Biss Tribe. And when I found myself here, I stayed."

Esmerelda glows with peace. "So for now, just think of the crown as symbolic. In everyday life, you'll wear a crown of GoddessPower that's physically invisible, but conveys your sovereignty over yourself and your life, and people will respond accordingly."

Biss nods, standing behind her throne. "Are any of you wondering why we're starting our journey at our destination? Or why you're sitting on a throne at a RoundTable, staring at a crown?"

"To get us excited?" asks Bianca, who was lifted by her Concierge into her throne.

"Close," Biss says. "We brought you here to see, feel and touch our destination at the end of this week-long experience. And we brought you here so you can know where we're going, to imprint it in your mind, heart and soul, then reverse-engineer how to navigate back here, and stay."

Esmerelda gets seated in her throne and adds, "The objective is to envision your dream life, write out a strategy and script to make it real, record it, and take it home to make it happen."

# Introductions & Intentions: Baring Your Soul in The Biss Tribe Class #88

Biss smiles, walking around the table and making eye contact with you and each woman as she talks. "Goddesses, it's time to officially express why you're here. You're here because you're tired of sacrificing your time, your energy and your dreams under the pressures of all that's put on us, and that we take on, and that we allow to suck the life out of us until it's too late to do anything about it.

"You're here to *finally* make a change that catapults you up and out of the drudgery of your current reality, even if it sparkles on the outside, so that you're living and loving as the Goddess who loves herself, her life and the mission she's leading in the world."

The women are silent, watching Biss and looking around at the grandeur of the ballroom.

"So, let's learn who's in your class of The Biss Tribe here on Infinity Mountain," Biss says, "starting with introductions. Look around at this group of 22 amazing women. You are the very auspicious class number 88 of The Biss Tribe. The number eight is the infinity symbol, so that's double infinity for all of you. So I expect extraordinary things from each one of you."

Biss looks you straight in the eye, then scans the group. "This is your sisterhood, a secret sorority, where you're bonding, exposing your deepest selves in *complete secrecy*. Remember, you signed an NDA as part of your registration."

Several women nod.

"That Non-Disclosure Agreement is just a piece of paper," Biss says. "Because what happens in The Biss Tribe, stays in The Biss Tribe. It's a karmic thing. Anyone who violates the trust of our sisters here in this room, by *ever* speaking a single word about any of us out in the world, will not only be in legal violation of the Non-Disclosure Agreement, but worse, you will be in violation of the spiritual laws that bind us."

Biss casts a threatening stare at each woman. "Remember Newton's Third Law of Physics, which says that for every action, there's an equal and opposite reaction? Think about that in everything you do. And when you're dealing with Spirit, you don't want to mess with that."

## Sunday, Day 1

"Whoah, whoah!" Andi runs a nervous hand through her hair. "Biss, that sounds like a threat. Like you're a witch or something, casting a spell on us. Freaks me the hell out, man."

"True that," Zeusse says as several women nod and whisper, "Yeah."

Biss casts a hard stare at Andi, then glances at the women. "Take it how you want. I didn't make this up. I'm just stating the metaphysical laws. A few years ago, a woman violated the NDA by doing a national TV interview that exposed incriminating information about her Biss Tribe sisters. Before this woman left the TV station, she collapsed and was rushed to the hospital. Her appendix had burst, and emergency surgery saved her life. That was karma, baby."

The women are silent and still.

"Creepy!" Marla whispers.

"Scary AF," Jade says.

"So," Biss says, "if you want a safe space to heal and grow, then honor the rules and cultivate an environment of absolute trust. Think about this: Do you want to expose yourself and get the help you need here, if you know someone will expose you?"

"Hell no!" Zeusse exclaims. "One wrong word and social media blows up and every sportswriter out there would chew me up and spit me out. It's happened too many times."

Marla raises a hand. "My ethics professor in college always said, 'Integrity means doing the right thing when nobody is watching.'"

Sammie nods. "Yeah, and karma isn't a bitch, like they say. Karma is actually a mirror reflecting all the bad shit you did in the past that's coming back to kick your ass."

"Amen, sista!" Celeste exclaims.

Biss still looks serious. "Does everybody understand the importance of confidentiality and trust here? Let's go around the table so each of you can say 'yes' out loud."

Marla quips. "This feels like kindergarten."

Biss casts a hard look at her. "Do it anyway."

Marla crosses her arms. "Women have fucked me up in the past. Trusting strangers, especially women, is not a thing for me."

Several women moan in agreement.

"Your GoddessPower activation requires teamwork," Biss says. "The magic of our method here is to harness the collective energy of everyone in this room, as well as the spiritual vortex here on Infinity Mountain."

"Use it or lose it, bitches," Sammie says, eliciting a few nervous laughs around the table.

Marla huffs. "I feel like I'm fucked if I don't do something drastic to change myself. So I'll *try*."

"To try implies potential failure," Biss snaps. "Your answer should be yes."

"Yes," says. Sammie high-fives her, then says, "Yes."

Biss nods at Delaney, who's beside Marla, and says, "Delaney?"

"Yes."

"Now let's go around the table, starting to your left."

"Yes," Bianca says. Then every woman says, "Yes," ending with you.

Biss walks slowly around the table as she talks. "Now it's time for each of you to share why you're here. Tell us what vexing things you need to conquer here in The Biss Tribe. Those inner demons within that you need to slay, by finally cracking the code on yourself that's been robbing you of Power, Pleasure, Prosperity, Protection and Peace all these years. Then state the intention for who you want to be—the happiest, most liberated, wildest version

## Sunday, Day 1

of yourself and your life—and what your empire entails. Who wants to start us off?"

Zeusse buries her face in her large hands and exhales loudly. "OK, I got this," she says, raising her head and wiping her eyes with her fingers.

"First, who is the most liberated version of myself that I want to bring out of my head and heart and into the world? I already *was* her when I helped our team win the WNBA Championship. That moment on live TV when I was holding the trophy in my hand and the team was lifting me up in the air, I felt like I had conquered the world. My confidence was through the roof. I felt fierce."

Zeusse shakes her head. "But now, my problem is confidence. For some reason, out on my own, tryin' to start my girls basketball academy to create the next superstars, I'm scared as hell. Procrastinating. Paralyzed from taking action."

She glances at the other women. "I survived some bad shit in my life. That ball in my hand pulled me up from the dirty bottom to the top of the world. Now God is telling me to help other girls do that. But I'm frozen. With fear. So why is this so hard?"

**Zeusse sits up straighter. "Bottom line, I came here to get my courage and confidence to build my empire: The Zeusse Girls Basketball Academy. I want at least one in every state, then we'll expand internationally."**

"Excellent!" Biss exclaims, standing near Zeusse and looking directly at her. "What's coming to mind is, perhaps you work better with a team in business as well, so you could assemble a team of trusted women, maybe former players, to achieve your goal."

Zeusse's eyes widen and her face glows with revelation. "Day-um, Biss, I never thought of that. My whole body feels like I just got struck by lightning."

"Welcome to the magic of The Biss Tribe at SeaGoddess Castle," Biss says, beaming.

## Welcome to The Biss Tribe

"Now Zeusse, open your *PowerJournal* to the GoddessMission page. You'll see lines for writing. Write a brief summary of the mission you just described," Biss says. "Everybody, do the same, and be ready to write after you speak."

You turn to the page that says "My GoddessMission."

"Zeusse," Biss says over the sound of turning pages, "write every detail that's coming to mind right now for the team you need to start your academies, and keep writing for the duration of the trip. That's for all of you."

Biss extends her arms. "You're in the GoddessVortex, which is a powerful dimension that heals and empowers you."

"Is the vortex the mountain or the castle or what?" Marla asks.

"All of the above," Biss says. "Because the crystal beds under Infinity Mountain elevate your vibration to tap into your divine guidance, as does our collective energy. So like Sammie just said, 'use it or lose it.'"

Biss winks at Sammie, who smiles.

Zeusse starts writing in her *PowerJournal*. "Hold up, though. I don't always trust working with females in business. I've been burned—"

"Then you ask God/Goddess/Spirit/Universe to bring only women you know, like and trust to join your team," Biss says. "Ask Spirit to reveal these women to you. Goddess Zeusse, you have the power to make that magic happen here in The Biss Tribe!"

Jade raises her hand, which is shaking along with her voice: "I don't know why I'm so wrecked right now. Like so raw inside. And hurting. Sad. Hopeless. Zeusse summed me up, too. When I play in my girl band, I'm on top of the world. As guitarist for The Star Chix, I am *that bitch*. She's my alter ego. My GoddessPower self. It *is* supernatural, because the music comes from somewhere bigger than me, and it does feel magical."

## Sunday, Day 1

Jade sniffles. "But as soon as I put down my guitar and step off stage, I feel like I have no purpose in life. I'm just another disillusioned Millennial working a soul-sucking day job at a mortgage company." She reaches for the tissue box on the table.

"I literally wake up in the morning and wonder, *why am I even alive?* The world is so fucked up, and I'm doing nothing to improve it, except play in my band. I'm 35 fucking years old and feel like *suuuuuuch* a loser." She presses tissues to her eyes.

"And I just *haaayyyyyte* that my parents drilled into me that I need a quote 'real job.'" She makes air quotes with her fingers. "That I can't just be in a girl band as my full-time gig. That I can't be 60 years old still playing in a girl band. And I'm like, look at Stevie Nicks! Tina Turner! Diana Ross! Madonna! They've rocked it to 60 and beyond. But something inside me won't let me let go of my parents's day-job concept. And that being a creative isn't a legit life purpose."

Jade shakes her head. "My worst nightmare is ending up like my boring, conformist mom and dad and my classmates from the private school they sent me to, where kids grow up to be clones of their boring vanilla parents."

She runs her fingertips up the green vines and goddesses tattooed on her arms, then tugs at strands of her pink hair.

**"So I came here to find my purpose in life,"** Jade says. **"I need to stop feeling so lost and do something meaningful to help people. In a way that frees me as a creative. Pretty much, I want to quit my job and travel the world with The Star Chix and make our band something that is a positive force in the world."**

Biss nods. "It sounds like your music is your GoddessGenius Zone. So we need to explore what's blocking you from building your empire around that."

Jade nods. "I know, but I don't know how."

## Welcome to The Biss Tribe

"Stay tuned, you'll know soon," Biss says. "Goddess Jade, you have the power to make that magic happen here in The Biss Tribe!"

Celeste high-fives Jade. "Girl, you can do it! Zeusse, you too! As for me, Biss!? Can you please help me find the real Celeste up in this castle? I already filed a missing person's report on myself. Because she is *lost!* Somewhere along the way of the marriage, the kids, the career, the sorority, the boards I sit on, my church responsibilities, and taking care of my parents who both have dementia, I lost Celeste in the chaos of putting everyone and everything before me."

She closes her eyes. A tear rolls down her cheek. She wipes her puffy eyes with tissues.

"I am so damn exhausted. I feel unappreciated and unfulfilled. Yeah, my life looks fantastic on paper: big career, prominent husband and high-achieving kids. We have a fabulous home. We vacation in Fiji and Bali, places I didn't even know existed while growing up with lots of love but not enough money."

**Celeste shifts in her throne chair. "Now I'm 54 years old, and I'm terrified of getting to the end of life and feeling like I did everything for everybody but Celeste. So I came here to find myself, make self-care a top priority, and find the guts to retire from corporate life and open Celeste's Sweet Shop, a café and bakery specializing in cakes and pies."**

Biss nods. "Your Supernatural Self will tell you everything you need to know to make all of the above your blissful new reality. Goddess Celeste, you have the power to make that magic happen!"

Andi raises her hand. "Celeste, I'll be your first customer. I have a monster sweet tooth!"

Celeste smiles slightly with trembling lips, then presses the tissues to her eyes.

Andi's smile fades as she twists the rings around her fingers. "So, I'll be blunt. Never said this out loud to anyone, and I feel

## Sunday, Day 1

scared as fuck right now. I've been living a straight lie all my life. I told some of you, my husband of 20 years ran off with another dude. This, after I did the whole white-picket-fence-two-kids-and-a-dog routine and work-in-the-family-business thing to conform to what my family expected of me. My grandparents started the chain of hardware stores and it was the expectation that us kids all carry the torch."

Andi grimaces and shakes her head. "I feel like I wasted my life—all 61 frickin' years so far!—living for what other people wanted for me. Not my truth. Then I read this book that your company published, Biss. *Joyously Free! Stories and Tips to Live Your Truth as LGBTQ+ People, Parents and Allies* by Elizabeth Ann Atkins and Joanie Lindenmeyer. That gave me the final push to say *hell no* to living a lie for a single minute more, so I came here to figure out how to do me for the rest of my life. I wanna be *Joyously Free*, like the book says."

She clasps her fingers together. "I love my kids. They're grown and have their own kids now. But I never wanted a husband. I wanted a wife. Oh shit, saying that out loud feels so good, but man, I'm so worried about what my parents and aunts and uncles and cousins will think, even though living by their rules made me depressed as hell. Man, I hate that!"

**Andi exhales loudly. "So I came here to reinvent myself. To let the world know that Andrea Sullivan is now 'Andi,' who's proudly wearing the rainbow flag, and will only be with women from here on out,** *and* **will officially sell my portion of the family business to open my art studio on the beach and find my wife."**

"You got this!" Biss says. "Goddess Andi, you have the power to make that magic happen here in The Biss Tribe!"

Sunshine raises her hand. "Biss, can I go next?"

"Of course."

## Welcome to The Biss Tribe

"So, this whole time listening to all of you," she says, "I have chills. You've all said something that echoes in my soul for why I'm here. But let's start with that crown—" she points to the one in front of her "—it's like, how could *I* wear a crown? I don't feel worthy. And after all my struggles, with my business, with money, with men, with never knowing my mother, and as an Indigenous woman, how could I ever get to the place where I get everything that crown represents? I can fill my head with the fantasy of it, but my reality is that every blessing comes with a massive curse."

Sunshine's large, dark eyes—lined with perfect black-winged liner and thick, natural lashes—glisten with tears as she says softly, "People say I'm blessed with looking exotic, but that just attracts men who use and abuse me. People say I'm super talented as a life coach, but I've been struggling so long as an entrepreneur while I watch coaches explode on social media and make millions." She shakes her head. "I feel so overworked, underpaid, and desperate to find new clients, even though I get *amazing* results with people I work with."

A deep rose hue tinges her clear caramel skin, especially around her small nose, which she wipes with a clump of tissues.

"I'm so mad!" she exclaims, her deep voice echoing through the expansive, silent ballroom.

"I'm furious at life, and I take it out on myself. It's like I put myself on punishment, 24/7, spending so much time creating courses and content that I post—only to get ignored, or worse, harassed by trolls who say vile things to me as a Navajo woman. So much violence is targeted toward Indigenous women. So many are missing. And nothing is done about it. I know I'm a warrior in my spirit, but I'm so tired of trying and failing."

Sunshine glances at Marla and Sammie. "I know you girls are way younger than me—I'm 44, that's like twice your age!—but I

## Sunday, Day 1

don't know how you become social media influencers. I have all the skills, but I feel so ignored and invisible—"

"We can help you, mama," Sammie says eagerly as Marla smiles and nods at Sunshine.

"Thank you," Sunshine says, "but I think there's something inside me that's repelling success, and that's why I'm here." She fingers the hummingbird pendant on her turquoise necklace.

"Making it even worse," Sunshine says, "is that I'm a powerful spiritual being who can manifest in magical ways. Our last name means 'magic power.' My grandmother Nani was a healer in the Navajo Nation." Her voice quavers. "I miss her so much. She raised me after my mother died in childbirth. My mom was only 13 and had been—" she turns pale "—raped by a married man, a neighbor, who was 48. So, I was literally conceived in violence, in trauma, in a criminal act."

Sunshine sobs. "Nani prayed over me so much and used her healing powers on me, but she said it's an inside job, and that only I have the ability to heal my trauma. But I don't know how."

She wipes her eyes with tissues. "All this keeps a dark cloud over me, energetically, even when I can magically manifest something. Like the rich boyfriend who took me on luxurious trips, but then punched me while we were staying at a five-star resort in the Maldives."

Sunshine pulls her hair over one shoulder.

"Men!" she sighs. "My downfall. They always derail me. I mean, I *let* them distract and derail me, and it's so delicious while it's happening. Until it isn't, and it just destroys me." She glances around nervously.

"Maybe some of you can relate, but I'm an empath with an anxious attachment style and abandonment issues, and I attract narcissists. Being so intuitive, I always know the moment when they're cheating. I even get visions of them with other women, and it's so graphic, the visions wake me up at night."

Sunshine squeezes her eyes shut for a moment. "Then this horrible anxiety literally makes me sick, but I don't have the strength to walk away and go no contact, because I'm so desperate for love and attention. I let their love-bombing suck me back in, only to find myself sitting home alone crying the next time he's out cheating and ghosting me."

Several women groan.

Sunshine shakes her head, looking around sadly. "I'm sorry for this trauma dump, like I'm vomiting all this up on you. But I have no one to talk to. My gramma died last year. She left me her house, or I would be homeless. And my aunt gifted me with this trip. I feel like my dreams are now or never. Do or die." She sobs into tissues.

"Don't apologize here," Biss says, as she and Esmerelda walk to Sunshine and each touch one of her shoulders.

"Sunshine, we're going to help you," Biss says softly. "We have the tools. And these are your sisters. You—" Biss glances around at every woman "—are all safe to express your deepest pain, unapologetically. You're free to say things you've never spoken to a single soul."

Biss bends slightly to cast a loving gaze directly into Sunshine's eyes and says, "Leave the pain and all the disappointments of the past here on the mountain."

Then Biss addresses you and all the women: "All of you, feel the magic of Mother Nature suck the trauma and tragedy out of your blood and bones, right here, right now, and let's do the work to heal from the inside out, to activate your GoddessPower and shatter the outer shell that's imprisoning your Supernatural Self, so you can step away from this week and manifest all the best of what you're speaking today."

## Sunday, Day 1

**Sunshine grasps** Biss's and Esmeralda's hands on her shoulders, then closes her eyes with a deep inhale. "I'm ready to receive this. I came here to heal my ancestral trauma, find my self-worth, and activate my powers to be happy with myself, build a seven-figure coaching business, and attract a husband who's loving and faithful."

"Your story is so similar to mine," Biss says. "Believe me, your Supernatural Self is about to blaze and help you manifest everything you desire."

Sunshine sobs as Biss says, "Goddess Sunshine, you have the power to make that magic happen here in The Biss Tribe!"

Next, you raise your hand and share your story, and explain why you're here.

*Dear Goddess Reader:*
*Write the reason you're here, what inner issues you need to heal, and the huge goal you want to achieve:*

_____

_____

_____

_____

*Imagine that Biss looks at you and says, "Goddess _____, you have the power to make that magic happen here in The Biss Tribe!"*

Next, Bianca says, "Biss, I am so ADHD, hopping from one thing to the next, getting nowhere, spread too thin."

Bianca speaks really fast: "If it weren't for my assistant at work—I'm a therapist at a mental health clinic specializing in the anxiety epidemic among teen girls and young women—I would get nothing done. Paperwork, especially. I never finish what I start. Anything from reading a book to starting my nonprofit, it's called Amy's Oasis, to help girls with anxiety. Amy was my patient who chose suicide after she didn't get into Harvard like her parents wanted."

Bianca speaks even faster: "Inside my head is a hurricane, 'round the clock. Since the accident, the car crash, hit by a drunk driver—I've been in my chair for about 15 years now—I think my brain just went haywire to distract me from my daily physical pain and emotional rage that this happened to me. My husband divorced me because the accident crushed my pelvis and ruined my ability to have babies." She points to her cheek. "This scar was bright red as the stitches healed. He told me I looked like Frankenstein."

Bianca inhales deeply and lets out a long, sad sigh. "If it weren't for my career, losing myself in helping these girls, I'd be an absolute basket case. Or worse. So now, I'm here to find some mental peace. To slow down. Just to be OK with where I am in life. I love my job. My condo. My friends. My family. I'm good. On the outside."

**She exhales loudly. "On the inside, Bianca is a freaking tornado. Bianca needs to find peace and calm, and commit to finishing what I start, especially my non-profit center for girls, Amy's Oasis. Sounds simple. But it's been pretty damn impossible. Help me, Biss!"**

"You got this!" Biss says. "The Peace Garden will be especially healing for you. And Goddess Bianca, you have the power to make

## Sunday, Day 1

that magic happen, to find your inner peace and the power to open Amy's Oasis, here in The Biss Tribe!"

Bianca looks hopeful as tears stream down her face, just as a beam of light shoots through the high windows, illuminating her and Delaney beside her.

"My turn," Delaney says. "I'm a classic over-achiever who feels like nothing is ever good enough. I have five degrees, most of which are from Ivy League universities. I still teach one course on women's literature at Princeton University. I've traveled the world. I have a loving, long-term marriage with a man and we have an equal partnership. Our grown children and grandchildren are all healthy and thriving. But like Bianca, my problem is internal. I need to somehow convince myself that I am enough."

Delaney wipes her eyes with tissues. "I grew up with a narcissistic mother who always made me feel bad and wrong and utterly inadequate. Whether it was taking back my Hanukah gifts because I got one B on my report card, or telling me that I looked awkward and ugly as an excruciatingly self-conscious 13-year-old girl as I spoke in the synagogue at my *bat mitzvah*, or telling me that I married the wrong man and that our marriage would never last—" she dabs her eyes. "I still see and hear her in my head. But now that she's gone—"

**Delaney wipes her nose. "I came here to accept that I have done more than enough in this lifetime. I am 75 years old and want to enjoy mental peace and self-love."**

Delaney fingers her plain silver wedding band. "I guess what's eluded me all this time is true self love. Feeling good about who I am, what I've done, and what remains for the rest of my life. All the women in my family have lived independently past 100, in excellent health. **So hopefully I have a good 25 years—like this** *PowerJournal* **says—to make the rest of my life, the best of my life."**

## Welcome to The Biss Tribe

Biss smiles. "Goddess Delaney, you have the power to make that magic happen here in The Biss Tribe!"

Tears stream down Delaney's cheeks as she raises her hands in prayer position toward Biss.

Marla lets out a dramatic sigh. "So, Biss, thank you for threatening everybody about the confidentiality clause. It would kill me if the truth leaked out. Because I am the impostor syndrome queen. I would never admit this in public, but I came to you for help, Biss."

The room is silent with all eyes on Marla.

"I feel like such a fucking fraud," Marla says. "I have this wild and sexy brand as an influencer, and all my brand deals are for bikinis and clothing that show off my tits and ass and body. I get shit tons of cash just to show up for an appearance at a club or event. And I make millions. But the reality is that I'm a total prude. I'm 25 years old and I'm a virgin. Terrified to have sex. And I've never even had an orgasm, even by myself."

Marla casts a suspicious look at every woman around the table. "All you bitches better keep this to yourselves, like Biss said, because this could ruin me. And based on some of the things you've said, maybe you're looking at me like, *that bitch is such a spoiled idiot, complaining about nothing when she has everything.* But it's not nothing to me. I need to make the inside of me, match the outside of me."

She glances at Sammie, who's holding her hand as their forearms rest on the ornate silver and velvet arms of their throne chairs.

"What we do is so competitive," Marla says. "All I do is compare myself to other girls, other influencers, watching my numbers. Worrying about my brand deals. Compare-itis is horrible. It's all about the exterior. And I'm so fucked up inside, especially about sex, because my papa is a minister and my mother is the church's first lady. They're super Catholic, from the Philippines and our

## Sunday, Day 1

church community in LA that I grew up in is like that. They massively guilted me to stay a virgin until I marry. I had to pledge my purity and wear a promise ring. They said sex is a sin except if you're married trying to have kids."

Marla rolls her eyes. "Their favorite saying was, 'The devil loves to take God's little angel girls and turn them into whores who suffer in hell.' They said that girls who touch themselves are pushing a button in an elevator that takes you straight into a lake of fire and brimstone with gnashing of teeth and all that bullshit. They said whores get punished on earth, then burn in hell forever. I don't believe that stuff, but my body does."

Marla shakes her head and says, "So, when I grew up, I gave my parents and everyone in the church the ultimate 'fuck you' for fucking *me* up so bad. That's why I became a sexy influencer, to totally rebel against it. My parents disowned me, like I don't exist. But their brainwashing is still controlling me in a way that's really fucked up. And not literally."

Marla squeezes Sammie's hand and says, "I need to unlock my body from religious-guilt prison. That's why I'm here. I feel like this extreme experience is a last resort. Putting my phone in that little bag on the bus was freaking traumatic for me! Posting my pics and vids and vlogging everything I do every day is like eating and breathing. It's my job! And we're launching Samla Marmie, our skincare line, in two months and it has to be out-of-this-world successful."

Marla purses her lips. "This is so fucked up. So **I want my inner self to match my outer self. The biggest thing I need here in The Biss Tribe is to cleanse myself of the guilt and shame and threats from religious brainwashing, so I can free my mind and body to enjoy my sexuality and feel free to have sex if I want to, and actually enjoy physical pleasure. I feel like I have to liberate myself before Samla Marmie can really take off."**

## Welcome to The Biss Tribe

Biss casts an empathetic gaze at Marla. "I promise, you are in the best place to make this happen. Goddess Marla, you have the power to make that magic happen here in The Biss Tribe!"

Marla whispers, "Thank you, Biss." Sammie hugs her.

"I, on the other hand," Sammie says, "am the exact opposite. Chasing men is my favorite sport. But I always lose. As influencers, we go to the hottest parties from Miami to Monaco to Paris and Rio and LA. We meet the most gorgeous men, and I want them all. They're like yachts, sailing into my world, and I want to sail on every one of them."

Sammie shrugs. "I have zero shame in my game. I see a guy I want. I get him. And I love it. I am soooo happy when he's showering me with attention and gifts and wining and dining me in a new dress every night."

Marla nudges her and says, "Until!"

"Until the cycle starts," Sammie says. "I latch on like a hungry puppy. I have no boundaries, and get mad when these guys don't honor the boundaries I never set. They start to treat me like the bitch of the day. I'm like a new toy that they play with until they get bored with it, then throw it in the toybox while they go find new toys. I see their posts with hot girls... I'm so jealous and possessive... I text and call them a million times. I cry, I scream, I just go crazy. I become that crazy bitch who can't control herself."

Sammie buries her face in her hands, the glitter on the tips of her pink-pointed fingernails contrasting with her perfectly arched eyebrows.

She looks up. "These assholes, they cancel me like I don't exist. I'm so devastated. Then the next crush is my life raft, until I float into another storm and sink again."

Sammie glances around. "I was raised as a Southern Belle in beauty pageants and all that stuff. You all probably think I'm just a stupid spoiled brat. And I feel like my issue is so frivolous

## Sunday, Day 1

compared to what some of you are here for. But it's *my* issue. And it's making me sick. Literally. I just got diagnosed with an autoimmune disorder that my therapist says is triggered by my chaotic dating style. But I can't stop!"

Marla grabs a tissue box and thrusts a handful of tissues at Sammie, who blots her eyes, never smudging her perfect makeup.

Sammie sobs, her whole body shaking. "I have *massive* Daddy issues. My dad was always gone, working, and left me and Mom in our giant house. She made me into like her little doll, making me prance across pageant stages and perform until I quit so I could focus on college. Maybe that made me an attention whore. Because I missed the spotlight and got a new kind of attention from the hot frat guys and athletes on campus."

She sniffles loudly and wipes her eyes and nose. "I swear, men are my drug of choice. I feel so intoxicated when I get their attention. And I'm just like, sick, when they abandon from me. Literally vomiting in withdrawal, like our friend, this gorgeous model, when she quit heroin."

**Sammie sniffles and raises her head higher. "So Biss, I came here to recover from my man addiction, get centered with myself, and create a peaceful and intentional dating style to find my husband while Marla and I 100-X our brands and businesses and launch Samla Marmie."**

Biss nods. "As a former man addict who had an anxious attachment style that also made me ill, I'm proof that you can recover and take your power back. Goddess Sammie, you have the power to make that magic happen here in The Biss Tribe!"

Hope sparkles in Sammie's tear-filled eyes as she gazes up at Biss.

Kiki raises her hand. "Mine is short. As I've already said, I'm like a little boat that's sailing with no navigation system and no destination. Just randomly showing up here and there, stopping

## Welcome to The Biss Tribe

for awhile, feeling happy for a minute, then storming away, drifting to nowhere in life." She strokes her long braid that's draped over one shoulder, fastened in a way that allows the white tips to explode in loose waves.

"I'm the fugazi queen," she says.

"The foo what?" Andi asks.

"Fugazi. It means fake," Kiki says. "My social media makes me look like I'm living the glamorous life with these two." She points to Sammie and Marla. "But the reality is trash. My mom secretly paid for this trip with the threat that it was the last time she'd support my unstable lifestyle. She calls me a bad investment. That's why my dad refuses to help me anymore. And my brother, I live with him and his wife in Miami, he says if I don't get my shit together, they'll kick me out."

Biss casts a comforting look at Kiki and says, "Goddess Kiki, you can find your purpose and create your best life. You have the power to make that magic happen here in The Biss Tribe!"

Kiki sobs into her hands.

"Let it out," Biss says, bending down to give her a hug.

After the remaining women share their stories and goals, Biss says, "Let's get up, stretch and hydrate."

Concierges appear and direct you and everyone to silver fountains flowing with flat water, sparkling water, kombucha and iced tea.

Helping to serve the refreshments are Panther, the tall, jet-black-haired woman with a sparkling nose ring who checked you in at the bus, and the bus driver, Vee, whose emerald-green hair matches the colorful mermaids tattooed on her arms.

You and the women enjoy the offerings during a short break before returning to your thrones, feeling refreshed and energized.

*Sunday, Day 1*

# GoddessAwakening: The Biss Tribe's Origin Story

Biss looks at you and each woman and says:

"You're here to transform your pain into power, by tapping into supernatural energy. That's how I created all of this for you. It started decades ago, with my GoddessAwakening. I want to share this story with you as an example of how my GoddessPower was activated to make magic and miracles happen for you here in The Biss Tribe."

Everyone is rapt as Biss slowly circles the table and speaks:

> Let's go back many years, when I broke up with a man after a relationship. He retaliated with verbal attacks. To cope, I went to the gym and jumped on a stair-climbing machine.
>
> But his words kept replaying in my mind like a vicious dog that wouldn't stop barking.
>
> "$*#@!" he had growled earlier.
>
> "These guys are gonna *@#! %&*!) #@!(&*% and toss you out like yesterday's trash. You'll be so sorry you left me!"
>
> I frantically pumped my legs...
>
> Trying to run from his voice in my head.
>
> Getting nowhere.
>
> "You are a *@#+ %&*) #@!"
>
> But his words kept chasing me down...
>
> Chewing me raw inside.
>
> My whole body prickled with anger.
>
> I tried to climb up and out of this feeling, literally, because I was climbing stairs.

## Welcome to The Biss Tribe

*God, please help me!* I prayed silently amidst the humming exercise machines, music and people working out around me. *God, please help me!*

My muscles were trembling. I wanted to burst into tears in the middle of the gym. That was my sanctuary where I sweat, pumped and punched out my anger with cardio, strength training and kick-boxing. The more stressed I was, the more intense my workouts became.

Especially on this night.

He cursed my ambitious career aspirations and life dreams while insulting my character.

Though this man lacked evidence to substantiate any of his accusations, he was attempting to "slut-shame" me, which means trying to degrade and intimidate women who are sexually liberated.

This experience inspired me to vent my feelings in my journal, and to pray for harmony and peace. When I was born, my father baptized me and asked God to make me a "Princess of Peace." But my peaceful responses to this man did not bring the harmony that I was praying for.

Still, I maintained a Jesus-like "turn the other cheek" response, preferring not to add fuel to the fire. I believed that would only continue and worsen the argument.

And once, when he yelled insults, I shouted profanities back at him. That only made the argument grow more heated.

Now, as I exercised, my heart pounded. Sweat poured. And his voice thundered through my head:

""%&*! #@$!"

## Sunday, Day 1

My mind's eye kept replaying the words, the feelings, the urgent prayers for harmony and the dramatic plunge from romantic bliss to *this*.

His condemnation of my talent and dreams was totally baffling. Why did he think that I would suddenly take my Ivy League master's degree in journalism from Columbia University and my bachelor's degree in English Literature from the University of Michigan, and my successful career as a journalist and author, and suddenly make prostitution my new career path?

And so what if I did!? I've always thought that sex work should be legal everywhere, as long as women are in charge of how it happens and with whom, and that the women are safe and can keep the money they earn.

But what would happen to me and my career amidst this chaos? Fear slithered through me. Would this conflict ever end?

How could I get through this ordeal without—as I had unfortunately seen happening to too many women—crumpling under the pain and pressure, succumbing to excessive alcohol, overeating, engaging in self-destructive behaviors, or allowing stress to etch premature wrinkles on my face and gray my hair?

Would this experience cast a permanent shadow over my sunny disposition and crush my spirit? Would I ever achieve my dreams as a bestselling author whose books are made into movies? Would I ever move to California as I had always dreamed?

Would I ever have my own TV shows? Would I ever trust the idea of romance and love again?

Or would this man smash my dreams?

That night in the gym, hot waves of sadness and fear and anger began burst up and out of me in a sob. But I didn't cry. I channeled the emotions into my legs as they attacked the exercise machine.

His name-calling reverberated through my mind, but I refused to cower.

I countered with my own exclamation:

"No, QUEEN! I'm a queen!" I declared this over and over, out loud, to silence his voice and erase his face from my thoughts. I didn't care how I looked, talking to myself and praying in the noisy gym.

*God, please help me feel better...*

Suddenly, out of nowhere, my mind filled with the vision of a small silver box. It was positioned inside the middle of my head.

And those foul words were flowing—like letters dancing through the air—into my right ear, through my brain, into the silver box. Then, as if it were a word-processing program, the silver box rewrote his insults, and a new word streamed out from the other side:

*Goddess!*

Euphoria rippled through me with the shivery deliciousness of an orgasm. It pushed a reset button on my frazzled emotions, and a geyser of joy exploded inside me.

Something deep within felt like a starburst of energy that sent sparkles through every cell in my body, glowing around me like an aura of light that was creating a forcefield of protection, like a giant bubble. My body felt strong and inexhaustible as I climbed the stairs with a sudden surge of energy.

As the word "Goddess" echoed in my mind, my spirit seemed to dance.

"Goddess!" I announced out loud.

Then a voice within me—a voice that was not mine—declared clearly:

"You are Goddess, Elizabeth. Know that. Be that."

"Goddess!" I declared out loud. "Yes, I am Goddess!"

In that moment, I felt like I had just been given a secret password that connected me to a supernatural network of divine wi-fi—that's just as invisible and powerful as the Internet connections on our devices that enable us to phone anyone, anywhere, or access any information we desire.

By simply saying, "Goddess," I plugged into an infinite and divine Source of power and peace. It was as instantaneous as flipping a light switch that sent an energy surge through my entire being. It jolted my brain and body with confidence that:

*Yes, I have the power to make all my dreams come true, including transforming this terrible situation into harmony while my career and family flourish.*

I felt limitless, protected, powerful—and thankfully—peaceful.

All from a single word.

Goddess.

That moment in the gym so many years ago was my GoddessAwakening. It happened a split-second after I prayed for help.

Spirit didn't say, "You are a Goddess."
Spirit said, "You are Goddess."
Like, you are divine. You are powerful.
The female version of God.

I believe that every human carries a spark of Creator-Source-Universe-Spirit-God energy inside us, and that spark is our spirit. Therefore, the female version of that energy inside girls and women is most accurately described as GoddessPower. Hence, "You are Goddess."

One more thing: when Spirit spoke at the gym, none of the goddesses of ancient mythology and global cultures came to mind, nor did movie stars who were revered as "screen goddesses." Instead, Goddess showed up as pure *energy* whose power transformed me in a blink.

I'm sharing this story because it inspired my mission to help you, now. I called out for help, and Spirit spoke, helping me transform my pain into power, and create this transformative experience for you here The Biss Tribe.

This is my empire, my realm, my SeaGoddess Castle.

Now it's time for you to take everything I've learned, and use it to create *your* empire, exactly as you please.

Who's ready for *that!?*

"Holy shit," Andi says as the women cheer, "I don't think I took a breath during that whole story. The bastard."

## Sunday, Day 1

Sunshine wipes tears from her eyes. "My exes have all been like that. And they all cheated on me, too. But I didn't know how to cope. So I just suffered. I felt mentally and physically ill from their gaslighting and lies to my face."

"No more, Goddess," Biss says, gazing down at her. "You've got the power now, and that will elevate you to set new standards for yourself to attract the loving, loyal man that you want, while you build your seven-figure business."

Biss pauses. "There's more to the story. My GoddessPower has helped make miracle healings happen. The man in my story had a catastrophic experience, and in the midst of it all, I forgave him. This was my first understanding of how forgiving someone lifts the anger and pain from your heart and soul and helps you heal. Now he thinks I'm an angel, and we have the harmony that I had prayed for."

"Amazing!" Sunshine says.

"It truly is a miracle," Biss says, "and the peace and power that I've received from Spirit by using the four GoddessPower Activation Tools, enabled me to experience this."

Biss holds up a *PowerJournal*. "OK my Goddesses, I shared my GoddessAwakening. Now it's time for you to write about yours."

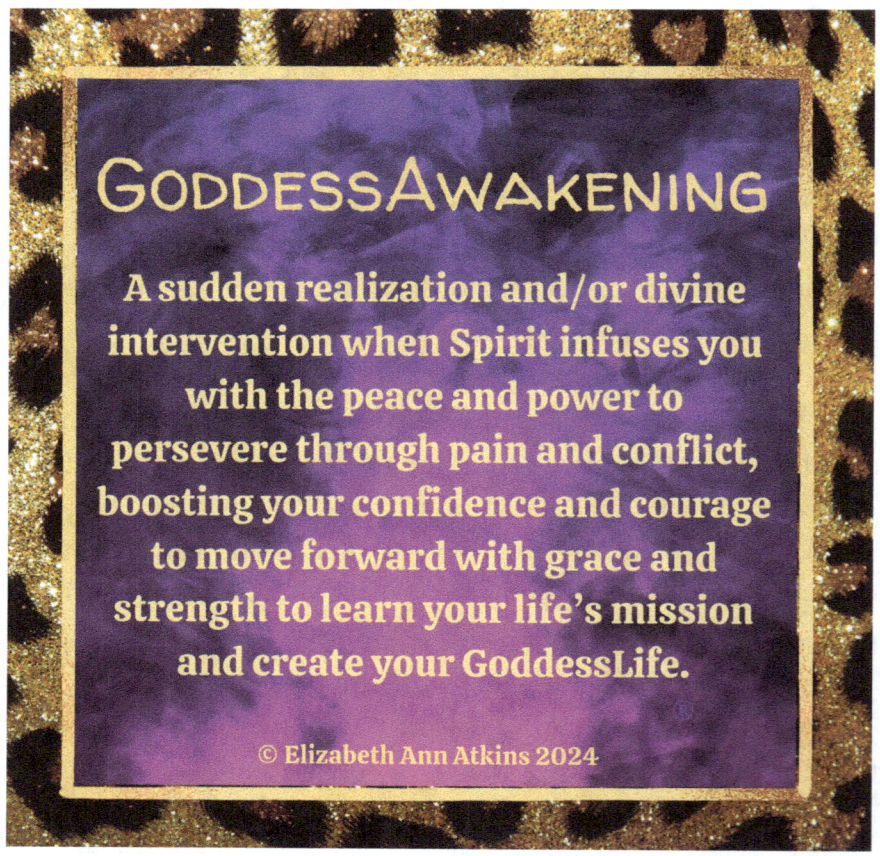

Words stream across the screen as Biss says:

"Your GoddessAwakening is a sudden realization and/or divine intervention when Spirit infuses you with the peace and power to persevere through pain and conflict, boosting your confidence and courage to move forward with grace and strength, while envisioning your best you and your dream life, which inspires an action plan to live your GoddessLife in 3-D reality."

Biss looks at you, then the group. "Quick, somebody tell me your GoddessAwakening."

"I haven't had mine yet," Andi says.

## Sunday, Day 1

"Oh yes, you have," Biss says. "Your decision to come here and leave your old life behind and create a new one, that was your GoddessAwakening."

Celeste raises her hand. "Mine was clear as day. It happened just before I signed up for this retreat. I broke out in eczema from stress over our board of directors's decision that compromised the integrity of our company. Plus, I was overwhelmed with my family. I was crying, itching, and driving to the dermatologist. So in the lobby of the doctor's office, I snatched up one of their brochures, and in the blank spaces, I started writing out my Auntie Rose's recipes for pecan pie and peach cobbler. That calmed me. I knew right then, Celeste is about to leave corporate America—which is making her skin bubble and bleed—and become a baking boss. An entrepreneur."

"Celeste," Biss says, "tell us how you got from there to here."

"Oh, I got some divine affirmation," Celeste says. "While I was writing, my girlfriend texted me out of the blue. She said her new hair salon, which she had planned out while on The Biss Tribe retreat, just hit $500K in sales."

"Riviera Wilkes-Wilson," Biss says. "Biss Tribe Class #80."

"Yes!" Celeste exclaims. "Granted, she'd been raving about her experience here, and telling me to come. But at the time, it just didn't click that this was for me. So while I was on the exam table waiting for my dermatologist, scratching my skin raw, I called my friend, found out how to register, and here I am."

"A Goddess, awakened as you can be!" Biss says with a smile. "So happy you're here."

Bianca shakes her head. "So could my GoddessAwakening be when I realized in a split second that if I don't change, and don't get my non-profit up and running, and stay stuck in the Bianca Tornado, it would just kill me?"

## Welcome to The Biss Tribe

"Yes!" Biss says, glancing at Bianca, then all the women. "It's that 'do or die' moment. Even if you're lacking confidence right now, something deep inside you knows you have the power to achieve your wildest dreams, or you wouldn't have invested the time, energy and money to come here."

"True that," Zeusse says, then starts writing in her *PowerJournal*, as do several women.

Biss glances around. "Some of you look overwhelmed and confused. Just start writing; let it flow. There are no wrong answers. If you feel stuck, ask the question directly to your heart, then listen and write whatever comes to mind. It's in there. It's screaming to come out. So my Goddesses, listen and write."

*Dear Goddess Reader, write about your GoddessAwakening. When did it happen? What did it feel like? How did it change you?*

_____

_____

_____

_____

# Sunday, Day 1

## Step into Your GoddessLife

Sunshine shoots through the high, stained-glass windows, illuminating Biss in colorful beams of light as she paces around the table, always making eye contact with the next woman.

"Goddesses!" she exclaims. "Get ready to write a new script for your future and play the starring role into your most limitless life."

"Can't happen soon enough," Jade quips. "But I know it won't be easy."

"True that," Zeusse adds. "I'm try'na write 'the end' on my struggles and get back into champ status like when I was on the court, but now in business."

"That's actually as easy as stepping through a gateway," Biss says, standing behind her throne, "leaving your current reality and experiencing your dream life, your GoddessLife."

A huge white smartboard slowly and silently drops on invisible wires from the ceiling, suspended behind and above Biss, who holds a clicker and aims a purple dot of light on the screen. A leopard print pattern and smoky purple background appear on the smartboard as words pop up and stream across the video screen.

"The definition of GoddessLife," Biss says, "is the mindset and lifestyle that you create by activating your supernatural GoddessPower to become the best version of yourself who's living your wildest dreams, every day, while ruling your personal and professional empire with Power, Pleasure, Prosperity, Protection and Peace."

The sound of each word seems to suspend in the air in the colorful bands of sunshine beaming down from the high, stained-glass windows.

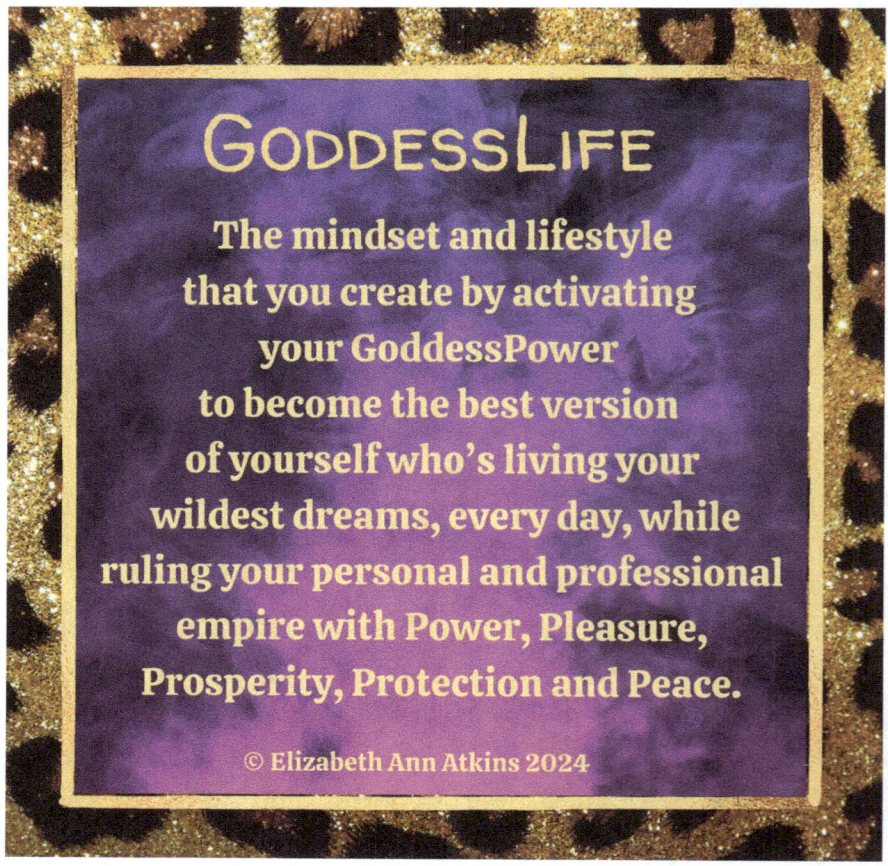

"This is the essence of why you're here," Biss says. "Somebody tell me if this is resonating with you."

Zeusse raises her hand. "Well, my whole thing is confidence, or the lack thereof, to open my academy. So I love what you said, but I just don't know why it scares the shit outta me if I lack the confidence to live up to that goal."

"Ditto!" Andi exclaims.

Sunshine raises her hand. "I have the fantasy life so clear in my mind. It's like the movie of the life I want, but bringing it out of my head and into reality has been impossible."

# Sunday, Day 1

Biss nods. "Look at that word. Impossible. It's actually, 'I'm possible.' But something is blocking you. Our mission is to identify your blocks and limiting beliefs."

Jade shakes her head. "I am the definition of both those things."

"My Goddesses, listen carefully," Biss says. "As someone who writes books, I'm here to teach you how to write a new story for your life. And **every story needs a star character.** You need to create the starring role for the feature film of your life. Just like when I write a novel and create a character, which comes from the supernatural source of Spirit, you're going to do that, and write the plot, describe the setting, identify the villains, and equip your character—who is Goddess YOU—to **slay every demon** who dares to hinder, stop, slow, sabotage, delay, derail, or destroy your mission to build your empire and rock your realm in ways that blow your mind on a daily basis."

Celeste's arms shoot up and she shouts, "Hallelujah! I receive that!"

"You'll write this script five times," Biss says, "one for every P as we ascend Infinity Mountain, for each of the five pillars of GoddessLife: Power, Pleasure, Prosperity, Protection and Peace. Today we're going to work on your GoddessPower, because that activates your Supernatural Self and enables you to experience the four other pillars of GoddessLife. So let's do it!"

Andi crosses her arms and sits back, looking angry. "You're a writer, Biss, this is easy for you! My writing sucks. I've been selling hammers and saws and lawn mowers for 40 years. Not writing like you."

Biss glances at you and the women. "Who also feels that way?"

Most of the women raise their hands.

"So here's how we'll do this," Biss says. "Everybody count one, two, starting with Andi, around the table until everyone is counted."

"One," Andi says.

"Two," says Jade beside her, followed by every woman.

"Now, every set of two is a team," Biss says. "You're going to verbally describe your two scenes to your partner."

As she speaks, Concierges appear and give each woman a palm-sized, silver device.

Biss says, "Record your scenes as you speak to your partner. These are mini recorders. We'll have your scenes transcribed for you."

"Why can't we just write?" Jade asks. "I don't want to tell my stuff to someone."

"Yeah," Zeusse says, "I've never told anybody the most private details of my personal fantasy life—"

Biss smiles. "Being scared and silent will keep every one of you stuck, stuck, stuck! Remember our talk about confidentiality among our Biss Tribe sisters?"

Marla shakes her head. "It's so hard to trust that."

"Without trust in this group, your GoddessMission will fail," Biss says. "Tell me, who here trusts herself? Do you trust yourself?"

The room is silent. Perplexed expressions flash on the women's faces.

"Exactly," Biss says. "If you truly trusted yourself, you would already be where you want to be. I know, because that was me. Some years ago, my sister Catherine—who you'll meet at the GoddessTreasure Cave, said, 'Biss, you can't trust another person, because you don't trust yourself!'"

Biss shakes her head. "Her words hit me so hard, because they were true. So I had to learn how to trust myself first. Trust that I would always do what's in the best interest of me. That meant stop being a people pleaser, putting other people's needs first, and never again saying yes when I meant no. Only when I started trusting myself did things start to change."

## Sunday, Day 1

Biss aims the clicker at the screen and reads the words that pop up: "The Merriam-Webster Dictionary defines trust as a verb, an action word, that means 'to rely on the truthfulness or accuracy of: BELIEVE.'"

She makes the little purple light dot circle the word "Believe." Then her eyes widen. "Believe! You have to take believing to the next level: knowing. You have to **know** that you're ready and that you can do this. And you have to **know** that others will help you, or you'll stay stuck as fuck. We're all aware that staying stuck is a nightmare, because it brought you here to escape it."

She glances back at the screen as another definition appears. "Trust also means, 'to place confidence in: rely on.' Rely on! That means, rely on each other! Rely on your Goddess sisters who are here to help you. By helping each other, you help yourself. Your transformation here requires trusting the women around you right now to help you discover and activate your power."

Marla and Sammie cast suspicious looks at each woman.

"Everyone is like, complete strangers, though," Sammie says. "And when we get back into the real world—"

"Anybody could put us on blast—" Jade adds. "I've been screwed over by female frenemies too many times."

Celeste nods. "We all have, but I'm ready to trust. I believe in karma. Like Biss said, if anyone betrays our trust, a nightmare will smash down on them with a mighty vengeance, in exact proportion to their betrayal."

"Agreed!" Delaney exclaims. "I'm ready to trust this process."

Biss exclaims, "YES! Anyone who's not on board with trust can leave now."

Bianca waves her hand. "Actually, I trusted the process and the people, sight unseen, when I signed up for this mysterious experience."

## Welcome to The Biss Tribe

"Truth!" Zeusse said. "Wouldn't have forked over so much dough to come here—and give up my phone!—if we didn't trust it on some level." She glances around the table, making eye contact with you and the other women. "So let's just go all in and do the damn thing. Go hard or go home!"

Biss raises her hands in prayer position and closes her eyes. "Music to my ears, beautiful ladies!"

She aims the clicker and fast-forwards to a picture of Sasha Maxwell. "Tomorrow at the GoddessPower Pyramid, when Sasha Maxwell speaks at the evening feast, she'll emphasize the importance of trust. In yourself. In your Biss Tribe sisters. In me. In the Universe. So—"

Zeusse flashes a big smile. "That female is truly a Goddess. A Queen. I watch her show and learn so much—"

"She's so *raw*," Sunshine adds with a grin. "I looooove it!"

Biss aims the clicker to show a silent video clip of Sasha in her dark pink-hued, animal print-splashed studio hosting her live video streaming podcast, *The QueenPower Show*. "Sasha hired women in her Biss Tribe class as her camerawomen and staff. Now that's trust."

Marla, Sammie and several women lean back in their throne chairs. They say nothing.

Biss smiles. "Yeah, baby, you hear me now! So, back to trusting the power of teamwork to make your dream work. Imagine that each of you is a lightbulb. Each of you individually glows brightly, but 22 lightbulbs will flood the room with light."

Biss casts a serious look at the women. "So, who here still wants to do our writing exercise alone? Raise your hand and you can go over in the corner and do your thing, your way, while we stay here at the Goddess RoundTable and vibe on each other's energy, using the foundation of trust in each other and belief in ourselves."

# Sunday, Day 1

The women are stiff and silent.

"I'm stayin'!" Sammie exclaims.

"Me too," Marla says.

"Everybody?" Biss asks.

"In!" Andi says as other women say yes.

"Now, the power of speaking your story out loud to another person," Biss says, "will force you to simplify it and make it exciting with the most interesting details to keep their attention. Like when you're telling your friend something that happened. You leave out the boring details and only share the most titillating ones."

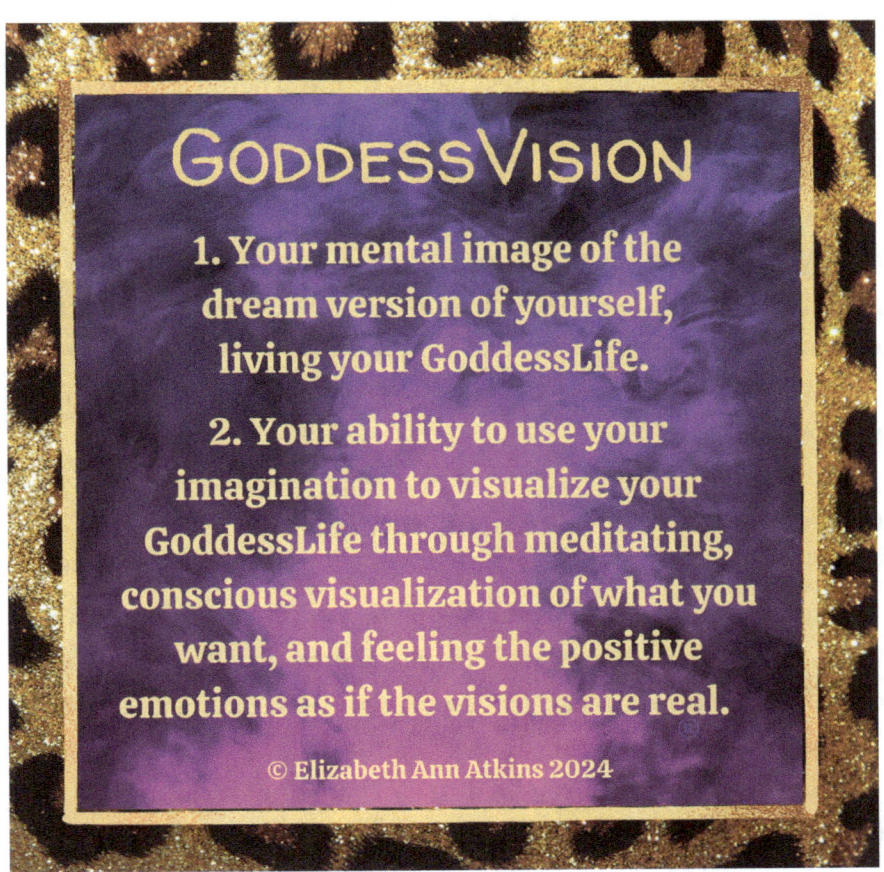

## GoddessVision

1. Your mental image of the dream version of yourself, living your GoddessLife.

2. Your ability to use your imagination to visualize your GoddessLife through meditating, conscious visualization of what you want, and feeling the positive emotions as if the visions are real.

© Elizabeth Ann Atkins 2024

## Welcome to The Biss Tribe

A graphic appears on the screen as Biss says, "Your GoddessVision is the dream version that you see in your imagination of yourself and your life that will become your reality."

"Your GoddessVision," Biss says, "is also your ability to use your imagination to visualize your GoddessLife by thinking about what you want, meditating, and feeling the positive emotions as you mentally rehearse your future in your present thoughts. Think of it like television. Tell-a-vision to yourself, then make it come true."

A movie director's slate appears on the screen, along with a movie screen, a spotlight and a golden Oscar.

"The way that we create our future," Biss says, "is to write a script that brings our GoddessVision to life. Then it's up to you to give your best performance—an Oscar-worthy performance!—to make it happen."

Andi huffs. "I'm no actress!"

"Actually," Biss says, "you especially, Andi, have been acting all your life. Playing the role that someone else wrote for you. Now it's time to let the real you take center stage."

"Whoah!" Andi says, dramatically dropping her pen on the table with a loud *clank*. "Mic drop."

"We've all been acting," Biss says. "You activate your GoddessPower when you take off the mask, stop acting and show your true character. Got it?"

"You are singin' my tune," Celeste says. "The unmasking of Celeste will send shockwaves around the world. Plus as a woman of color, we have a mask for every occasion, like Paul Laurence Dunbar says in his poem, *We Wear the Mask.*"

"Same!" Sunshine exclaims. "It's exhausting. Help me unleash my inner bitch. I hate playing nice all the time."

"Hang with us, mama," Marla says. "We got you."

Sammie adds, "We are masters—no, mistresses!—of bitchery."

## Sunday, Day 1

The screen shows a photo of Sasha Maxwell in this ballroom, writing her GoddessVision in her *PowerJournal.*

"Every woman who has a Biss Tribe success story," Biss says, "has used this process, and tomorrow evening, you can ask Sasha Maxwell about how she did it."

A movie theatre marquis appears on the screen and says: "Now showing: GoddessLife starring YOU!"

Biss continues: "Every feature film begins with a screenplay that starts as an idea in the screenwriter's mind. That's you, right here, right now. Writing your GoddessVision is the first step to the physical manifestation of ideas in your head."

# Write Your GoddessLife Script

The screen says "Your GoddessLife Script" and shows a worksheet:

Title: _____

Writer: _____

Executive Producer + Director: _____

Starring Role: _____

Heroine: _____

Supporting Cast: _____

_____

Plot: _____

_____

_____

*Welcome to The Biss Tribe*

Setting: _____

_____

External Villains: _____

_____

Internal Villains: _____

_____

Ending: _____

_____

One-sentence overview: _____

_____

Two-sentence summary—

Professional: _____

_____

Personal: _____

_____

# Sunday, Day 1

*Dear Goddess Reader: please complete the GoddessLife Script worksheet. You may want to keep reading and come back to it after you see how Biss and the 22 women complete theirs.*

Biss glances up and says, "You'll find this worksheet in your *PowerJournal*. Before you fill it in, let's do the exercise together. Who wants to volunteer as our example?"

Sunshine's hand shoots up. "Me, please!"

"Great," Biss says. "Tell me the answers. Title?"

"The Turquoise Experience: Sunshine Rising."

As Sunshine provides the answers, Esmerelda types on a laptop and Sunshine's answers appear on the screen.

Biss says, "You are the writer, executive producer, director and heroine. Next, who's your supporting cast? Include me, Esmerelda, and your 21 Biss Tribe sisters who each bring a talent and their support to the table. Who else?"

"My aunt," Sunshine says. "I need an assistant, a business team for marketing, accounting, and content creation, new friends, and of course my forever person. My man."

Biss nods. "Great. Plot?"

Sunshine says: "Oh here goes. A struggling life coach and narcissist magnet finds her power to create a seven-figure business and teaches entrepreneurs how to do the same. She finds her soul mate for love, travel, and a lifetime of devotion and happiness together."

"Sounds like a Hallmark movie," Delaney says.

"Setting?" Biss asks.

"Santa Fe, New Mexico," Sunshine says. "Where I live. Right now, I work out of my home, but I want to buy a house or building and transform it into my event and teaching space called The Turquoise Experience. I also want to hire a lot of Indigenous women entrepreneurs as my vendors, because I know what a struggle it can be. I want to be the support for them that I feel I've never had."

"I love that!" Marla says. "Can me and Sammie come and lead a class on how to become an influencer?"

Sunshine smiles. "Yes!"

"I'll supply the deserts," Celeste adds.

"Yes!" Biss exclaims. "This kind of creative synergy and cross-pollination helps build your dreams together. OK Sunshine, who are your external villains?"

"Hmmm," she says. "I'll say any man who comes along to distract me, rather than helping me achieve my dream. Including exes who randomly show up and try to tempt me back into their shitshow."

"Anyone else?"

"Yeah," Sunshine says. "A frenemey named Linda. Fake friend, real enemy. She's my main competitor in town. She smiles in my face, but talks bad about me to steal my life coaching clients."

Celeste scowls. "I think we all know at least ten people like that."

"Girl gang saboteurs!" Bianca says.

Sunshine looks disgusted. "Back when we were friends, I told her about a man I was crazy about, and she went and seduced him and told me about it. They actually dated for six months. He turned out to be a monster. I'm grateful; it showed that rejection is God's protection. But that made me distrust women."

Biss shakes her head. "We need a strategy to deflate any power she has to hinder your success, in business or otherwise, and learn to trust. Now, what are your internal villains?"

"Do you have three hours?" Sunshine says with a laugh.

"You can write more later," Biss says, "but tell us the main ones."

"Lack of confidence," Sunshine says. "My inner mean girl who says I'm not worthy and will never succeed or find my forever person. Negative thinking, fears that people will hate me when

## Sunday, Day 1

I'm really successful, not believing in myself, and self-sabotaging behaviors."

"You just described me," says Susie, who's been quiet until now, and has spiky black hair. "I'm all of the above."

Several women say, "Me too."

"These are universal problems," Biss says, "and fixable ones. So let's write your two-sentence summary. Start with professional."

Sunshine pauses. "A struggling life coach conquers her fear of success and financial lack to build a seven-figure business incubator for women entrepreneurs called The Turquoise Experience, where they get the coaching and financing they need to succeed."

"Perfect!" Biss exclaims. "Now your personal summary, one sentence."

Sunshine looks dreamy as she says, "A woman heals her inner wounds to find peace and self-love—and as a former narcissist magnet— attracts her devoted, loving soul mate for world travel and a lifetime of happiness together."

"Slam dunk!" Zeusse exclaims, smiling. "I'm impressed!"

"Whoah, Sunshine," Andi says. "All that just rolled off your tongue like magic. My words aren't coming so fast."

"Like I said, I have a clear vision of what I want," Sunshine says, "and I've been practicing this for years. But no results."

"This is an excellent start," Biss says. "Sunshine, thank you for serving as our example. Now you'll learn how to finally get those results. Everybody, does this make sense?"

"I've never been more clear," Celeste says as women say yes and nod.

"Scared, but clear," Marla says.

"Does everybody see how you're the screenwriter composing the script for the feature film that is your life story?" Biss asks. "That film needs a cast, and you play the starring role. Some people call this 'main character energy.' I call it superstar Goddess energy. You create the setting, the plot, and the supporting roles."

Some women shake their heads.

"I don't know if I can do this," Kiki says. "I mean, I came here because I have no idea what I want to do with my life. I've done everything from waitressing to starting an OnlyFans page to teaching Arabic dancing to working as a nail tech. I love everything at first, then I hate it, so I quit and look for the next thing. Getting nowhere in life."

Kiki purses her plump lips. Her thick black eyelashes flutter downward like a curtain over her eyes. In a flash of shiny purple pointed fingernails, she dabs tears from her eyes with her fingertips.

"Kiki," Biss says softly, "you can get clarity here in The Biss Tribe. Just be patient and gentle with yourself, and the answers will come."

Kiki's platinum-tipped dark hair gently dances over her shoulders as she shakes her head and does not look up.

"You have to know who your villains are," Biss says. "Villains are not just external people and forces who try to block your dream; they're also internal thoughts, bad habits, addictions, and self-sabotaging behaviors. Uncertainty, like Kiki just expressed, can be an internal villain. But to defeat them, we need to figure out who and what they are. You ready for this?"

"Never been more ready!" Andi says as Kiki looks up and nods.

"I should feel like the sky is the limit," Kiki says. "My family escaped being killed in Iraq. They brought my dad and his brothers and sisters to the U.S. for a better life. So I should feel ambitious like they were, when they opened their grocery stores and gas stations in Detroit with nothing in their pockets but a dream."

She sighs as tears drip down her cheeks. "But I feel like such a disappointment, like I'm just like sitting on my ass, wasting my

## Sunday, Day 1

life. Not honoring my grandparents for helping me be born in a country where anything is possible. In our culture, my family is all about hard work and making money. But my family is always shaming me for being confused and not being a good role model for Arab American girls."

Biss steps close to Kiki, who holds her hand and looks up at her.

"Kiki," Biss says, "just know that you have the answers within you and we will help you find them!"

Several women cheer her on.

Jade pulls her pink hair back into a ponytail, then releases it into a wild tumble as she lets out an exasperated sigh. "As much as I want it, I'm scared as fuck. What if I really make it happen? What if I leave all the shit behind and just flow with my girl band and travel the world and have all the money I need to live while making myself and my fans happy with our music?"

Biss almost jumps up and down as she says, "Then you're living your GoddessLife, baby! That is the key! You can do it! Starting now."

Esmerelda raises a hand. "Jade has a great point. Fear of success is a real thing. How many of you are feeling that?"

Almost everyone raises a hand.

"I feel it's like leaping off a cliff into the unknown," Sunshine says. "Like, how can I handle it? I'm so used to struggling in my own head, in my life, and in relationships, it's almost like my discomfort zone is my comfort zone."

"Because it's familiar," Delaney says. "I feel the same way. But I hate it and want to escape it. Now! I'm ready to step into the unknown."

Esmerelda asks, "Who else is ready to step into the unknown?"

Marla's hand shoots up. "I think the first step—my GoddessAwakening, right?—is being so freaking tired of feeling a certain way, that you can't stand it a minute longer."

Sammie nods. "We want relief from how bad we've felt. Help!"

Biss smiles. "Let's take five minutes to complete the worksheet, which will rev you up to describe your GoddessLife scenes with your partner."

# Write the Script for The GoddessPower Personal Life of YOU

Near the fireplace and in a beam of sunshine that's blue and green as it shoots through the stained glass windows, Vee and Panther help Esmerelda lay a plush lavender rug and assemble 14 brass bowls—big and small—along with a variety of wooden sticks that each have a ball on the end.

"Every script is made up of scenes that tell a story." Biss glances at the screen, which says, "The movie of your life" and shows video of her standing on the rear deck of a gleaming white, black and dark purple yacht whose name, *Sea Goddess,* appears on the back in gold letters as it cuts through turquoise waters and churns up frothy white waves in its wake.

"I'll share mine first," Biss says. "Remember, I'm coming from a place where I was struggling financially, having one wrong relationship after another, exploring identity issues as a mixed-race woman, and dealing with tremendous anxiety, frustration, struggles with food, fat and self-esteem, and even suicidal ideation."

Esmerelda sits facing you and the bowls with her legs crossed as Vee and Panther adjust the bowls to create a perfect half-circle in front of her.

"Writing the script for the new me," Biss says, "was the first step to physically manifesting it. As Napoleon Hill says in his book, *Think & Grow Rich,* whatever you can conceive in your mind, you can achieve in reality."

# Sunday, Day 1

Biss glances up at the video, which shows the wind blowing her hair and her white dress as she gazes out at a tropical beach in the distance.

"Remember, you're scripting your future, which will play out like a movie in your imagination until your GoddessLife becomes your daily reality. Listen to mine, and make yours bigger, better and bolder! Be grandiose! Delusional! And unrealistic!"

She holds up a *PowerJournal*. "Open your book to the page that says: **My GoddessVision.** We're going to write the vision from your conscious imagination, which is your thinking mind, right now. You're basically putting into writing what you described as your mission earlier today."

Sunshine lets out a panicked moan. "Why is my heart pounding? Like I'm so dreading making it real, even though it's everything I want?"

"Truth!" Zeusse says, holding up her pen. "My hand is shaking."

"All of a sudden, I'm having the worst craving for ice cream," Jade says. "To numb out and not face this."

Delaney looks anxious. "Is this fear of failure or fear of success?"

"It makes me want to escape from this table," Bianca says. "Because I've failed so many times, yet I'm obsessed with finally succeeding."

Marla huffs. "I'm so over-saturated with all the words! GoddessLife. GoddessVision. I'm trying to keep up with what everything means so I don't fuck it up."

Suddenly the most angelic song and unique musical sounds, like chimes and tones from heaven, float through the ballroom. You and everyone turn to Esmerelda, who's singing and holding in each hand a wooden stick that has a ball on the end. As she strikes and strokes the edges of the bowls, she creates a symphony of soothing sounds.

"Oh. My. Goodness," Sunshine whispers, closing her eyes and leaning back. "That is heavenly."

Esmerelda's wordless song and bowl sounds float through the air and into your ears like ribbons of satin. Jade bursts into tears, sobbing softly into her hands. Everyone stares in awe or leans back and closes her eyes or sighs or cries.

Biss says softly, "My beautiful Goddesses, the tones from the sound bowls are activating energy centers in your body, called chakras, which we'll explore tomorrow at the GoddessPower Pyramid. For now, Esmerelda's music will begin to activate your Supernatural Self, that all-knowing voice within you that speaks your truth."

Esmerelda hits a high note as if to punctuate Biss's words, while the bowl sounds vibrate through the air.

"In your mind," Biss says, "ask your Supernatural Self to help you write your GoddessVision. Ask her to quiet the noise in your head, so you're free to focus on composing the most grandiose vision for your life. Then ask your Supernatural Self to upload the images into an imaginary projector that makes your GoddessVision play like a film on your mental movie screen."

Biss points the purple dot on the screen, which says, "Describe a Scene from Your Personal GoddessLife."

She looks at you all and says, "Right now you're going to write a scene from your personal dream life, the one that plays out in your mind and may feel impossible, but it's your fantasy and our job is to work to make it come true. My Goddesses, here's when you really need to release all inhibitions and write with wild abandon."

Words scroll on the screen. "Here's what I wrote for myself," Biss says, "as an example of how to describe your own scenes. My scene shows the most blissful success in my **personal** GoddessLife. Here goes:"

## Sunday, Day 1

Standing on the rear deck of my yacht, *Sea Goddess*, I sway to the sultry global fusion hip-hop music that's booming as dozens of fascinating people dance, lounge and laugh on the plush sofas and mattresses, and enjoy the jacuzzi.

The scene is decadent, my body lulled by the gentle hum of the 144-foot yacht beneath my bare feet on the caramel-hued, polished-wood planks of the deck. I feel safe as my captain and crew safely maneuver through the infinite expanse of turquoise waters of the Caribbean Sea on this sunny afternoon excursion, after docking overnight in the harbor of SeaGoddess Castle, my home on Mermaid Island, the private island that I own.

I have never felt so profoundly peaceful and happy, with my entire being aglow with joy and gratitude that I am finally living this life of my dreams.

Beside me is my Man, his large hand gently resting at the small of my back, which is bare because I'm wearing only a thong bikini as the hot sunshine keeps my healthy glowing skin bronze and sun kissed. We are fit and healthy, thanks to the high-vibe eating and daily workouts in the gym here on the yacht, as well as in our homes.

"Bliss, more wine?" he asks, gazing down at me with the same passion burning in his eyes as the moment that morning when we'd awakened in our suite. We'd made love as our bodies tremored and our souls danced in the air around us, as we start most mornings and end most days, with frequent erotic interludes in between. Now, as he gazes down at me, I silently thank God for delivering—finally!—

my Man who loves and celebrates me the way I've always craved, and I reciprocate that to him, in an endless loop of giving and receiving love, affection and comfort.

"I'd love that," I say, my eyes sparkling up at him.

A waiter—a man in white shorts embroidered with the purple *Sea Goddess* insignia, showing off his buff physique, appears and my Man says, "The usual for Bliss, please."

"Yes, sir."

My Man and I watch the beautiful women in bikinis and men in swimsuits laughing, dancing and sunning themselves, cocktails in hand, as waiters and waitresses offer trays of fruit and charcuterie boards. The scent of garlic delights our senses as a waitress approaches with skewers of colossal shrimp—glistening with a spicy Szechuan sauce—adorned with basil and a chunk of sweet pineapple.

My Man and I each take one, savoring the spicy-sweet flavors as the salty sea air tickles our cheeks and keeps us the perfect temperature under the Caribbean sun. I close my eyes and moan as the tastes and tender textures explode on my tongue.

*This is GoddessLife, and I am so grateful.*

What's magic about this moment—and why it epitomizes everything I've ever desired—is that I received this gift of extraordinary, luxurious abundance by executing my divine life assignment. I followed my calling as Goddess to create the empire that helps women—and therefore men and children as well—to activate their infinite power, become the

## Sunday, Day 1

dream versions of themselves, then create empires that literally make the world a better place.

In this moment, I glance at my family members—healthy, happy, and harmonious, and thriving in every way as they lounge, eat and play games.

I love knowing that my trustworthy staff is handling all my business for my multimedia company, while I enjoy this well-deserved leisure time.

I'm also peaceful and confident because I have healed and released the issues that had plagued me in the past—anxiety, insecurity, lack, fear, doubt, and self-sabotage. I am secure and confident in my relationship with myself, knowing that I will continue to create and influence in ways that empower people everywhere. I also know that if/when any problems or conflicts arise, I am equipped with supernatural power to resolve them in ways that are better than I ever imagined.

And I'm secure and confident in my relationship with my Man, knowing that he's mine and I'm his, forever and always. I'm secure and confident in every aspect of my personal life, including the continued abundance, because it is my celestial reward for work well done by creating and sharing my Goddess empire.

As I teach the women in The Biss Tribe, I have slayed my most vexing inner demons, freeing me to rise into my rightful daily reality in my personal GoddessLife.

Zeusse claps. "Biss, that's dope as hell!"

"But Biss," Andi asks, "do you really have a yacht? Or is this a fantasy that you're trying to make reality?"

Biss nods. "Before it became reality, this fantasy was so clear in my mind, it felt real, man included. Now, thankfully, I do have a yacht. And all of you will enjoy a sunset dinner cruise during the festivities when we return here to SeaGoddess Castle at the end of the week."

"Sweet!" Jade exclaims. "I love boats."

Sunshine, almost bouncing with excitement on her throne, says, "I want to hear how you met your man. I desperately want that."

Biss smiles. "Spirit actually showed me this man in meditation many years before he actually showed up. I'll share that story in the Pleasure Tent. So, right now, you're taking us to a vivid scene in your personal life that shows your GoddessLife. And you write it like a movie scene starring you in the feature film of your life."

Bianca raises her hand. "What if I don't want anything that grandiose? What if I just want mental peace and I don't even want a partner?"

"Then do that!" Biss exclaims. "Your personal script can be as simple or as extravagant as you want. Because *you* have the power!"

A digital clock appears on the screen above Biss. "Let's take 20 minutes to describe a scene from your personal GoddessLife. First, turn to face your partner in our one-two pair-ups. You each get 10 minutes to describe your vision for your personal GoddessLife to your partner. Be excited

## Sunday, Day 1

about it. Hold nothing back! Unleash your wildest fantasy life! Share every detail. Feel the thrill of it as if it's already real. And record it into your device as you speak."

You and the women shift to face your partners, and excited chatter fills the ballroom as the sharing begins.

*Dear Goddess Reader:*

*Write a scene from your personal GoddessLife that includes vivid details showing your ultimate health and happiness. Describe the scene through your six senses: what you're seeing, hearing, touching, tasting, smelling and feeling. Also include dialogue.*

*Print and post the written version where you can see it every morning and night, and read it out loud. Also record it into the audio app on your phone and listen to your recording every morning and night.*

*If it's easier for you to verbally describe your scene, rather than to write it, then use the voice-to-text function on your phone's notes app, then use that to record the audio version. Read and/or listen to yourself describing your personal GoddessLife when you wake up and before you go to sleep.*

_____

_____

_____

_____

## Welcome to The Biss Tribe

After 20 minutes, Esmerelda makes a deep gong sound on her bowls, and the chatter subsides.

"My Goddesses!" Biss exclaims. "How'd that go?"

Sunshine raises a hand. "Mine flowed like melted butter."

"Impostor syndrome for me!" Jade complains. "It feels like a lie that will never come true."

"Believe that, and it won't," Biss says. "Have you ever watched a movie where people are leaping over rooftops and making it to the other side? When you know in real life, they would never make it?"

Jade nods. "Of course."

"Well, that's called 'suspension of disbelief,'" Biss says. "It's when you're watching a movie, and you suspend your disbelief and let your imagination just go with the flow of the movie magic. Do that with this exercise. Suspend your disbelief and believe in magic."

"Yes!" Sunshine shrieks. "I described my scene the whole time thinking of waving a magic wand to make my loyal loving husband appear while I feel peaceful and happy and secure, like Biss described in hers. And something deep inside me—it must be my GoddessPower?—I could feel it expand like warm light in my belly as I told my vision to Bianca. My vision that I've never, ever shared with anyone! I'm starting to feel like maybe I can really do this!"

Biss dashes around the table to high-five Sunshine.

"Jade, and anyone who's struggling with this, be gentle with yourself," Biss says. "You can do it!"

Esmerelda announces it's time for a quick break. She leads you all in a stretching exercise while the Concierges refill your water goblets.

"Okay my Goddesses," Biss says, glancing up at the screen, which says, "Describe a Scene from Your Professional GoddessLife. Here's what I wrote for mine, *before* this became reality. You'll notice that you're literally sitting in my vision that started with this writing exercise and is now a physical experience for *you.*

# Sunday, Day 1

So for any disbelievers here at The GoddessRoundTable, here's proof that this works."

Biss reads the words scrolling across the screen:

> No words can describe the overwhelming bliss, gratitude and fulfillment that make me tingle from head to toe as I observe the mind-blowing scene after The Biss Tribe Coronation in the SeaGoddess Castle ballroom.
>
> I'm watching 22 of the newest Crowned Goddesses of The Biss Tribe as they're dancing the night away to the hottest beats of DJ Panther. Each woman's eyes are sparkling as their bodies move freely and joyously under the flashing purple and pink lights that make the crystal chandeliers twinkle like the stars that these women are becoming.
>
> Even the women who began the week with the most pessimistic, hopeless, self-loathing despair are now beaming with confidence and belief in themselves. All because I shared the blueprint that helped me rise from exactly that, to Goddess of my GoddessPower empire called The Biss Tribe.
>
> I savor the thrill of this moment, feeling the weight of my crown on my head, which matches the gold shimmer of my backless, form-fitting dress and stiletto sandals. Esmerelda is beside me, dressed the same in silver.
>
> Our Goddess graduates are also wearing their crowns, which are now adorned with five stones symbolizing success at each Goddess Activation Station for the pillars of Power, Pleasure, Prosperity, Protection and Peace.

## Welcome to The Biss Tribe

Some women are triumphantly holding up their crowns and spinning or placing them on each other's heads. Their charm bracelets and crystal jewelry glisten in the light. And they're wearing custom-designed outfits that reflect their individual visions of GoddessGlam; some are adorned with feathers, pearls, rhinestones and sequins, while others are more simple or masculine, and everyone is loving their look.

At The Goddess RoundTable, women are still feasting on an endless dinner from a decadent buffet of jumbo crab legs, lobster, the finest steaks, lamb chops, gourmet vegetables, pasta, rice and vegetarian options. The scents of garlic and herbs waft through the air.

Nearby, the purple back-lit bar offers the best wine, mixed drinks and mocktails. Several women gather around a tall, silver champaign fountain, filling their crystal flutes.

Similarly, women at the dessert bar are selecting the sweetest treats and dousing them under the creamy stream of the gurgling chocolate fountain.

We're celebrating after the ceremony where each woman received her Biss Tribe Certification stating that she successfully completed the week-long course and is now ready to return to her everyday life to build her empire. Suddenly a woman approaches me.

"Biss, can I give you a hug?" she asks tearfully. "You changed my life. I know I can be and do anything now. Watch me!" Then she embraces me and half-laughs, half-sobs.

## Sunday, Day 1

I know that she'll achieve her Goddess Vision, because hundreds of women have already done so, after making proclamations just like hers, during this celebration.

As this woman's exuberance intensifies mine during our hug, I think about how Goddess is our Supernatural Self, and how I have followed the guidance of my GoddessVoice to create this life-changing experience for so many women. This understanding is between me and God, and I know that as I continue to execute my divine life assignment, I will help more and more people who are all making the world a better place.

This divine alignment with my Goddess Mission defines professional success for me.

Sammie's face tenses with worry. "That's amazing, Biss, but I feel super anxious. In my head, I see millions of girls everywhere using our Samla Marmie anti-aging skincare routine every morning and night, like they're addicted to our products, but putting it into words—"

"You just did!" Marla laughs. "Stop underestimating yourself, bitch!"

Biss looks around at each woman. "Now we'll do the same exercise, describing your empire: what it looks like, feels like, smells like, and sounds like. Take us there just as vividly as you're sitting here."

A countdown clock appears on the screen as Biss says, "Let's take 20 minutes to describe a scene from your professional GoddessLife. Face your partner. You each talk for 10 minutes and remember to record each other with your devices. Be as wild and free with your professional vision as you were with your personal one."

You and the women turn to face your partners, and voices boom through the ballroom as you all share your most extraordinary visions.

*Dear Goddess Reader:*

*Write a detailed scene from your professional GoddessLife and/or use the audio recording app on your phone to describe it verbally. Then read and listen to your description every morning and night.*

_____

_____

_____

_____

After 20 minutes, Esmerelda makes a deep gong sound, and the talking stops.

"My Goddesses!" Biss exclaims as the Concierges collect the recording devices. "Your scenes will be transcribed and provided to you in print-outs as well as in a digital format. You'll record a new scene at every Activation Station up the mountain, and you're free to write new scenes as frequently as they come to mind."

Esmerelda continues playing her soothing music.

"So, how'd it go, describing your professional GoddessLife?"

## Sunday, Day 1

Delaney raises her pen. "I was perplexed at first, but then I felt like I was getting a download from the universe, as opposed to my own mind providing the ideas."

"That's your Supernatural Self," Biss says, "connecting with the universal field of knowledge where all the answers await our discovery."

Andi adds, "I described my art studio, and it was so real, I could even smell the paint and the ocean air. I heard the waves crashing on the beach outside, and I heard my wife in the kitchen, singing as she made our lunch."

Marla crosses her arms and lets out an ugly sound. "The mean-girl voice in my head was telling me I already hit my peak and I'll never be more successful than I am now. And that girls will hate our skincare line and think the name is stupid."

"Look who's underestimating herself now!" Sammie exclaims. "Samla Marmie is pure innovation. Both our names chopped in half and blended together. That's wicked smart!"

Biss looks at Marla. "Do you believe the mean-girl voice?"

"No, or I wouldn't be here."

"Good," Biss says. "We all have the proverbial devil on one shoulder and angel on the other."

Celeste raises her hands in agreement. "Yes, we do!"

Biss says, "Our job is to distinguish which one is talking, and learn how to either ignore the negative voice or prove it wrong."

"That's what's up!" Zeusse says. "I heard that voice in my head, too, this whole time. But that B also told me I'd never make the WNBA team and that I'd never win the championship. So whatever she says, just makes me work harder to shut her down and do the damn thing better than I thought I could."

"Zeusse, yes!" Biss clicks the screen as the definition of Goddess appears. "Remember this? Part of activating our GoddessPower means slaying our most vexing demons."

"One hundred percent," Zeusse says.

Jade sighs. "One of my demons has a name: chocolate chunk ice cream, and it calls my name every night."

A few women laugh.

"That's a legit demon," Biss says. "I used to be addicted to sugar, and ice cream was my drug of choice. All that sugar changed my entire physiology, from my mental health to my hormonal balances to the color and texture of my skin, and it made me depressed. I considered it spiritual warfare from forces that were holding me back from my GoddessPower for so many years as I struggled with food and fat. But I beat it, and you can, too. With all the tools you're learning here."

Biss glances around the table. "Ladies, Jade has a great point. Something that might seem silly, like an ice cream craving, can actually be as destructive as I just described. So don't blow off anything as frivolous or unimportant."

Sunshine shivers. "I don't like the word demon."

"Me either," Zeusse says, "but I consider it a blessing because it pushes me beyond my limits."

"But that word, demon, scares me," Jade says. "Even though that's exactly it."

Biss nods. "Because GoddessPower is supernatural. It's the light of our creator within ourselves. Since we live in a universe of dualities, the opposite of our supernatural GoddessPower is actually evil. We're here to counteract it. This is a big mission, ladies, and you're ready for it."

Andi glances at the security guards. "We're facing evil inside ourselves and in the world, apparently."

"True," Biss says. "For now, we're working on the internal demons, evil and blocks. So let's identify what's been blocking you."

"Mountains!" Andi quips.

"Myself," Bianca moans.

Sunday, Day 1

# Find Your POWER by Identifying How You Feel POWERLESS

A diagram appears on the screen as Biss says, "Please look at this diagram in your *PowerJournal*."

| | | | |
|---|---|---|---|
| **With MYSELF** | How do I feel **powerless**? | What would make me feel **powerful**? | How to find my **power**. |
| | | | |
| | | | |
| | | | |
| **With Other People & in the World** | How do I feel **powerless**? | What would make me feel **powerful**? | How to find my **power**. |
| | | | |
| | | | |
| | | | |
| **With Spirit** | How do I feel **powerless**? | How would I feel **powerful**? | How to find my **power**. |
| | | | |
| | | | |
| | | | |

Biss continues: "We all know, if you want to clean your house, you have to clearly see the dirt, and have the right supplies to remove it. The same goes with power."

"Huh?" Jade says.

"You need to know exactly how you feel powerless, so you can strategize how to empower yourself in that area," Biss says. "This exercise helps you do that in terms of yourself, with other people, and with Spirit.

"Let's take five minutes to write whatever comes to mind. Leave the 'how to' column blank. We're going to meditate on that tomorrow."

"Then why are we doing this now?" Tish asks.

"So these ideas can start percolating in your mind," Biss says.

After five minutes, Esmerelda makes a gong sound.

Biss smiles. "Yes! That's our cue to get up, stretch, use the bathroom and get a drink and a snack."

Vee and Panther welcome all of you to the buffet for veggies and dip, fruit, cheese, crackers and tea, coffee, kombucha and flat or sparkling water. As you and the women stand at tall tables and sit at café-style ones near the buffet, instrumental Middle Eastern music booms and four belly dancers twirl into the ballroom, electrifying the air with their jingles, chimes and sensuous movement.

"Holy shit!" Andi exclaims.

"Oh I love belly dancers!" Sunshine says.

"Look at their eyes," Jade says with awe. "So intense!"

"Everybody get up!" Biss says. "It's time to dance!"

# Take a Break to Belly Dance

The belly dancers perform as the gold coins on their ornate outfits jingle. One wears an orange satin bra and long skirt adorned with sparkles, and the others wear turquoise, yellow and purple tops and skirts or harem pants with flowy, sheer fabric. Wonderful chime sounds ring from their finger symbols.

As you and the women dance, and Tish raises her arms and shimmies her shoulders, shrieks of joy and cheers explode through the ballroom.

## Sunday, Day 1

"OK, my Goddesses," Biss says as the music volume lowers. "Who wants to learn a quick belly dance?"

"I'm a terrible dancer," Marla says.

"Let's try it!" Sammie orders, pulling her hand.

The dancer wearing orange says, "Every Goddess must know how to move her body with sensuality and confidence. These movements can help activate your feminine energy and release any tension in your bodies. I'm going to demonstrate a few simple moves, and you can follow me."

Esmerelda appears with a basket of colorful waist scarves that are covered in gold coins. "This is optional," she says, "but it's more fun when you can hear yourself jingle as you shake your hips."

Most of the women tie a scarf around their hips, then follow the dancer's lead. Soon the music booms louder and everyone is dancing—some succeeding at the belly dance moves and others—like Zeusse and Andi—moving to the beat in their own way.

Biss and Esmerelda join the dancing, as most of the women are smiling and cheering. A short time later, Biss says, "OK my Goddesses, let's thank these lovely dancers for our energy-boosting break."

You and the women return to your throne chairs feeling refreshed and energized.

## *Let's Step Through the GoddessGateway*

Biss stands behind her throne chair as the screen shows a gate overgrown with thorny vines reminiscent of those around the castle in *Sleeping Beauty*.

"Something is stopping you from entering your GoddessLife," Biss says. "It could be that your limiting beliefs, fears, bad habits, people, lack mentality, and other circumstances are blocking your GoddessGateway. So your most important job right now is to identify these blocks and find the keys to unlock the entrance to your best future. Until now, it's been padlocked, chained, barbwired, barricaded, covered with prickly vines, cemented over, and hidden by forces that don't want you to know or use your power that's on the other side."

Celeste laughs. "Is there a Goddess locksmith up in here? I need her to bring some jumbo wire cutters, dynamite sticks, and a damn bulldozer to bust open my GoddessGateway."

Several women laugh.

## Sunday, Day 1

"Add some tanks and nuclear bombs for mine," Andi says.

Kiki grimaces. "Mine is like, not even a gate. It's like one of those secret doors that are hidden in a wall that looks like a bookcase, and you can't open the door unless you can find the secret button that activates the door."

"That's really clever, Kiki," Biss says. "We will find that button for you!" Biss smiles at everyone. "And fortunately, for all of you, I'm about to help you tap into some supernatural energy that's stronger than all the cement and barbed wire and barricades you could ever imagine."

Marla sighs. "If it were that easy!"

"Shush, mama!" Sammie says with a play-swat on Marla's forearm. "At least we have a new way to think about it. I like this gateway idea."

"Me too," Kiki says. "It's like an escape—"

"Escape hatch!" Celeste exclaims. "Girl, I've been trying to find mine for a long time!"

Celeste and Kiki share a laugh.

"I need you to become obsessed with this concept," Biss says. "Of seeing yourself stepping through this GoddessGateway and into your GoddessLife where you live bigger, better and bolder and manifest your heart's wildest desires, personally and professionally."

Words pop onto the screen and Biss reads:

"The GoddessGateway," Biss says, "is the dividing line between your current, undesirable reality and your dream life. This metaphorical gateway is locked until you find the keys to the bulldozer that crushes/demolishes/removes what's blocking you, so you're free to step through the gate and into your GoddessLife. You can access the keys through your Supernatural Self."

Biss points up at the screen, which shows a diagram that says, "How Biss Created The GoddessGateway."

Welcome to The Biss Tribe

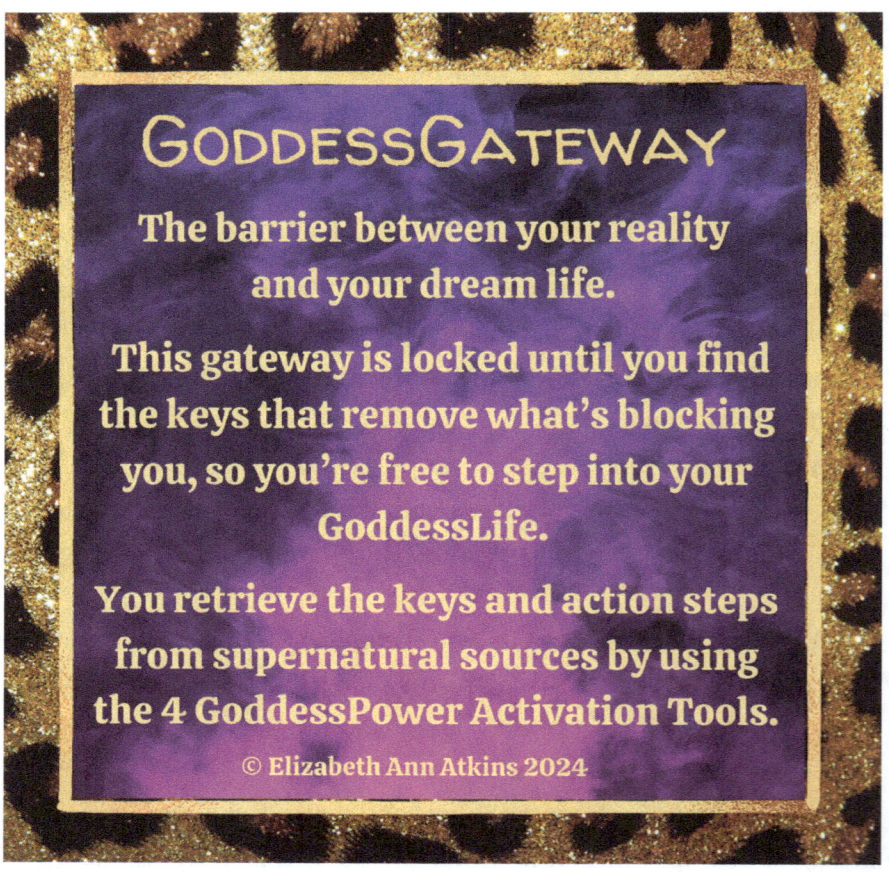

"I drew this during a meltdown," Biss says. "I was very upset, so I meditated, and Spirit showed me a vision of a gateway that I could step through, leaving my then-reality of feeling like a failure, and stepping into my GoddessLife. This amazing moment happened on August 8th, during the Lions Gate Portal, a time every year when the planets align a certain way to create very potent cosmic energy that helps us manifest our dreams."

Biss points to the screen. "So, I laid a giant pad of paper on my back porch, grabbed a purple marker, and drew an archway. On the left, under 'past,' I wrote all the bad things I was feeling. Powerlessness. Lack. Depression. Frustration. Rage. At the time, I

## Sunday, Day 1

was struggling with too much work and not enough compensation, as well as one failed romantic relationship after another—with the same person showing up with different names and faces. All while feeling like my dreams would never come true."

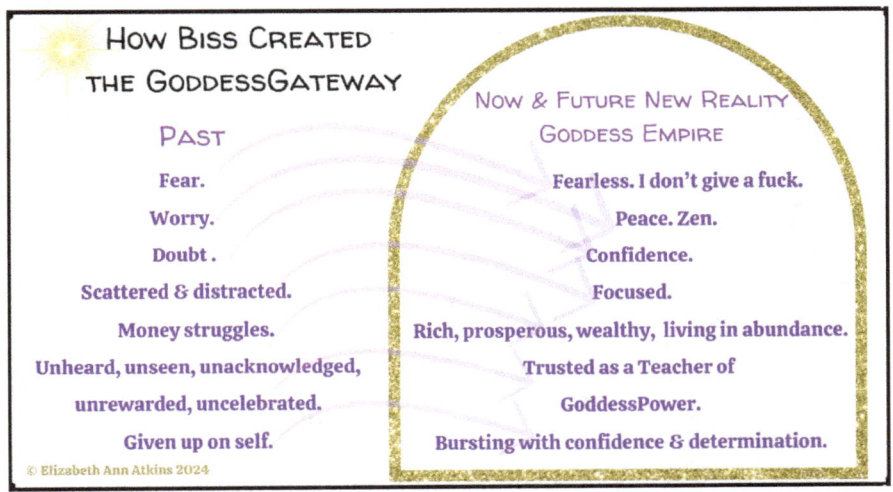

Many women shake their heads.

"You're telling my story," Sunshine says.

Tears sparkle in Biss's eyes and her voice quavers: "Believe that anything is possible. You can do this!" Biss puts her hands in prayer position under her chin, closes her eyes, and tilts her head up toward the ceiling.

"Then on the right side of the paper, I wrote 'Now & Future New Reality: Goddess Empire.' I took the Lions Gate Portal concept and renamed it The GoddessGateway. That rough description in this original diagram evolved into my GoddessLife."

Biss points her clicker. Another diagram pops onto the screen.

"Then I made the gateway concept into a worksheet for myself, which I started teaching in my GoddessPower Retreats."

## Step through the GoddessGateway into your GoddessLife!

### Action Steps
- Action Step 1
- Action Step 2
- Action Step 3
- Action Step 4
- Action Step 5
- Action Step 6
- Action Step 7
- Action Step 8

### GoddessLife
- confidence & believing in yourself
- bliss
- riches
- safe & secure
- serenity
- wellness
- success
- loving relationships

### Current Reality
- powerlessness
- punishment: self-sabotage, self-criticism, wrong relationships, miserable work
- lack & struggle
- fear, worry & doubt
- anxiety
- poor health, low energy
- career failure

### The Biss Tribe Retreat

© Elizabeth Ann Atkins 2024

Bianca raises her hand. "Biss, how do we know what to put for the Action Steps? I am totally clueless."

Several women groan in agreement.

"If I knew what to do," Jade says, "I'd be doing it and I wouldn't need to be here."

"Yeah, how do we figure out how to get the keys and open the gate?" Marla asks.

"With meditation," Biss exclaims with a smile. "My Goddesses, we can best hear our Supernatural Selves when we get silent and still, clear our energy, and connect with the infinite power of the divine, which means the Universe, God, Spirit, your Higher Self, or whatever higher powers you believe in. Then we create two-way communication that provides all the truths you need to know about yourself and your life."

Bianca groans. "I can't meditate! My ADHD makes my head spin in a thousand directions at once. It doesn't work for me."

"Same!" Jade groans.

"I'm fucked!" Andi crosses her arms. "I can access supernatural sources like I can walk on the moon right now. I can't—"

"We don't say that word here," Biss says, shooting a hard look at Andi, then Bianca. "What you think, then speak, is the first act of creating your reality. And we're here to create dreams, not perpetuate the nightmare of stuckness that brought you here."

Andi glares at Biss. "You make it sound so easy."

"It's *not* easy," Biss says, "but it's possible. Look at me! I did it! It wasn't long ago that I wrote this."

She glances up at the chandeliers and grasps the back of her throne chair. "All of this—the castle, the experience, and being here with you—it started in my imagination. And through this process, it became real. Fast!"

"I've never meditated before," Celeste says.

Several women echo: "Me either."

Sunshine scowls. "I've tried so hard, but my brain is like a blender. Spinning constantly."

Bianca cringes. "The Bianca Tornado won't let me quiet my mind!"

Zeusse lets out a defeated sigh and points to her head. "I got a hurricane up here. Category 100."

"Meditation is a myth!" Marla says. "It's fake. All these influencers say—" she switches to a high-pitched, mocking voice: "—just calm your mind and meditate. It's my morning routine. I'm such a spiritual being. It's so simple."

Marla rolls her eyes and returns to her own voice. "Yeah, bitch, 'cause you just did a gummie to mellow your ass out."

Delaney and Bianca chuckle.

Sammie play-swats Marla's hand. "Stop. Be nice. Listen and learn."

Discouraged chatter fills the room.

Biss raises her hands. "Everybody! Calm down! You can do this! You signed up for it! The retreat description on your contract clearly states that meditation is a major tenet of your transformation in The Biss Tribe. Remember?"

Esmerelda strokes the bowls and sings a long, sorrowful note.

"When I first tried meditation," Biss says, "it was awful. Mental chaos, noise, anything but peace. But I kept at it, every night. And soon it was *magic*. It made me psychic. And it gave me psychedelic experiences that helped me create this, for you. So trust me. And chill!"

Soft groans of dread rumble through the group as another diagram appears on the screen:

Sunday, Day 1

# Step through the GoddessGateway into your GoddessLife!

## Action Steps
Identify blocks and action steps to break through & fly.

## GoddessLife
What you want in your dream life.

## Current Reality
What you want to leave behind.

**The Biss Tribe Retreat**

© Elizabeth Ann Atkins 2024

## Welcome to The Biss Tribe

*Dear Goddess Reader: please fill in the worksheet and leave the third column blank until we meditate at The GoddessPower Pyramid.*

"It's time to do some work, my Goddesses. Turn to this diagram in your *PowerJournal*."

As the women flip through their books, Biss says, "Notice how I wrote more about feelings than things. Because our emotions are energy, and energy either attracts or pushes away what you want. So, let's spend five minutes filling in the worksheet. Write whatever comes to mind first. And leave the column on the right—the action steps—blank."

Esmerelda sounds her gong; you and the women stop writing. "How was that?" Biss asks. "Anyone want to share?"

"I need five more pages to list what I'm leaving in the dust," Bianca says.

"Use the blank pages at the back of your *PowerJournal*," Biss says. "Let it all pour out. Ladies, you can revisit these exercises this evening in your rooms, after the GoddessPower Feast. In your room, you'll also find a blank Biss Tribe journal so you can pour out your heart and soul. If you fill that up, ask your Concierge to bring you another one."

Delaney raises a hand. "My ideas have never flowed so effortlessly while I'm writing."

"That's because this is a spiritual vortex here on Infinity Mountain," Biss says. "The energy here awakens your heart and soul and makes it easier to connect with Spirit, where your GoddessGenius is free to come out and create with wild abandon."

## Sunday, Day 1

Sunshine, who's writing furiously in her *PowerJournal*, barely glances up. "I feel like I want to write constantly while I'm here because this doesn't happen at home. All these worries crash the party in my head and I make an excuse to stop believing in myself."

Several women nod and comment in agreement.

"Writing is one of the most powerful tools you'll use here," Biss says. "And here are more enhancements for your GoddessPower."

Vee places a GoddessTreasure Chest on the table in front of Biss, who opens it and holds up a clear crystal wand that's the length of her hand, along with two shiny purple stones.

"Now my Goddesses, please open your Treasure Chests," she says. "Inside you'll find your clear quartz crystal wand and two amethyst crystals. These stones carry powerful vibrations that help you activate your GoddessPower and as a result, your Supernatural Self."

You hold the crystals, fingering the smooth textures and studying the patterns and colors.

"Crystals can turbocharge your manifesting powers," Biss says, "especially amethyst and clear quartz. You can work with them by holding them, or placing them on different parts of your body, to amplify this power."

Biss walks around the table as she talks.

"Now open the black satin pouch in your Treasure Chests." The clink of beads tumbling on the table echoes through the room. From the bag, you behold a necklace of luminescent white crystals anchored by an egg-shaped, black crystal that has a silvery shimmer.

"Biss, these are just like your necklace," Zeusse says.

"Yes," Biss says, fingering hers. "The white beads are moonstone—a very high vibrational crystal that helps activate your GoddessPower. In ancient times, people believed that these crystals contained moonbeams, and even named the stones

Aphroselene, a combination of the Moon Goddess Selene and the Love Goddess Aphrodite. Moonstone also illuminates your life path and helps you discover your purpose."

Concierge helps you put on the necklace that hangs to the center of your chest.

"The large stone," Biss says, "is black tourmaline, which blocks negative energy."

Silver charms dangle over the black stone. One is The Biss Tribe logo; the other is a starburst inscribed with your name. You finger the beads and feel the cool stones on the back of your neck.

"These crystals will help power you through the week and beyond," Biss says. "So my Goddesses, our time at the RoundTable is over for now. Follow me!"

# A Preview of Your Personal Podcast in The GoddessPower Studios

As Biss leads you and the women out of the ballroom, she says, "At the end of the week, everything will come together here at SeaGoddess Castle, starting in the GoddessPower Studios."

You follow Biss down a spiral stone staircase that has a lift for Bianca's wheelchair. Walking through a long marble hallway, you pass a beautiful wine cellar whose glass doors reveal hundreds of bottles around a large, chandeliered table and chairs. At the end of the hall glows a sign: The GoddessPower Studios.

Biss leads you through the double doors into a plush lobby where The Goddess Power Show with Elizabeth Ann Atkins® in silver block letters glows in purple light against a white marble wall.

Below it, zebra-print pillows adorn the tufted black velvet sofa facing a tall silver reception desk. The ON AIR sign is dark as Biss leads you through a door into a long hallway with many doors. She opens the first one, and you follow her into a dark studio.

## Sunday, Day 1

The soft lights flicker on, illuminating the silver The Goddess Power Show letters on the purple backlit wall facing a high silver table. Surrounding it are four silver stools with tall backs and purple velvet seats. A silver microphone hangs in front of each chair, and headphones sit on the table for each person.

Facing the table is an elevated engineer's area, kind of like a DJ booth, with all kinds of lighted panels and video monitors.

"Damn, this is dope!" Zeusse exclaims, looking around.

"This is one of our studios," Biss says. "We also have studios in Detroit, New York, LA, and at SeaGoddess Castle Caribbean on Mermaid Island, as well as a studio on my yacht, Sea Goddess."

Marla runs her hands over a velvet stool and almost shrieks to Sammie: "I am so in withdrawal from my phone. This is epic! I need pics and vid of us here!"

"Biss, can we be guests?" Sammie asks. "We want to talk about our skincare line."

"Yeah!" Bianca exclaims. "How can we be guests? I want to talk about my nonprofit."

"Didn't you read the contract that you signed to come here?" Andi asks.

"I feature a Biss Tribe Goddess on the show every week," Biss says. "You're not invited until after you become a Biss Tribe success story."

Andi glances around at the women who are standing shoulder-to-shoulder and facing Biss. "We have to qualify by showing proof of the empire we've built and sustained for at least two years *and* that we've created our GoddessLife in our personal lives, too."

"Correct," Biss says, leading the group back into the hallway. "We'll share the criteria before you leave at the end of the week."

As you walk, several women chatter about past show topics.

"Biss, one of your shows inspired me to find the courage to come out as polyamorous and bi," Jade says. "I just can't do the traditional hetero-monogamy thing. It's so restrictive and unnatural. Not that I have *anybody* in my life right now. I'm in the most solo dry spell *ever*. But it's giving me space for self-discovery."

"Truth," Zeusse says. "Same here. I call it 'lover noise.' I love being in love—or at least in lust and infatuation, but I feel like it takes over my mind, like warm and fuzzy fog. I can't perform at my optimum ability when a female is pullin' at my attention and time, and I'm pourin' it all into her—at my own expense, energetically. So right now, I need every synapse in my brain firing on my how to make my girls basketball academy a global success. Nothing feels better than that."

Biss stops in her tracks and turns to face everyone. "Did everybody hear what Zeusse just said?"

"No," Jade says.

"Zeusse, please repeat what you just said for everyone to hear," Biss says.

Zeusse repeats.

"That is GoddessPower!" Biss says. "Having the ability to pull all your energy back and focus on yourself and your mission. So sear this concept in your head, heart and body, and apply it to your own mission. I'll talk about this more at The Pleasure Tent, during our training about how to avoid derailing your dreams in ManLand or LoverLand, depending on your preferences."

Biss's expression goes from grim to grinning. "This is one of my favorite topics!" Biss turns to quickly stride through a door that says The GoddessPower Studio.

You and the women follow her into a white marble hallway lined with 22 numbered doors. Esmerelda opens one so that you and the women can see a recording booth. It's all silver, with a desk, video monitor, microphone, headphones, and a camera facing a plush purple, high-backed chair whose top is embroidered with the Biss Tribe logo. Soundproofing foam covers the windowless walls.

## Sunday, Day 1

Biss steps inside, pointing to the equipment. "After you complete the five Activation Stations this week and compose your GoddessLife scripts for Power, Pleasure, Prosperity, Protection and Peace, you'll each enter one of these booths and record the audio and video versions of your script. You'll also record The GoddessPower Promise, which includes sections for each P that you'll learn as we ascend Infinity Mountain."

Sunshine groans. "I get so nervous on camera."

"I don't love the sound of my own voice," Bianca says. "It's too squeaky."

"Oh man, I don't want to be on camera," Andi says. "These girls—" she points to Sammie and Marla "—are photogenic and natural at it. I'm not."

"Neither self-criticism nor compare-itis are allowed here," Biss snaps. "And this exercise is not about looking cute or sounding like a professional broadcaster. It's about looking yourself in the eye and convincing yourself that you're the most bad ass version of yourself that you can be, and that you're here to do the work and be unstoppable about it."

Esmerelda, who's standing beside Biss, says, "For those of you who are anxious about your voice and video recordings, we'll provide a coaching session before you hit the studios. That will help you sound energetic and enthusiastic as you record your personal GoddessPower podcasts—for your eyes and ears only!—that you'll watch and listen to every morning and night, and hopefully in-between, after you go home."

"That sounds like so much work!" Sammie complains.

"Do we *have* to do this?" Jade asks. "Twice a day?!"

Biss scowls. "Absolutely! This is how you reprogram your brain and get into autopilot to create your GoddessLife. Up until now, your thoughts have been stuck in mental ruts, like a car stuck in the snow, spinning your wheels, burning the engine, wasting time and gas, inhaling toxic exhaust fumes, getting nowhere, and possibly threatening your life, depending on where you're stuck."

"That's quite grim," Delaney says woefully.

"It's the truth, one hundred percent," Zeusse says. "I'm ready to do whatever it takes to get outta my rut. Or die tryin'."

"Speak what you want!" Biss snaps. "Zeusse, de-activate those words and say, 'succeed' or 'make it happen'."

Zeusse looks stunned for a moment, then exclaims: "The Zeusse Girls Basketball Academy will be a global success!"

Sammie whispers, "This is turning into The Zeusse Show."

"Right?!" Kiki snickers, as do several other women.

"Oh hell no!" Biss exclaims, glaring at Kiki and Sammie, then looking you and every woman in the eyes. "Jealousy, resentment, mockery and the wrong kind of bitchery will stop your success! Here and in the world. Because the metaphysical laws of the universe give you back, what you put out. So, one more comment like that, and whoever says it will be escorted out of here by security. You will not poison our tribe with hate."

The women are silent. Zeusse has a poker face.

"I'm sorry," Kiki tells Zeusse, who stoically responds, "All good."

"If one of you says something brilliant that everybody needs to hear," Biss says, "I *will* shine the spotlight on you. All day long. Now, back to the power of language."

Biss steps out of the booth and into the hallway, speaking as she walks backward toward the staircase.

"My Goddesses, your words program your mind and create your reality! Your brain makes the sentence. Your mouth speaks it. Your ears hear it, and that reinforces the thought in your head, which inspires action that either holds you back or helps you soar. Which do you choose?"

Celeste looks distraught. "But the devil on my shoulder is always whispering some discouraging trash to me. Louder than the angel on my other shoulder is encouraging me."

Zeusse pretends to flick lint off her shoulder and cuts a split-second look at Kiki. "You need to knock that motherfucker off. That's what I did on the court. That bad voice inside my head was loud! So I cut the volume on it. I went into my zone where every thought in my head was the image of me shooting three-pointers, or jumping up above all the females on the other team, like superhuman, to win that game for my team."

Celeste flicks her shoulder and says, "Devil be gone!"

"Let's head back to the Inn," Biss says. "Who's ready to feast?"

# The Goddess Feast:
# On Being a Goddess Bad Ass

You're back in the ballroom at The Biss Tribe Inn, seated at one of two long tables, enjoying your favorite dinner that's prepared exactly as you like it. You and the women have freshened up in your rooms and changed into all-black evening attire that matches your personality.

"That music is so unique," Jade says, swaying to the sultry sounds of three women in black lace gowns as they play a harp, an electric violin, and a flute on stage.

"Ladies!" says Biss, sleek in all-black leather pants, stiletto sandals and a form-fitting lace halter top whose strings zig-zag up her back. "Who's ready to be a bad ass!? Say it!"

"BAD ASS!" everyone chants. "BAD ASS! BAD ASS!"

As the chant subsides, Sunshine glances down at her filet mignon and says, "But I'm so scared of being called a bitch."

"I love it when people call me a bitch," Marla says, dipping a sourdough roll in a saucer of herbed olive oil. "It means I'm speaking up for myself."

"That fear," Biss says, "is society's conditioning to keep us quiet and compliant. It's time to be bold!"

The screen over the stage drops and "BAD ASS" appears against a smoky purple background framed by sparkly leopard print.

"A Goddess does something every day that makes her feel like a Bad Ass," Biss says, pointing to the screen. "But first, let's define Bad Ass. As you know, here in The Biss Tribe, we're trailblazers, and we define things in ways that work best for us. That's why I rejected the online definition of Bad Ass, years ago when I looked it up."

Biss scowls. "The first definition said: 'A man who…' I stopped reading, because you can be born with a vagina and still have more balls than many people who have a penis. Women are bad assess, too. And I didn't like the common spelling that merges two words into one: badass. That looks weird. So, creating my own definition is an Act of Goddess; I'm a Bad Ass writer who makes up her own words. As a result, here's my Biss Tribe definition of a Goddess Bad Ass." The words stream across the screen:

"A woman with the utmost confidence and courage to think, speak, live, love and work however she wants—without hurting anyone—in ways that celebrate her talents, interests and authenticity—so she can experience her ultimate Power, Pleasure, Prosperity, Protection and Peace."

"I want to be that!" Celeste exclaims, holding a lamb chop close to her mouth. "24/7!"

## Sunday, Day 1

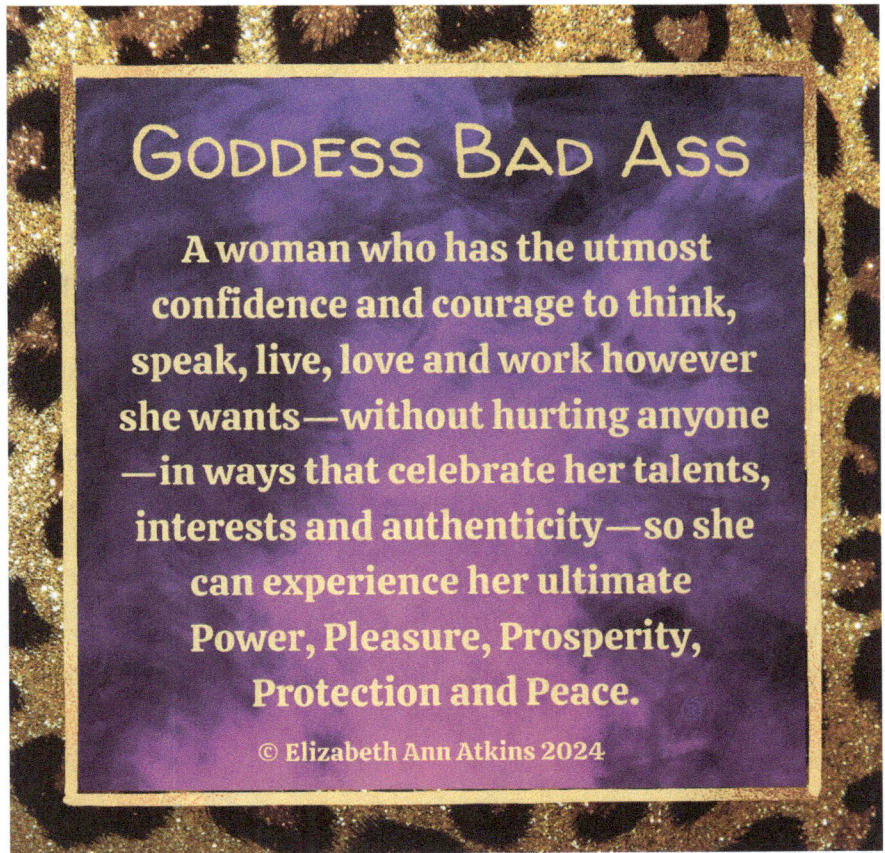

Biss smiles. "But there's a catch to our special Goddess way of being a Bad Ass. Every day, you need to do at least one thing *by yourself* without seeking any approval, accolades or concern about what anybody thinks, even if they would clap, cheer, like, follow, share and make your moment go viral. Nope!"

Marla drops her roll. Sammie clanks down her pink cocktail. And they ask in unison: "Then what's the point?"

Biss shakes her head. "You're doing this for *yourself,* to boost your confidence and self-esteem. And to flex your sovereignty over yourself. That means doing things to please yourself first and *not* being performative."

Sammie groans. "That's wasting a selfie opp, big time!"

Biss shakes her head. "Selfie, emphasis on *self*! Girls and women grow up in 'performance mode.' We're coached and critiqued and criticized for how we talk, speak, stand, sit, dress. Often to please the male gaze."

Jade says, "It made me so mad when I realized that girls are always saying sorry and sitting in a way that takes up as little space as possible while manspread is a thing." Wearing a plain black sleeveless sheath dress that shows off her tattoos, Jade pushes her chair back, sits with her legs wide, and throws her arms out.

The women laugh.

"Jade, you woke up to this," Biss says. "Many women, unfortunately, go through life so programmed to comply with these rules, that they never become aware of it."

Marla and Sammie, who like Bianca and Kiki, are wearing bodycon dresses adorned with rhinestones and feathers, raise their hands at the same time.

"We always feel like we're on trial for not being ladylike," Marla says.

Sammie adds, "I call it being punished in 'girl court' where the rules are more strict for us than for guys and men."

"I agree entirely," Delaney says, "and when I was your age, the punishment was far more severe."

Biss looks directly at you and the other women. "So this exercise on being a Goddess Bad Ass forces us to celebrate ourselves, regardless of what anyone else thinks. It's about you and only you knowing and celebrating that you are extraordinary—without needing or wanting approval or affirmation from anyone but yourself."

Marla and other women look perplexed. "I don't understand," she says. "Everything we do is to get likes, followers, sponsorships and brand deals. We're always performing."

## Sunday, Day 1

"Understood," Biss says. "But activating your GoddessPower means doing behind-the-scenes work on yourself. How you feel in private about yourself will make your more charismatic, radiant and successful in public."

Zeusse, who like Andi is wearing tuxedo pants and a buttoned dress shirt, raises her hand. "This is like, the crowd can be goin' wild while I'm on the court, and we're winning, but I know I can do better. So even though they're cheering for me, I can't receive that unless I know I'm doing my best. And if I'm doing my best, but the crowd doesn't react, it doesn't matter. Because I'm in competition with myself to be my best, every time, no matter what the fans are doing or not doing."

"I grew up as an approval junkie," Bianca says. "But you're always chasing the next high, and when it doesn't come, it sucks. You spiral into panic and lack the self-esteem to fill yourself up first."

Sammie and Marla nod. "That's us. With dopamine hits on our socials."

Celeste, whose fitted satin dress forms a dramatic V over her cleavage and flares at her shoulders, raises her glass of red wine. "Biss, *please* tell us how to level all the way up to being a Goddess Bad Ass."

Delaney nods. "I desperately want to stop thirsting for approval outside of myself."

"This is so contradictory to social media culture," Sunshine says, "which is all about external approval. And that's the point, right?"

"GoddessPower is *within!*" Biss exclaims. "We have to go inside ourselves to find it. And your daily Bad Ass Goddess Moment helps you do that. Here's an example."

Biss walks back and forth, never breaking eye contact with you and the women.

"One day, I was stressed out," she says. "The gym always pushes my reset button, so I chugged my Green Goddess Smoothie and went to my favorite spot: the squat rack. It's a square metal arch supporting a barbell, and you add weight to the barbell with metal circles called plates. I was listening to sexy hip-hop music, with the heavy bar on my shoulders, as I squatted into a seated position, then squeezed my glutes and abs while pushing up with my quads and hamstrings. I did this 15 times. The upward push against the pressure creates an amazing release of tension from my whole body."

The screen shows video of Biss doing squats in the gym, wearing a purple sports bra that says *The Biss Tribe* across the front and down one leg of her leggings.

She glances up at the video with an ecstatic expression. "In the wall of mirrors, I could see my arm and shoulder muscles flexing as I gripped the bar. My leg muscles were toned and strong and bursting with energy. And I remembered times when I had once felt so bad about my body and myself, I would look in the mirror and say, 'You fat, disgusting cow!' This moment in the gym was a celebration that I had stepped into my GoddessPower and transformed my mind and body with self-love, self-care and high self-esteem. It was *bliss!*"

Biss makes eye contact with several women. "In that moment, sweat popped from my skin. My heart pounded. I was breathing hard. It felt so good! Goosebumps danced over me from head to toe. I closed my eyes to savor the sensation. I shivered. I might have moaned. Then it was like, 'I'm having a *squat-gasm.*' My leg muscles were trembling so hard, I felt wobbly. This was my Bad Ass Goddess Moment. I didn't care what anybody thought. Or if anybody was looking at me. Because this was for *me.* I felt strong and accomplished for challenging my body to look and feel my best."

Esmerelda, wearing a chiffon jumpsuit that ruffles at her wrists, steps beside her. "Biss, just to be clear, that was *your* moment. The

## Sunday, Day 1

gym was crowded. The people around you—mostly men—probably noticed you. But it didn't matter. You were making a deposit in your Bad Ass Goddess account, to withdraw anytime you needed a boost of confidence during the rest of the day."

Marla gasps. "Oh! I get it now. It's the opposite of my whole life! But I get it."

Biss smiles. "My beautiful Goddesses, tell me some of *your* Bad Ass Moments."

Celeste flashes a mischievous smile. "When I make my husband feel so good during sex that he starts crying."

"But that involves another person," Jade protests.

"So does Zeusse's story when she's playing in front of a crowd," Andi says. "I don't understand."

"The Bad Ass element here is how Zeusse and Celeste feel inside because they did their best and felt great about it. It's not about how someone else reacts."

"I need to practice that when my girl band plays," Jade says. "Definitely feel like a bad ass when I'm practicing my guitar all by myself."

Sunshine adds, "My Bad Ass Moment is when I make a delicious spinach, provolone and pesto omelet. Just for me."

"Mine," Delaney adds, "is when I do a yoga pose perfectly and my whole body feels in flow."

Andi nods. "For me, it's painting. I just get lost in it. And when I shred the bullseye on the paper target at the gun range. And when I ride my Harley home."

"Yes!" Biss exclaims. "How many of you have had a Bad Ass Goddess Moment, and you were so excited to share it with someone, but when you did, their lack of excitement—or criticism—burst your bubble?"

Sunshine's hand shoots up. "Never should have told that stupid MF. My ex. He was always shooting down what made me happy."

"Pop!" Jade moves her hand like she's holding a knife and stabbing the air. "*Pop! Pop!* Goes my excitement when the bubble burster pierces it with their venomous fangs. My ex-best friend was the queen of that."

"That's why you don't have to tell anyone," Biss says. "They might try to diminish your joy or accuse you of bragging or showing off."

Zeusse, who's enjoying a tomahawk steak with broccolini and garlic mashed potatoes, says, "I stay quiet until folks prove worthy of knowing my moves."

"I like that," Bianca says.

Biss stands behind her empty chair at the head of the table, while Esmerelda does the same at the other end.

Esmerelda says, "Ladies, check the little crystal box nestled in the flowers on the table in front of you."

You and the women open the boxes. Inside is a charm of the yin-yang symbol, a circle with a black swirl and a white swirl, like two commas—one upside down—and a dot of the opposite color in the wide part.

"Your Concierges will attach them to your charm bracelets when they return," says Esmerelda, walking between the tables.

"The yin-yang symbol represents the feminine and masculine energy that's naturally within us," Biss says. "GoddessPower requires a balance of both, but most of us need to awaken our masculine energy. Having a daily Bad Ass Moment helps you do that."

Bianca asks, "Does our masculine energy mean acting like a man?"

"No," Biss says. "Just like a man who's able to express his emotions, show empathy and give affection is in his feminine energy, a woman who is assertive, aggressive and ambitious is flexing her healthy masculine energy."

"I feel super yang in my girl band," Jade says.

## Sunday, Day 1

Sammie groans. "I'm on feminine overload. Hate it!"

"But we don't want to be like dudes," Marla says. "Can we be both?"

"That's the goal," Biss says. "But for most of us who have been conditioned to stay in our feminine energy and fear our masculine energy, we need to awaken that side of ourselves."

Celeste drops her lamb chop and says, "Oh, honey talk to me! To me, feminine means playing nice and I'm sick of that."

"Where does sex fit into all this?" Sammie asks.

"Great question," Biss says. "To truly unleash our desires and enjoy pleasure in ways that fulfill us and allow our wildest expression, we need to unleash our masculine energy. It will also help you excel in business."

"It seems like feminine energy," Sunshine says, "is all about being quiet, playing small, feeling scared to speak up, and not creating conflict."

"That's wounded feminine energy," Biss says, "because we fear being punished for not following the rules of how a girl or woman should behave. Here on Infinity Mountain, you're healing your feminine energy and learning to unleash your masculine energy, so you have balance."

Biss points to the symbol on the screen. "The yin-yang symbol represents perfect balance. And your daily Bad Ass Moment helps you activate your masculine energy. So tonight or tomorrow morning, please write in your *PowerJournal* seven things you can do every day to feel like a Bad Ass. It can be anything. Grilling the perfect meal. Growing beautiful flowers in your garden. Being an awesome parent. Staying in your GoddessGenius Zone while refusing to succumb to fear, worry, doubt or distraction. Doing what you want to do, and not caring what anyone thinks. It's time to flex your yang!"

The Concierges serve plates of the most delicious desserts. As excited chatter erupts over the rich array of chocolate cake, cheesecake and other treats customized for you and each woman's unique preferences, the Concierges attach the yin-yang charms to your bracelets, creating a festive jingle.

"OhmyGod," Sammie exclaims, "this chocolate soufflé is insane!"

Zeusse looks up from the French vanilla ice cream melting over her warm peach cobbler. "This is the bomb, almost as good as my grandmother's down South." She closes her eyes to savor another bite.

The sultry music plays louder.

"My Goddesses!" Biss exclaims as you and the women enjoy your desserts. "Who's ready for some fun?"

Everyone cheers.

"The Concierges will escort you to your rooms," Esmerelda says, "to change into bathing suits or loungewear."

"Then we'll re-convene on The Goddess Playground out back," Biss says. "You can swim in the pool, sit in the hot tubs, relax around the fire, dance under the stars, get a fireside massage, and most of all, have fun."

## Quiet Time in Your Room

When you return to your room and relax in the spa-like bathroom that offers both a shower and a large sunken bathtub, along with an array of your favorite candles, soaps and self-care products, you retreat to the cozy bed and write in your *PowerJournal*.

## Sunday, Day 1

*Dear Goddess Reader:*

*Write 8 Bad Ass Goddess activities—one for every day—that you can easily incorporate into your lifestyle. If more come to mind, write them here. Refer to this page as a reminder to do one of these things daily to flex your yang and be your most authentic YOU, living in your fully activated GoddessPower.*

- I feel like a Bad Ass when I:
_____

  Because it makes make me feel like:
  _____
  _____

- I feel like a Bad Ass when I:
_____

  Because it makes make me feel like:
  _____
  _____

- I feel like a Bad Ass when I:
_____

  Because it makes make me feel like:
  _____
  _____

- I feel like a Bad Ass when I:
_____

## Welcome to The Biss Tribe

Because it makes make me feel like:
_____
_____

• I feel like a Bad Ass when I:
_____

Because it makes make me feel like:
_____
_____

• I feel like a Bad Ass when I:
_____

Because it makes make me feel like:
_____
_____

• I feel like a Bad Ass when I:
_____

Because it makes make me feel like:
_____
_____

• I feel like a Bad Ass when I:
_____

## Sunday, Day 1

Because it makes make me feel like:

_____

_____

That night, you sleep better than you have in a very long time, and your dreams are so vivid, you want to stay in them. They're a wild mix of the day's experiences, and you can still hear Biss's voice—

"Wake up, Goddess!" she says with a gentle tone. "It's the dawn of a new day! You have infinite potential to create the GoddessLife of your wildest dreams."

You open your eyes. You're alone in the room. *Oh wait, that's actually Biss talking.* She's speaking through the intercom system:

"Before you rise," Biss says, "today and every day, keep your eyes closed, and your body still. Imagine at your very center, a ball of yellow light, like the sun glowing within you. As you're waking up, see that sunburst of energy gently expanding through you, tingling into every cell in your body, infusing you with supernatural immunity, restoring your DNA to perfection, surrounding you with a forcefield of protection, and filling you with energy, excitement and enthusiasm for the day ahead. Let it make you be confident, courageous and fearless, going after your heart's wildest desires. This sunburst of energy within you is your GoddessPower. Let nothing dim it. Make it blaze!"

You lie still, allowing her words to sink in. Then you write about it, and your dreams, in the Dreams & Ideas section of your *PowerJournal*. You feel that, despite the lingering fear that you could fail at implementing the amazing lessons learned here after you get home, you're eager to try.

Concierge delivers a silver tray with morning beverages, including coffee, tea and a Green Goddess Smoothie, along with a basket of fruit.

Then, after the invigorating exercise of your choice—a mountain hike or bike ride, a garden walk, yoga, strength training, a swim, or a jog—you shower, dress and join the women for breakfast, enjoying your favorite entrees prepared exactly as you like them. Next, dressed in your preferred style of comfortable clothes and shoes, you board the bus that will transport you and your Biss Tribe sisters to the first stop up Infinity Mountain: The GoddessPower Pyramid.

# Monday Day 2

## GoddessPower Activation Station #1

*The GoddessPower Pyramid*

# Welcome to The GoddessPower Pyramid

After an ear-popping ascent up the pine-shrouded mountain, the bus turns onto a level dirt road.

"Holy shit!" Jade exclaims from the seat beside you. "Why is the bus heading straight into a stone wall?"

Zeusse laughs. "Chill, sweetheart. It's a stone-covered gate. See, it's opening."

Inside the gate, as the bus passes through thick woods, Esmerelda stands at the front of the bus near Vee, the driver.

"Ladies," Esmerelda says, "welcome to the GoddessPower Pyramid."

When the bus stops, and you step off, you're facing a huge glass pyramid in a clearing on a plateau on the mountainside.

"This is Isis Peak," Esmerelda says, "named for one of the most powerful and revered goddesses ever, Isis from ancient Egypt."

To your left is the rugged stone mountain. To your right is a line of pine trees alongside a railing and a steep drop-off to the vast valley below. Tall trees shroud the front and back of the pyramid. Sunlight gleams from its gold metal points and beams, while the sun's reflection off its glass panes obscures the interior.

"Come," Esmerelda says, leading you through a tunnel-type vestibule that opens onto a sun-filled atrium filled with tropical trees, plants, and a stream gurgling over rocks. "Please get comfortable in your rooms, enjoy a light snack, and we'll see you shortly in the sanctuary."

Your Concierge escorts you up an elevator to your room, whose slanted glass window offers a stomach-flipping view of the valley. The room's Cleopatra-esque style is tasteful and extremely comfortable. You change into loose-fitting clothing made of fabric that feels as light as air against your skin, and cushioned sandals that seem to massage your feet.

You enjoy your favorite snacks and beverages from a mini buffet, then Concierge Jami escorts you down the elevator.

## The Meditarium

The elevator doors open and a tantalizing scent—like sandalwood and rose—greets you at the doorway to an expansive underground room where soft, spa-like music plays.

"Look at *this!*" Celeste exclaims, as you and the group enter and look up at a domed ceiling whose recessed lighting glows softly with alternating pink and purple.

"Whaaatttt?" Jade says. "We get to sit in flower chairs?"

Arranged in a half circle on the plush, blue-green carpeted floor are 24 round, velvet ottomans shaped like giant lotus flowers. Each has an emerald-green base from which rise eight cobalt-blue "petals" curving upward, high enough to provide back and head support.

"Welcome to the Meditarium," says Esmerelda, who's wearing a flowy crepe lavender tunic over leggings. "As your Concierges guide you to your pods, please get comfortable. These individual meditation stations are designed like blue lotus water lilies, which grew on the Nile River in Egypt, and the lotus flower carries a sacred message for your journey here."

Your Concierge guides you to your pod. You climb through the gap between the flower petals; the opening provides a clear view of two pods at the front of the room where Esmerelda is standing.

## Monday, Day 2

You sink into the cushioned velvet, luxuriating in comfort with a tasseled pillow, a plush blanket and your GoddessTreasure Chest.

"This is so fun!" Marla exclaims. "I am like fiending for my phone to take pics."

Celeste has a euphoric expression as she leans back, extends her legs and closes her eyes. A Concierge lifts Bianca from her wheelchair and places her in her pod.

Jade glances up at the domed ceiling, then down at the chairs. "Wow, a planetarium where you meditate. The Meditarium. That is freaking genius."

"That's what's up," Zeusse says, stretching out in her pod.

The plush surroundings absorb the women's excited chatter as they take their places and Biss sprints in, wearing cream lace leggings over a satin poet's shirt that exposes one shoulder.

"Who's ready to activate your superpowers?" Biss asks.

"Let's do it!" Andi shouts as the women cheer.

Biss stands beside Sunshine's pod and rests a hand on one of the velvet petals.

"First, let's talk about the lotus flower," Biss says. "It's deeply symbolic of rebirth, because it grows in water from roots in the mud. It blooms beautifully on top of the water. But every night, it retreats back into the murky river, only to pop up in all its glory—sparkling clean—at sunrise. We are *that*."

Esmerelda nods. "Open your GoddessTreasure Chest, and lift the latch labeled Power."

You find a yellow beaded bracelet, a bottle of rosemary essential oil, and a lightning bolt pendant.

"Place the citrine bracelet on your right wrist," she says. "These yellow crystals carry a vibration of power."

Concierge attaches the pendant to your bracelet, which joins the jingles as all the women do the same.

Biss walks between the pods, making eye contact with you and each woman. "Your GoddessPower is a survival tool. It's often activated during the most difficult moments of your life. During duress. Stress. Sadness. Grief. Pain. Trauma."

Delaney says, "Pressure in rocks makes diamonds."

"Exactly!" Biss smiles. "Wait 'til you hear what I say about diamonds tomorrow at the Pleasure Tent."

"Diamonds in a Pleasure Tent," Sunshine says. "That sounds luscious."

"Our struggles help us grow and enjoy pleasure more intensely," Biss says, "just like the lotus takes root in a shifting river and blooms into a beautiful flower."

## Your GoddessPower Activation Begins

The lights dim and the ceiling dome turns purple, flashing with white and gold lightning bolts.

"Ladies, use the remote in your pod," Esmerelda says, "to recline one of the pedals so you can lean back and watch the video screen on the ceiling dome, like when you're in a planetarium."

You and the women lean back and gaze up at the lightshow, which illuminates each woman's face in colorful flashes.

"Welcome to your GoddessPower Activation," Biss says, leaning back in her pod and gazing up at the screen. It shows a woman's silhouette with golden light pulsing from the sky, through the top of her head, down her body, and into the earth.

"Let's talk about energy for a minute," Biss says. "Come with me, all the way back to high school physics class."

Words pop onto the ceiling screen as she talks and points upward; you lean back to watch a cartoon of a dynamite stick whose wick is sparking.

## Monday, Day 2

"Energy can be neither created nor destroyed, but it can change form," Biss says. "Remember that? My science teacher gave the example of a dynamite stick that's just an object sitting there keeping to itself, until a spark is applied, and BOOM!"

The cartoon dynamite stick explodes with a flash of red, orange and yellow light across the screen.

"It sets off the stick's dormant energy," Biss says, "which explodes with enough force to blow up everything around it. We are THAT! Our GoddessPower is already inside us. We just need the spark to set off that dormant power. Pain is often the spark, and you're about to learn how to keep it blazing."

You and the women are quiet, watching the screen.

"Everything in the universe is made of tiny particles that are vibrating, even in objects that appear solid, like your lotus pods and your jewelry," Biss says.

The domed ceiling flashes with lightning bolts as video shows rock boulders tumbling down a mountain.

"Some energy is dense, like rocks," Biss says. "Some energy is light, like lightning. It's all made of electrons and protons that are whirling around inside atoms that make up everything. This registers as a vibrational frequency, which radiates through and out from the object. Dense, solid things vibrate at a lower frequency, while the invisible energy of the universe vibrates at the highest frequency."

The screen shows a waterfall with a rainbow glowing in the mist as the sunshine hits it.

"When sunlight hits moisture," Biss says, "the moisture splits the white light into colors that make them visible. This enables us to see the light that is otherwise invisible."

The rainbow morphs into a woman's silhouette; light glows within her and sparkles around her.

"This high-frequency light is invisible, yet it's inside and around our physical bodies," Biss says.

The screen shows a monitor with squiggly lines zig-zagging and printing on paper inside a machine.

"The synapses firing in your brain are electrical impulses that can be measured on a mechanical device in squiggly lines on this EEG from an electroencephalography machine," Biss says.

Then the screen shows a rotating model of a human head highlighted in areas with splotches of red, green, yellow, blue and purple. Biss says, "Electronic brain energy can also be measured in heat maps that show up on a computer screen."

The screen shows the outline of a woman's form with a glowing red heart in her chest, pulsating bigger, then smaller, to replicate a heartbeat.

"Electricity keeps our hearts beating," Biss says as the heartbeat stops. "If you need proof, then think about what reverses cardiac arrest."

On the screen, paddles connected to coiled wires appear on each side of the woman's chest. With a deep *buzzzzz* sound, bolts of electricity jolt into her heart from each paddle, and her heart resumes beating—big, then small, big, then small.

"An electric jolt from a defibrillator restarts the heartbeat," Biss says. "Why? Because the electricity pulsing through you is your spirit. When a person dies, their soul, this energy, leaves the body, taking the electrical impulses with it. A defibrillator reactivates the electricity and life—the soul—returns to the body."

"Whoah!" Andi exclaims. "I never thought about it like that."

The screen shows a woman's form that glows with light expanding from her core into a huge bubble around her.

"This energy is so big and bright, it creates your aura, your energy body—a forcefield that can extend 18 feet around your physical body."

"GoddessPower" forms in the golden ball of light at the center of the woman's torso.

"But how do we activate this GoddessPower that we're all born with?" Words form on the screen, then flow into the woman's silhouette, swirling in the yellow ball. Biss reads as they appear:

"Meditation... high-vibe living... Pranayama... energy clearing... journaling... rituals... The GoddessPower Promise... your GoddessVoice... your GoddessVision... your ascent up Infinity Mountain... and your initiation into The Biss Tribe."

The words condense into a red-orange swirl inside the yellow ball. Suddenly, with a loud *crackle-sizzle-geyser-whoosh* sound—letters explode out in a starburst of red-orange-yellow words.

"Say them with me, my Goddesses!" Biss exclaims as the words form on the screen. "Power! Pleasure! Prosperity! Protection! Peace!"

The 24 voices exclaiming these words electrify the air.

"OK, the science lesson is over," Biss says playfully as Vee and Panther help Esmerelda spread out a plush lavender rug and arrange the 14 brass sound bowls and wooden sticks.

# The Four GoddessPower Activation Tools That Awaken Your Supernatural Self

The soft crackle of electricity fills the air as lightning flashes dramatically around a woman on the ceiling screen.

"Now let's talk about the four GoddessPower Activation Tools that awaken your supernatural self," Biss says. "These tools attune our energy with the power currents, also known as the frequencies, of God/Goddess/Creator/Universe/Spirit."

You can't see her, but Andi sounds discouraged: "Wait, I'm a nuts-and-bolts type person. Not used to relying on anything that's invisible. I need to touch it and hold it in my hands."

Celeste laughs. "Shock *me,* baby! Bring on *all* the currents and electrify my ass. I need it every bit of it."

"Yeah, let's plug in and power up, bitches!" Marla says.

Andi groans, "Man, I don't know."

Several other women make sounds of self-doubt.

"If this sounds bizarre to any of you," Biss says, "please just follow along. I'll guide you every step of the way."

Esmerelda's angelic voice and unique musical sounds fill the room as the ceiling screen shows sparkling golden light cascading over the woman's silhouette.

Biss says, "I'm going to teach you four simple techniques right now, that will change your life. The first GoddessPower Activation Tool is a breathing exercise called *Pranayama.* Then an energy clearing. Then a guided meditation, followed by journaling."

Moans of protest rumble through the women.

"Like I said yesterday, meditation terrifies me," Andi says. "I am so fucked."

"Let's just try," Celeste says.

"Yeah," Sunshine says, "maybe being in the GoddessVortex will make it easier. And with Biss leading us, hopefully meditation will finally work for us."

"I'm down," Zeusse says.

A collective groan rumbles through the Meditarium.

"That groaning doesn't sound like GoddessPower," Biss snaps. "That sounds like quitter vibes. And we don't have quitters here."

Esmerelda's music becomes louder and more beautiful.

"Trust me," Biss says. "I'll guide you every step of the way. So I need everyone to set the intention to experience the magic of meditation. Say it with me: I'm setting the intention to experience the magic of meditation."

## Monday, Day 2

You and the women repeat that as the screen shows a transmission tower beaming signals to cell phones, which light up when the signals hit.

"Meditation activates your GoddessPower by attuning you to the infinite energy of the universe," Biss says. "And we connect with that energy and tap into divine guidance—and have two-way communication with God, Spirit, Angels, Ancestors, and all of the divine—the same way we use our cell phones."

Sounds of protest erupt from the shadowy pods.

"Wait, what?" Kiki snaps.

"I don't believe that," Andi quips. "It can't be that easy."

"Why have I never heard this before?" Bianca demands.

"Because it's the ultimate power!" Biss shouts over the noise. "And it makes us unstoppable and supernatural!"

Bianca sounds furious: "Why isn't this taught in schools?"

"Yeah!" Kiki says. "Why isn't it common knowledge?"

"Ladies, calm down!" Biss shouts. "Most humans lack the desire and the discipline to do the work to activate this power, even if they know that it exists and that it can grant their greatest wishes."

"Oh, there's the catch," Andi says, "it takes work!"

"What sets us apart as Goddess thought leaders, innovators, influencers, and entrepreneurs," Biss says, "is that we tap into this energy and allow it to guide us into our infinite potential. And no, it's not as easy as turning on your cell phone and typing in the wi-fi password. At all!"

"Darn it!" Sammie sighs. "That would be amazing!"

Biss continues with a threatening tone: "So only those of you who are willing to do the work, diligently and daily, will truly achieve your GoddessVision and live your GoddessLife."

The room goes silent.

## The GoddessPower Pyramid

"Now that I've got your attention," Biss says, "let's think about activating your GoddessPower the same way that you use your cell phone. If you're in a place with no cell towers, you get no service. If you're in an area with spotty wi-fi, your connection goes in and out."

The screen shows the sun and stars and outer space radiating golden beams to silhouettes of people, which glow when the beams strike them.

"Think of the energy that activates your GoddessPower as divine wi-fi," Biss says. "With your phone, you trust that the wi-fi is there, and you trust that it will wirelessly connect your device to an invisible network where you can access people and information everywhere. All you need is the password."

"That's dope," Zeusse says, "but what's the password to the GoddessPower network?"

Esmerelda's satiny voice floats through the air with a deep tone, "OOOOooooohhhhhmmmmmm." At the same time, the *Om* symbol floats across the domed screen above.

"That's the password to the GoddessPower network," Biss says. "That sacred sound, *Om*. O. M. Electricity used to be measured in ohms. When we say this tone in an elongated way, like *Ooooohhhhmmmm*, it creates a vibration and sound bath that clears our energy and connects us with the universal field of knowledge where our GoddessPower is pulsing right now."

Andi groans, "Help! I'm lost in the cosmic fog!"

Jade asks, "Why doesn't it just come into our heads by itself?"

"Because!" Celeste exclaims. "Our human brains are so full of noise and self-doubt and everybody else's opinions and all the rules we have to play by."

Sammie huffs. "Why do we need cosmic guidance? It seems more realistic for GoddessPower to be about helping women use our own brains to guide ourselves."

## Monday, Day 2

Marla lets out a cynical laugh. "Uh, excuse me, but where has that gotten you, besides lost in Man Land. We wouldn't be here if we had figured that one out."

Biss turns on the lights. The women shield their eyes and groan in protest.

"GoddessPower is not realistic!" Biss shouts, standing in front of her pod facing you and the women. "It's not normal. It's not easy. It's not common or commonly known!"

"Biss," Celeste says. "I know you're about tired of us whiny broads. But what if my mind stays on fast-forward, always thinking about work, my family and all the other chaos that's swirling around up here?"

She points to her head, and glances at several women who are anxiously nodding. "My mind is a hungry monster that craves worry, fear and doubt."

"Same!" Sunshine sighs.

Jade says, "I am so in panic mode right now."

Celeste asks, "What if we can't get into your meditation groove?"

Biss walks to Celeste's pod. "Think about the clarity of when you started writing the recipes in the doctor's office. You were getting a divine download. Your GoddessPower—which was activated by your emotional and physical pain that day—was connecting you to the supernatural source that was giving you instructions on how to change your life. You blocked out any- and all chatter in your mind and you were in your GoddessGenius Zone."

"I was?" Celeste asks.

"What's a GoddessGenius Zone?" Jade asks.

"Something we'll explore later," Biss says, "but basically it's when you're totally tapped into what you love. You lose track of all time and space, and it feels like an out-of-body experience, because you're in your flow state. Celeste, it's when you're baking.

Jade, when you're playing in your band. Zeusse, when you're playing ball. Andi, when you're painting. It's the thing you do best and love the most, and that's the magic space where your GoddessPower explodes."

Biss climbs into her pod and crosses her legs, her spine straight and her head in perfect alignment.

"So let's just get to it," Biss says as the lights dim and the ceiling casts soft pink and gold light over the women. "Right now, you're going to learn a simple spiritual practice that includes the four GoddessPower Activation Tools: breathing, energy clearing, meditating, and journaling."

Andi nods. "OK, my heart is saying, 'I think I can, I think I can,' but my heart is pounding like crazy. I am freakin' terrified."

"Feel the fear and do it anyway," Biss says. "Just sit back, relax, follow my voice, and believe—*know!*—that you're full of infinite power that's waiting to explode up and out of you."

Zeusse smiles. "That's what's up!"

Biss smiles. "OK my Goddesses. Let's do this!"

# A Goddess Practices Daily Spiritual Hygiene

## GoddessPower Activation Tool #1: Pranayama

As Esmerelda's wordless song and music continue, Biss says, "Let's start with a breathing exercise called *Pranayama*. This is tool number one. It primes your brain and body for meditation. It also calms you and energizes you all at once, so use it any time you need to reduce anxiety or rev up for great mental focus."

Biss speaks as her words stream across the screen:

"*Pranayama* is a pretty word for 'Alternate Nostril Breathing.' *Prana* is Sanskrit for 'breath' and *yama* means 'control.' The goal is

## Monday, Day 2

to infuse your brain and body with oxygen and expel the old air, which releases toxins and promotes mental and physical wellness."

Biss presses her thumb to the left side of her nose.

"Press your thumb to one nostril so it closes," she says, "and inhale so deeply through the other nostril that your belly expands, as if you're filling yourself with air. With each inhalation, savor the sensation of cool, fresh air entering your body and invigorating you."

You and all the women follow her instructions.

"Then lift your thumb and press your ring fingertip to your other nostril," Biss says. "Exhale through your open nostril, until all the air is expelled. Think about expelling the old, stale air and energy with each exhalation. Let's do this several times."

You and the women follow Biss's lead to repeat the exercise four times. Biss lets out a soft moan. "Mmmm. Anybody else have an oxygen buzz?"

Marla says, "It feels awkward."

"But good!" Sammie adds. "It made me chillax!"

*Dear Goddess Reader: You can watch a video demonstration of Pranayama on the YouTube channel for The Goddess Power Show with Elizabeth Ann Atkins® by using this QR code:*

# The GoddessPower Pyramid

GoddessPower Tools

# Let's Cleanse Our Energy in a Shower of Light and a Sound Bath

### GoddessPower Activation Tool #2: Chakra Clearing

Biss looks excited as she says, "Let's bask in a cascade of sparkling light that cleanses our energy, then clears our chakras. This is tool number two. Ready?"

The lights are dim as Esmerelda's music softens.

"Please lie back and look at the dome," Biss says with a soothing tone. The screen shows the silhouette of a woman's body with colorful balls of light glowing along her spine, from her tailbone to the top of her head.

"Our bodies have seven main energy centers that play an important role in our mind-body-spirit wellness. Are any of you familiar with the chakra system?"

"The what?" Andi asks as several women say yes.

"The chakra system comes from ancient Hindu traditions," Biss says and more small lights glow in and around the female silhouette. "It's a network of energy centers in and around our bodies."

# Monday, Day 2

The words, "Stress and trauma are toxic," stream across the screen.

"We all know," Biss says, "that negative energy from stress, trauma, fear and other emotions can cause a headache or stomachache, diarrhea, rashes, chronic illnesses like colitis, conditions like eczema, and even cancer and fatal heart attacks."

Biss continues: "Stress is bad energy that stays in our bodies and makes us sick. So we need to cleanse our energy bodies of trauma and stresses to prevent emotion-induced ailments and to feel peaceful. One way to cleanse that negative energy is to do a daily practice to clear our energy centers, our chakras."

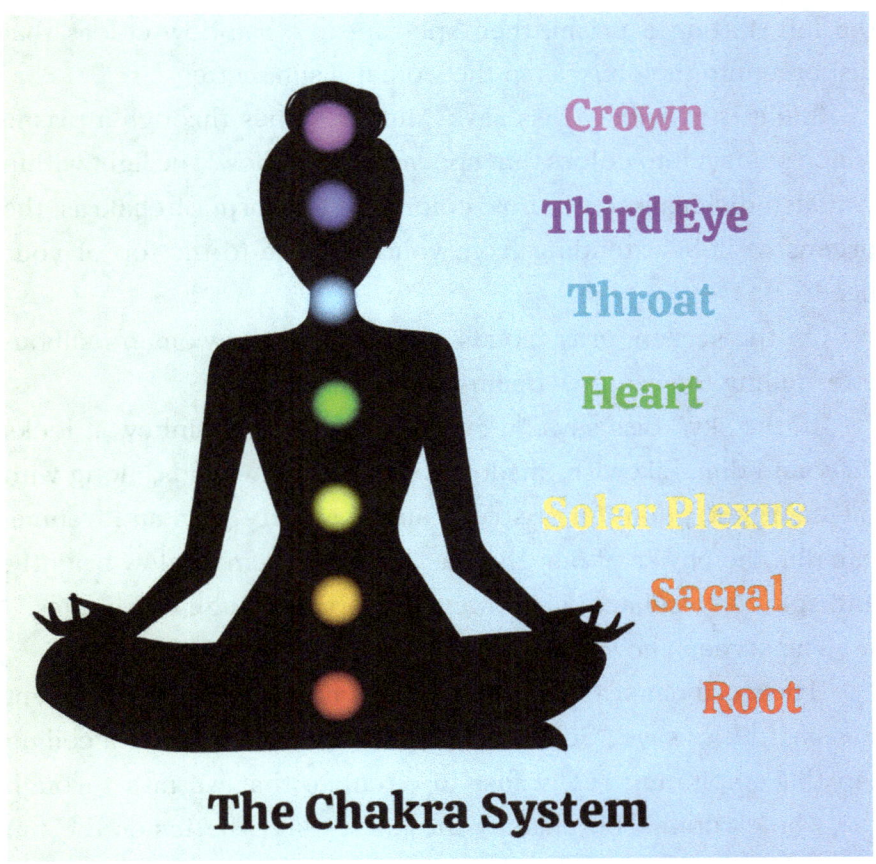

## The Goddess Power Pyramid

The colorful lights in the woman's silhouette glow brightly, one at a time, from her tailbone to the top of her head.

"Just like a high-fat diet causes cholesterol to clog the arteries that can cause a fatal heart attack," Biss says, "the accumulation of negative energy on the chakras can block the positive attributes of each energy center from flowing in your life. So, just like when someone eats a low-fat diet to prevent clogged arteries, or eats more fiber to cleanse their digestive systems, or takes a shower every day to remove dirt from their hair and skin, you can clear your chakras to remove the negative energy that accumulates on them every day, over a lifetime, and even from past lifetimes."

On the left side of the screen, a beam of light shoots in from the left, hitting a prism, then splitting into rainbow colors that disperse into the chakras in the woman's silhouette.

"Light is invisible," Biss says, "until it shines through a prism, which splits it into colors that appear as a rainbow. The light within you also divides into rainbow colors—in the form of chakras, the organs of light extending from your tailbone to the top of your head."

On the screen, gray clouds rumble over the woman's silhouette, dulling the rainbow beams and light orbs.

"In the sky," Biss says, "if smog is blocking a rainbow, it looks dirty and dim. Likewise, shadows of ancestral wounds, along with the energetic pollution of stress, anger, anxiety, pain and trauma, can dim the power of our chakras. We want them to glow brightly, and spin to circulate their powerful energy through our bodies."

The screen shows a ceiling fan with a light attached.

"The word chakra means 'spinning wheel of energy' in ancient Sanskrit," Biss says. "So think of a heat lamp attached to a ceiling fan that's spinning really fast to circulate that warmth through the whole room. The cleaner the blades are, the faster the fan can spin and the more brightly the light can glow and radiate its energy. Since each chakra rules a different aspect of your being, you want them all on the fastest and brightest settings."

Biss pauses. "Everybody with me?"

"Kinda airy-fairy," Andi quips, "but I'm trying to hang on."

"Good," Biss says. "Because this internal power system can turbocharge your quest to manifest your GoddessLife. And if you don't do regular cleaning and maintenance, you could be holding toxic energy that blocks your connection to Spirit and causes discomfort, disease and even death."

Celeste laughs. "My chakras need a power wash!"

"Mine too," Sunshine says. "I think mine look more like a gumball machine; they're so heavy with shame and pain that they fell down into my belly, all on top of each other."

Marla sounds worried. "How much time does it take every day to use these tools?"

Sammie adds, "Oh my God, it sounds like a full-time job."

"Just like you allocate time in your day to exercise because you know it gets results," Biss says, "you can prioritize time to flex your GoddessPower muscles. I'd say start with 30 minutes a day to use these four tools."

Several woman groan. Biss sounds annoyed. "There is no magic pill. Shortcuts often get us lost. And avoiding the work gets us nowhere. This is why most people never maximize their potential. They're not willing to do the work. You decide."

The women are silent as Biss looks up at the screen, where a red ball of light glows at the base of the spine on the woman's silhouette.

"Each chakra has a name, a corresponding color, a prayer and a sound that clears it," Biss says. "For example, the ruby-red **Root Chakra** represents physical survival, safety, money and sexual health. If this chakra is blocked or unbalanced, we experience problems around our physical survival, safety, money and sexual health. The same goes for all the issues with the other six main chakras."

Sunshine asks, "Can I just get a Root Chakra replacement? Mine has obviously been malfunctioning for a long time."

Biss laughs. "That's a fun way to think about it. But the beauty is that you can unblock your chakras and bring balance to these areas of your life. I'm about to show you how. It really works. Remember, though, it takes *work*. Every day. That's why your GoddessPower Activation is rooted in a spiritual *practice*. But the results are worth the effort."

Biss announces a break for everyone to stretch and use the rest room. Afterwards, as you and the women settle back in, the Concierges offer crystal goblets of water and Green Goddess Smoothies, as well as pink and purple fruit smoothies.

"Enjoy an energizing smoothie," Biss says, "before we take a shower of light and a sound bath, then meditate and journal. It's important to stay hydrated as we do this."

# Connect with Spirit and Your Supernatural Self

## GoddessPower Activation Tool #3: Meditation

After the break, Biss holds up a *PowerJournal*. "Keep this handy, because you're going to journal about any guidance that you receive during the meditation. Turn to the page that says GoddessVision Meditation number one."

The room is silent as Biss speaks in a soothing tone:

## Monday, Day 2

*Dear Goddess Reader: Please use this QR code to hear or watch Biss leading this energy clearing, meditation and journaling exercise.*

GoddessPower Tools

Sit with your spine straight. Close your eyes and become very aware of your breath, your face, and your body. Notice any tension in your forehead, your jaw, your neck, your back, and anywhere else. Then envision those muscles as if they're butter, growing warmer and softer, melting away all tension into a warm, sweet flow circulating through your body.

Now focus on your breath. Let's breathe in through the nose, and exhale through the mouth. Inhale so deeply that your belly pokes out slightly, and become aware of the sensations of that delicious, fresh air flowing into your body, followed by the old air leaving. Continue to inhale and exhale.

Breath is our life force. Infusing our brains and bodies with fresh oxygen enables us to relax, rejuvenate and activate our greatest GoddessPower. Now let's inhale peace, and exhale anxiety. Inhale joy... exhale worry. Breathe in faith... exhale fear. Inhale confidence... exhale conflict.

## The GoddessPower Pyramid

Let's set the intention to clear our energy, get into a deeply relaxing state of meditation, connect with the divine, and learn the guidance we need to bring our GoddessVisions into 3-D reality.

Now imagine you're walking outside, onto the grass. As you look up at the sky, a golden beam of sparkling light shoots down to consume your entire being. This powerful pillar of light pulses all around you and through you, glowing like a crown of light above you, then pouring its warm, golden glow—like a shower of light—into your head, cascading down your throat, through your chest, your arms and out your fingertips, extending into your abdomen, then surging down your legs and shooting tiny lightning bolts from your feet into the ground.

Envision this light shooting from your tailbone into the earth, through the mud, rocks, and water, then anchoring to the core of Mother Earth. Now imagine that this pillar of light is surging up from the center of earth, through your body, and up into the infinity of sky and space.

As this luminescent beam pulsates up and down, creating a crystalline column of light anchored in the earth and plugging you into the infinite energy of the universe, you are the connecting point between heaven and earth, with your heart at the very center.

Now in your heart space, envision someone whom you love more than anyone. Savor that feeling of pure love and joy. See the light shower pouring through you and illuminating that love, expanding it outward from your heart, filling your entire

## Monday, Day 2

body, then bursting into a joyous bubble around you.

Imagine this love brightening the light inside your body, illuminating every cell. See the light that's infused with love going into every cell in your body like tiny sparkles, burning away any bacteria, toxins, viruses or mutations. See that light and love restoring every cell in your body to perfect health and repairing your DNA to perfection. Again, see this love and light shooting like laser beams into your cells to deactivate and destroy any toxins, bacteria, viruses and mutations, restoring every cell to immaculate health.

Imagine this sparkling-bright light from heaven pulsing through your veins and arteries, purifying your blood, your muscles, and your bones. See it surging up into your brain, where it makes your synapses fire with perfect precision, restoring and maintaining perfect chemical balance for your mental health, and enabling all your body functions to operate in perfect synchronicity.

See the love and light illuminating your brain's left lobe, right lobe, pineal gland, prefrontal cortex, reticular activating system, subconscious mind, brain stem, and your spinal cord.

Now this light infused with love expands through your skull, your scalp, into your hair, then into your eyes and ears to protect your vision and hearing. Next, this cleansing light flows into your respiratory system, to infuse your nose, mouth, throat and lungs with supernatural immunity. Yes, your respiratory system is filled with this beautiful and powerful light, making you immune to any bacteria, toxins, viruses or mutations.

Next, this light cascades into your heart, where it heals both heartache and physical ailments. See this light flowing into your stomach, pancreas, gallbladder, spleen, liver, kidneys, intestines and reproductive organs.

Witness how this light floods your nervous system, your adrenal glands, your lymph nodes, even your fat, before it expands outward to restore your skin to perfect health.

See this light glowing around you, then circling the entire world with peace and love to bless every person with nourishment, safety, shelter, education, clean air, clean water, freedom of speech, freedom of religion and all good things.

See this light making the leaders of the countries doing good things for the people and the planet, while Mother Earth is restored to her majestic glory. Then see the light swirling back to your home country, blessing every person with peace and love, safety, equality and justice. Then see this light surrounding your loved ones like tiny tornadoes of light that infuse them with supernatural immunity while creating a forcefield of supernatural protection around each one. See their faces glowing with health and happiness.

Now see all that light pouring into the top of your head like a shower of golden sparks, cascading through you, and washing over the energy centers throughout your body. Feel this light clearing away negative energy and opening the channels to

## Monday, Day 2

connect to the universal field of knowledge and the divine, while boosting your immunity and cultivating wellness in mind, body and spirit.

See this light pooling at your tailbone, swirling around your ruby red Root Chakra. Spirit, please cleanse and clear our Root Chakras, to empower our ability to survive and thrive with courage and success in physical, sexual and financial health. The tone is *Lam*. Inhale and say it with me. The tone will create a vibration that is a sound bath that clears the energy on your Root Chakra. Imagine that this sound bath is removing any smudges, smog or dimness around your ruby red Root Chakra, while making it spin and circulate its powerful energy through your entire being.

Biss, you, and all the women inhale and join a long, loud, extended chant of: "Laaaaaaaaaaahhhmmmmmm." The vibration is loud and powerful in your ears as it reverberates through your body.

"Above our ruby red Root Chakra and below the navel is the orange **Sacral Chakra**," Biss says. "It represents creativity and sensuality. Spirit, please cleanse and clear our Sacral Chakras, so that we may enjoy emotional balance, creativity and pleasure. The tone is *Vam*. Inhale and say it with me. Imagine that this sound bath is removing any smudges, smog or dimness around your orange Sacral Chakra, while making it spin and circulate its powerful energy through your entire being."

Biss, you, and all the women inhale and join a long, loud, extended chant of: "Vaaaaaaaaaaahhhmmmmmm."

"Next," Biss says, "our yellow **Solar Plexus Chakra** above the navel rules personal power and action. Spirit, please cleanse and clear our Solar Plexus Chakras, to empower our ability to take action in the world with confidence and knowing. The tone is *Ram*. Inhale and chant it with me. Imagine that this sound bath is removing any smudges, smog or dimness around your yellow Solar Plexus Chakra, while making it spin and circulate its powerful energy through your entire being."

The Meditarium vibrates with the women chanting in unison: "Raaaaaaaaaaaahhhhmmmmm."

"Next is the emerald-green **Heart Chakra** at the center of the chest, and it rules unconditional love and healing," Biss says. "Spirit, please cleanse and clear our Heart chakras, so that we can give and receive unconditional love and healing. The tone is *Yam*. Inhale and say it together. Imagine that this sound bath is removing any smudges, smog or dimness around your emerald-green Heart Chakra, while making it spin and circulate its powerful energy through your entire being."

"Yaaaaaaaaaahhhmmmmmm," everyone chants.

"Above that is the turquoise **Throat Chakra**, which rules communication," Biss says. "Spirit, please cleanse and clear our Throat Chakras, to empower our ability to express our highest truths with courage and confidence, and to demand honesty from others. The tone is *Ham*; inhale and chant together. Imagine that this sound bath is removing any smudges, smog or dimness around your turquoise Throat Chakra, while making it spin and circulate its powerful energy through your entire being."

"Haaaaaaaaaahhhmmmmmmm," echoes through the Meditarium.

"Next, your indigo **Third Eye Chakra** between the eyebrows rules intuition," Biss says. "Spirit, please cleanse and clear our Third Eye Chakras, to empower our ability to see into the divine realm and receive wisdom. The tone is *Sham*. Inhale and say it together. Imagine that this sound bath is removing any smudges, smog or dimness around your indigo Third Eye Chakra, while making it spin and circulate its powerful energy through your entire being."

Everyone chants: "Shaaaaaaaaaahhhmmmmmm."

"Now, at the top of your head is the lavender **Crown Chakra**, which represents divine connection," Biss says. "Spirit, please cleanse and clear our Crown Chakras, to empower our spiritual awakening, self-realization and unity with Source, humanity and all divine guidance to bring our GoddessVisions to life. The tone is *Om*. Inhale and let's chant together, three times. Imagine that this sound bath is removing any smudges, smog or dimness around your lavender Crown Chakra, while making it spin and circulate its powerful energy through your entire being.""

"Ooooooooooohhhmmmmmm."
"Ooooooooooohhhmmmmmm."
"Ooooooooooohhhmmmmmm."

The room is silent as Biss says:

"Now that we're in a very relaxed state, I'm going to guide you on a meditation to connect with Spirit and learn more about your GoddessVision, as well as the action steps you need to take to step through the gateway and make your GoddessLife your daily reality."

# Finding Your GoddessPower in the Divine Dimensions

As Esmerelda uses a drum to create a deep, steady beat every 4.5 seconds, Biss speaks in a soothing tone:

> The drum beat serves as a "sonic driver" to help you get into a trance-like state and has been used by healers since ancient times. The beats "drive" your brainwaves into the Theta zone, which is just above a dream state and is the best way to connect

with the infinite energy of the Universe. You can call this energy God, Goddess, Creator, Spirit, Source, your Higher Self, or another term that resonates with your beliefs. I'm going to say Spirit during this meditation.

Keep your eyes closed and your bodies still.

First, let's set the intention to journey into the divine realms where we can connect with Spirit and learn what we need to know to get clarity on your GoddessVision, along with the action steps that will open the gateway into your GoddessLife.

Let's begin by imagining a golden beam of light shooting down from the sky like a supernatural elevator shaft that will transport you into the spiritual dimensions.

You start this process with your imagination, but at some point, you'll transcend into a multi-sensory experience that doesn't feel like it's coming from your own mind. You may see, hear, and encounter beings, ideas, spoken messages, and visions that are unexpected or unfamiliar; this indicates that the information is coming from Spirit rather than your imagination. Listen, observe, and allow the experience to unfold.

As the light beam surrounds you, call out to your spirit guide to escort you. This guide may show up as a powerful spiritual being such as Jesus or the Hindu Goddess Lakshmi. An angel may wrap you in their wings. A Pegasus may tell you to get on its back. An ancestor may take your hand. Your Power Animal may show up to guide you, symbolizing characteristics that you need to adopt, such as

## Monday, Day 2

a lion teaching you courage, or an eagle showing you how to soar above the ordinary and look at the big picture.

In your mind, greet your spirit guide and thank them for escorting you into the spiritual dimensions. Then state your intention: "Please show me the details of my GoddessVision and the action steps to manifest it."

Next, allow your spirit-self to detach from your physical body and ascend up this beam with your guide. As you ascend, know that you are safe and surrounded by an army of angels. You may feel a floaty sensation. Keep going.

Just as an airplane passes through a layer of clouds as it ascends toward the infinity of sky and space, you also pass through a lavender veil that separates the divine dimensions and the physical world. So feel yourself gently floating upward, up, up, light as a feather up this golden beam with your spirit guide, until you land in your "power spot," a space that is your unique portal to enter and leave the divine realms.

With your spirit guide at your side, know that this experience is different for everyone. There's no right or wrong. You may see, hear, feel or simply know new information that comes in the form of spoken words, images, feelings, symbols and scenes as if playing on a divine movie screen. Likewise, you may enter into a vivid world that looks like outer space, a garden, an enchanted forest, or even a golden palace in the clouds. Be open to what you experience.

> Next, ask Spirit: "Please show me the details of my GoddessVision and the action steps to manifest it."
>
> You may see, feel, hear, or sense a presence. The spiritual being or beings that show up to help you may take you somewhere—to a throne, an altar, a forest, a house, or anywhere. You may hear words, see symbols, or be shown visions. Ask questions. Listen. When the interaction concludes, thank God and/or the angels and/or other beings who helped you.
>
> Now I'm going to give you some time to journey in the divine realm and learn what you need to know to bring your GoddessVision to life.

Biss is silent while Esmerelda continues her drumming every 4.5 seconds. After five minutes, Biss resumes:

> It's time to thank the divine beings who showed up to help you. Make sure you imprint everything in your mind so you can remember it and write about it when you come out of meditation.
>
> With your spirit guide, make you way back to your power spot. From there, slide down the golden beam of light, ever so gently, floating like a feather in the breeze.
>
> Just as the airplane passes through the layer of clouds to return to earth, you pass through the lavender veil that separates the divine realms from the physical world. Then continue to float down like a leaf in the wind, down, down, back to yourself.
>
> Notice the stillness in your body and the slowness of your heartbeat and breathing. Slowly "come

back" by wiggling your fingers and toes. Take some deep breaths, and when you're ready, open your eyes.

What did Spirit tell you? Were your questions answered? Did you receive instructions? Notice how you feel now. Describe your experience in your *PowerJournal*. Make sure you record any action steps that Spirit provided to make your GoddessVision real.

I'm going to give you 10 minutes to journal. Spirit will speak through this intuitive writing, so let it flow. Don't think about it or process it. Just keep writing until every detail is on the page.

The light brightens just enough for you to write in your *PowerJournal*. Sniffles and soft sobs punctuate the silence, along with the sounds of crinkling paper and pages turning.

"OK ladies," Biss says, "that was 10 minutes. You can keep writing. Or you can share what that experience was like."

Celeste sniffles. "My Auntie Rose showed up. She was my guide and she's the one who taught me how to bake. That woman put a rolling pin in my little three-year-old hands and the rest was history. So in the meditation, she took me into this beautiful commercial kitchen, it was like I was really there, I could feel the heat and smell the apple pies baking as my employees, they were all wearing pink uniforms embroidered with my cupcake logo, they were working and Auntie Rose was showing me my business plan and a TV crew was coming to interview me and the lobby was packed with customers. Eating in and picking up orders. It was so real! She told me to give my resignation at my job as soon as I get home and go straight to the bank to get a loan and start shopping for commercial kitchens that I can rent with the goal of buying my own building within a year."

Celeste sobs. "Auntie Rose said to tell you, my Biss Tribe sisters, we should never worry about the money when we're on our missions. She said trust that all the resources will come when we need them. And for me, she said someone famous will taste my carrot cake and rave about it on TV. Biss, now I know I can do this!"

Biss smiles. "Congratulations! Make sure you write down every detail of what you need to know."

"I'm blown away," Celeste says. "I've always felt Auntie Rose's presence since she passed 15 years ago, but this felt like it was really happening. She was glowing so much, she looked luminescent and her eyes were happy."

"That is beautiful!" Biss says. "Who else wants to share?"

Andi runs a hand through her hair and exhales. She speaks with a quavering voice: "I'm freakin' out, man. I can't believe it actually worked. I saw it. I saw my art studio. And I saw a woman. Petite, brunette and happy like a kid on their birthday. She was bringing me lunch, my favorite homemade tacos—the fried kind—with lots of guac, and we both had on matching rings. She's my wife. Her name is Billie."

Andi buries her face in her hands and sniffles. "This person showed up to escort me. I couldn't see them. They just felt warm and had a deep, soothing voice. Said their name is Nell. They told me five specific things I have to do to get my art studio on the beach. Including what realtor to call. And they said, don't buy the blue house. Get the one with the hot tub. Man, if somebody else told me this happened to them, I'd call them a liar."

Biss smiles. "The amazing thing is, Andi and everyone, you can use this meditation to learn what you need to know any time, in any situation. This divine guidance is always available and it's free. All you have to do is tune in, ask, and listen."

"Biss, you were right," Andi says. "That my human brain thinks too small, and that we'd see stuff in meditation that's even bigger.

## Monday, Day 2

Well they showed me this building that has a front gallery and event space for the public, with my studio in back overlooking the beach and my—our!—living space upstairs with a balcony and view of the water. Holy shit, my mind is blown right now."

Biss walks over to Andi and casts an excited look at her. "Andi, write down every detail."

Biss looks at you and scans the group. "All of you Goddesses, I can't emphasize this enough. Write everything while it's fresh. Especially if it feels fantastical and like something you've never thought of yourself. Then, if doubt starts to creep in as you go about your life, you can read it and remember, 'This is what Spirit told me and showed me.' Understand?"

The women nod and say, "Yes" or "Yeah," while many continue writing. Zeusse looks up from her *PowerJournal* and says:

"Mine was so fast! At first during the elevator ride up, I was in a purple tunnel and it felt like I was being sucked into outer space. I could see streaks of light and stars in the distance, and I was cold. But my guide, my spirit guide, it was a giant angel—" Zeusse lets out a low chuckle as Biss steps to her pod.

"I can't believe this," Zeusse continues. "This angel wrapped me in the softest, warmest feeling. I couldn't really see them. It was blurry, but I just knew. They said their name is Gabe, Gabriel, Gabrielle?"

"Archangel Gabriel!" Biss exclaims, smiling at Zeusse. "The archangel of power and strength, and communication. Wow! The archangels are like the superheroes of angels, and they're gender-neutral."

"For real?" Zeusse asks, pressing a clump of tissues to her eyes. "Dude, this is some psychedelic shit, and I'm totally sober right now."

"Psychedelic," Biss says. "Yesssss! Zeusse, did Archangel Gabriel or any other Spirits tell you about your GoddessVision to open your girls basketball academy?"

Zeusse looks up and nods. "Yeah, once we hit the power spot and were in this whole outer space vibe, I was on an airplane with my girls, our own plane, and we had big trophies, and we were celebrating a championship, and that five girls had college scholarships to play ball, and that some of the graduates from my program were already WNBA stars. I hadn't even thought that far ahead; I was just dwelling on how to start the business."

Biss nods. "Did they give you guidance on how to do that?"

"Gabriel, I mean Angel Gabriel, said to call Venecia P. Morton, a retired coach who's a consultant on business and basketball. I met her once at a reception, and she's cool people. And she's a boss that folks know not to fuck with. The angel told me, 'You can trust her. She's your point person to the money and people to start your academy.'"

Zeusse holds up her *PowerJournal.* "I wrote down *everything.* Including the names of my partners, and I asked Gabriel about them, and the angel told me what jobs and skillsets each woman will bring. And that there's an empty school building in my old neighborhood in Harlem that I can buy for my academy." Zeusse starts writing again. "Aw snap, I got more."

Sunshine sits on her knees and rises higher above the petals on her lotus pod. "At first, mine was horrible. It was like every bad thing that ever happened to me was playing as a video on the walls of a tunnel while I went up with my guide, a giant brown bear, and I was riding on his back. He said his name is Medicine Bear."

She sniffles. "Oh my God, I sound so crazy saying this out loud. A bear was talking to me! But it wasn't with words, it was telepathic, and there was so much love coming out of the bear to me. And the bear said he's always with me, even when I'm not in

## Monday, Day 2

meditation. And he said I won't find my husband until I do more work to heal myself, and he told me the name of the best therapist in Santa Fe who was coronated in The Biss Tribe and specializes in women's self-esteem and healing from trauma."

"Princella DuVay," Biss says.

"Yes!" Sunshine says. "As for my GoddessVision, the bear took me up the beam, which finally turned into golden light, and said, 'You've passed all those tests. You are strong now. You are Goddess. I'm here with you to help you believe in yourself.' Then the power spot was like a swing in the sky, a big pretty swing with flowers on the ropes and a velvet cushion on the seat, and I—"

She sobs softly. "I literally felt like God was pushing me. I couldn't see who was pushing the swing to make me go so high. But I just knew it was God. And I felt so free and happy, like a little kid. I was giggling and thinking about nothing but the pure joy of the moment. And I kept swinging higher and higher, until in the clouds around me, these pastel clouds, people started popping up and saying, 'Thank you, Sunshine, you saved my life,' and one was writing an online review that says, 'The Turquoise Experience transformed me from meek, terrified and hiding, into a seven-figure business owner with confidence through the roof. *And* I lost 40 pounds along the way!'"

Sunshine looks up at Biss, who's standing beside her pod, gazing down. "Then it was like I was writing words that were streaming in the clouds, and it was a business plan. A description of my business. My marketing plan. My team that includes Indigenous women like me. Same with my vendors. My revenue for the first five years. My website that ranks first. Oh! And—"

Sunshine looks over at Marla and Sammie. "The bear told me to work with you two, and that I will become an influencer, and that I'll have the money to pay you to teach me and that you'll be creating a new stream of income with your online course teaching women like me how to attract clients, build our businesses, and make money through social media."

Marla and Sammie both pump a fist into the air.

"I got that, too!" Marla said. "We've been talking about this, and we even want to host retreats, like influencer boot camp, at a sexy resort on the beach in Hawaii or the Bahamas, where we teach you everything you need to know. I saw it in my meditation."

Marla speaks softly: "But first, my spirit guide showed up in this blinding glow of like sparkly-white light. I couldn't see her, but I could feel her magnetic pull, and she said her name is Lady Hope, and she's here to help me heal my shit with my parents. She said I have to forgive them and release my anger toward them, and heal our relationship. She said I can't bring my GoddessVision to life on a foundation of anger and resentment, or it will crumble."

Biss, who's standing between Marla's and Sammie's pods, asks, "Did she tell you how to heal?"

"Did she!" Marla exclaims. "For a long time in my meditation, she had me in this little room with a bed and gray walls. It was so dreary! She said I was a cloistered nun in another life and that my vow of celibacy was still stuck on my soul, and that I chose to come into this life with these parents as my soul's lesson to break free—" she lets out a nervous laugh "—I sound so cray-cray right now but this is what she said! The way to free myself from it and enjoy sex with a man I love is to break the vow of celibacy like, inside me—"

Marla's eyes fill with tears. "It makes sense now. It's not my fault. She said my dream man will show up after I like vomit up all my feelings about my parents and guilty fear of pleasure that comes from a past life. In that little room, she showed me writing and writing and writing, like pouring it all out, and starting every line with forgiveness."

## Monday, Day 2

Marla shakes her head. "I don't fucking understand forgiveness. But she said, write, 'I forgive myself for XYZ,' and 'I forgive my parents for XYZ,' and to do that for any- and everything that comes to mind that's making me so mad and holding me back."

"Wow, girl," Sammie exclaims. "Who knew?"

Marla shakes her head. "So then she finally took me out of the little room and took me in this giant control room, it was like at NASA when they're about to launch a rocket into space, and you see all the people watching monitors and flipping switches with blinking lights, and giving directions. I was the boss! I was standing on a little platform talking into a headset microphone, telling everyone what to do. And all my social media was playing on the screens, and the numbers were exploding on the monitors and beeping and flashing."

Marla looks up at Biss. "In my mind, I was thinking, *bitch, you're making this shit up. It's wishful thinking.* But it wasn't, Biss, not at all! I've never thought of anything like this and I've never heard of Lady Hope. It was soooo real!"

Biss nods. "That's when you know it's Spirit. All of you who've shared, this is tapping into your supernatural GoddessPower. When the ideas and visions are so unique and far beyond your imagination, that's confirmation that it's from Source because it's way bigger than what our human minds would conceive."

"Mine was all that!" Sammie exclaims. "I was in a whole nother life. My dream life! I had escaped Man Land, and I was walking down the aisle in the dreamiest wedding gown, and my husband was standing under this altar of yellow flowers, and Marla was my maid of honor, and I was like floating with happiness and my brain was empty of anything except pure love and peace. I didn't want to come out of the meditation. I wanted to jump into that moment—"

"Beautiful," Biss says. "Did Spirit give instructions on how to get there?"

"Did they!" Sammie says. "I don't like it, but if that's my reward, then I'm game. This lady, she looked like an Egyptian queen, she took me to like a spa bath and I had my own pool which had pink flowers floating on the water, and it smelled like roses. These women were around me, washing my body and my hair and someone was singing and playing a harp on pillows while incense was burning." Sammie looks around and lets out a nervous laugh. "This sounds so whack!" She looks up at Biss. "You promise nobody will repeat this out in the world? I would just *die!*"

Biss casts a reassuring look down at Sammie, then glances at you and all the women. "That's our promise to each other here. Trust is the foundation of our transformations. If it's betrayed, then the Laws of Karma will take effect."

Sammie wipes her eyes. "So this Egyptian goddess, she said I have to quit men and sex for a year to cleanse my energy and change my thinking. She said my energy field is like a graveyard of all the dudes I've dated, and I have to cut the cords and soul ties? Whatever that means."

She glances up at Biss with questioning eyes.

"Cords," Biss says, "are energetic connections we have with people who stay in our heads and hearts and even our souls, for good or for bad. When we become aware of these cords, and we need to release these people and the energetic hold they have on us through memories, feelings, and heavy emotional baggage that you may not even realize is coming from them but is holding you down, you can metaphorically cut the cord by asking Archangel Michael to do it or envision a giant pair of scissors cutting a long rope that's connecting you to someone."

"Somebody get me a chain saw," Celeste says playfully. "I got a lotta cords to cut!"

"Make that two," Kiki says.

## Monday, Day 2

Sammie continues: "The women bathing me, they were using some kind of oil on me, and they said it would break the soul ties I have from all my sex partners. But what are soul ties?"

Biss nods. "When you're intimate with someone, it's not just your physical bodies that are connecting. Your energy bodies, your souls, are intertwining. The emotions, the pleasure, the chemical reactions in your bodies, and the spiritual connection all form a strong imprint on your energy. You can't see it, but it's like an imprint on your spirit that you carry around. And, we'll talk more about this in the Pleasure Tent tomorrow, but when a man ejaculates inside a woman, he is literally injecting his DNA into her body!"

"Gross!" Marla exclaims.

"Talk about male dominance," Jade says.

"It's beautiful if your goal together is to create a baby," Biss says. "That's the biological function of intercourse. However, one study showed that male DNA was found in the brain of a 90-year-old woman. Which means the sperm had somehow traveled through her body and lodged in her brain. So when you think about the idea of a man, especially if he's a casual sex partner, and his DNA getting into a woman's brain and staying there for life, that is deeply disturbing."

Groans echo through the Meditarium.

"Of course, using condoms can prevent this, and they're the smartest choice for casual sex," Biss says. "However, condoms can't protect you from STDs, Sexually Transmitted Demons. This is the bad energy that fuses with yours during sex. And if the man has a lot of partners, all of those people's energy is transferred to you through his, so you're now infused with the chaotic energy of him and countless other people, often low-vibe people who are not honoring their bodies or their energy, all swirling inside you, which can trigger anxiety and general bad feelings in you."

## The GoddessPower Pyramid

"No wonder I'm so fucked up!" Sammie exclaims. "That's exactly how it feels, and it makes me crazier with every guy! All their bitches's energy is making me cray-cray!"

Biss nods. "It's real. A very important disclaimer here, which we'll discuss in the GoddessPleasure Tent tomorrow. Every woman has the right and freedom to enjoy sex with whomever, and however many people, she desires. But when we learn about intimacy in terms of energy—and how it can deplete yours and potentially infuse you with toxic energy from another person—we can decide to channel our energy into our missions and only share it in sacred relationships that enhance our energy. That is GoddessPower."

Sunshine moans. "Oh, I love that."

Biss turns back to Sammie and asks, "Sammie, did the spiritual beings share more details on how to stay celibate and how this can help you manifest your GoddessVision to find your husband and build your business?"

Sammie nods. "They said I have to exercise more, to burn off my sex drive, and to put all that energy into my work. It was wild, but they like lifted this heavy energy and noise out of my head and off my calendar, showing how much time and energy I waste chasing men and obsessing over them and having meltdowns. It made me feel so light!"

Marla asks, "What about how to 100-X our skincare business?"

"I asked that so many times," Sammie says. "The Egyptian goddess said first, I have to detox from my man addiction because it's blocking my success in business."

"Holy shit, what?!" Marla exclaims. "I'm the opposite. But it's blocking both of us. We can do this, mama!" Marla and Sammie high-five.

"Thank you to everyone who has shared so far," Biss says, glancing around. "Anyone else?"

## Monday, Day 2

Delaney tucks her silver curls behind one ear and says, "I want to say that mine was as spectacular as all that, but it wasn't, and maybe that's the point. I simply felt the purest sense of peace that I've ever felt. I was floating in a warm sea of nothingness and I absolutely loved it. I didn't want to leave. I was in the sea, and the sky above me was blue, and I was floating effortlessly, and the warm water was silky on my skin, and I was naked, and I felt no need or want for anything except the solitary bliss of being with myself in this watery cocoon."

"That's what's up," Zeusse whispers.

Biss nods. "Did Spirit give you any instructions on how to cultivate that feeling when you get home?"

Delaney wipes her eyes with a tissue. "The four tools," she says. "My spirit guide was a lady on a white horse. She rode me up to this sea in the sky, and told me to walk into the water, then float. It reminded me of the weightlessness I felt when swimming in the Dead Sea in Jordan, only better. And then she was talking to me; I could hear her in my mind, even though she was on the beach with her horse. She said, use the four GoddessPower Tools every day, and they will bring you back here."

Delaney sighs. "I am so undisciplined with things like this. So I asked her how I can stick to this. And she said, 'Close your eyes and remember the joy of now. Crave that like a person craves chocolate or sex or any other pleasure. And meditate after yoga. It primes your body and brain for spiritual connection.'"

"Wow," Biss exclaims. "I suggest that you create a space in your home where you can go every day, undisturbed, to breathe, clear your energy, meditate and journal, and do it at a set time, perhaps every morning."

Biss glances around. "That's for all of you. You need to schedule your daily GoddessPower Activation time, and fiercely protect it."

## The GoddessPower Pyramid

Delaney nods. "I'm pledging to you, Biss, and all of you here in our Biss Tribe sisterhood, that I will do the breathing exercise, clear my energy, meditate and journal every morning at home."

"Me too!" Sunshine announces. Most of the women exclaim a similar commitment.

Bianca looks anxious, and talks fast: "I'm so embarrassed to share mine. I literally was in a tornado, the Bianca Tornado, in my meditation. A giant dog, a beautiful dog that was as big as a pony, I think it was a labradoodle with super soft caramel-colored fur, showed up and I rode up on him. It was really fast, like we were flying through a wind tunnel and then we were up in this storm, and everything in my life was whizzing past me through the air. And the dog was running really fast, and I held on, and I saw the accident and the crushed car and the drunk driver and people and papers and babies and my ex-husband and my clock when I can't sleep... everything that swirls in my head every day. And then finally after the dog kept running a long way, we arrived at this Victorian gingerbread house; it was lavender with flowers and a pretty porch and a sign out front said Amy's Oasis: a sanctuary for girls. And on the porch were adolescent and teen girls, talking and laughing, playing board games, sitting on a swing reading, and it felt like such a happy place."

Bianca sobs and her voice quavers. "Oh my God, it was like I was there. I never had a clear vision like this. And there it was. And the dog took me through the front doors, and the house smelled like baking cookies, and I had an office, and in the foyer that had an open staircase with the most beautiful carved banister and stained-glass window on the landing, was a picture of Amy, my patient who chose suicide after she didn't get into Harvard like her parents wanted."

Bianca blows her nose in a clump of tissues. "In every room, there are girls. Taking a cooking class in the kitchen, then serving

## Monday, Day 2

the food to other girls in the dining room. In the basement, they're playing ping pong and watching a movie in the theatre. In upstairs classrooms, they're learning about self-esteem and finance and how to be an entrepreneur, and they're having private sessions with therapists."

Bianca pauses. "And get this. The dog, which didn't actually talk, but communicated with me without words, told me to teach the girls the four GoddessPower Activation Tools."

Tears drip down Bianca's cheeks as she looks at Biss. "Biss, I don't know how to thank you—"

Biss smiles. "You, and everyone here, you can thank me by going out and doing the work to make all of this your reality. It's your dream, but it's also going to make dreams come true for all the people whose lives you touch."

"That's what's up," Zeusse says.

"Bianca?" Biss asks. "Did Spirit provide any action steps for how to start the non-profit, purchase the house, and actually make Amy's Oasis operational and sustainable?"

Bianca nods. "The dog, his name is Noah, said to call someone named Joe Faizzon in my town, who has an incubator for non-profits and has scholarships to pay for his program that takes me through the step-by-step process."

"Perfect," Biss says.

Jade raises her hand. "My turn! I was really pissed when this started, because I couldn't latch onto the spirit guide idea or the light beam elevator. So I concentrated really hard on making my brain focus on calling in help. Then it was so wild, this chick showed up, she looked like me! Tatts everywhere, piercings, blue hair. 'I'm Ellie,' she said. 'Let's go!' I know this sounds crazy, but I hopped on the back of her motorcycle! I couldn't really see it, but we were *flying* up! My stomach was flipping and I was scared as fuck, because we were going at like a 90-degree angle, just straight up!"

Jade lets out a soft laugh. "The whole time, she was talking so fast, it was faster than a human can talk, and all the words were registering in my head, and music from my band was playing; I don't know how. But anyway, she said she's my angel and my muse, and that she's with me all the time, and she named all the songs I've written, and said she helped me write them, but she won't help me write any more until I quit my office job and go back to being a music tutor, which I used to do during college. And as soon as I do that, our band will take off."

Jade hugs herself and rocks slightly. "I was like, 'Ellie, how can I talk to you every day?' and she said, 'Just like this. I'll talk through your GoddessVoice, but you have to practice hearing me.' Biss, what's a GoddessVoice? Did you already teach us that?"

"It's your inner voice," Biss says, "your divine voice within. The voice of your soul, which speaks through your intuition. We'll talk more about it this afternoon. What happened when Ellie took you into the divine dimensions?"

"Studio time!" Jade says. "We were in a music studio, me and my band, recording an album. And someone ran in and said we had just hit number one on the charts, and that our world tour was almost sold out."

Several women cheer.

"Excellent," Biss says. "What about how to heal the rift with your parents?"

"So when we went up in the clouds," Jade says, "my grandparents were there and they said something like, 'forgive them for they don't know what they do,' and that they're only doing what they think is best for me. So my grandparents said just be chill with my parents and do my thing, and they'll see that I'm on my

## Monday, Day 2

right path. It's all about money for them, and when they see that I'm successful, they'll finally understand me."

Biss smiles at Jade, then steps to your pod. She looks at you and says, "Tell us about your meditation, and what you learned about how to manifest your GoddessVision."

*Dear Goddess Reader:*

*Please describe your meditation experience, including: your encounter with your Spirit Guide; what happened in the divine realm; what you learned about how to manifest your GoddessVision; and specific action steps that you need to take:*

_____

_____

_____

_____

After you share your experience, Biss looks around and asks, "Any final thoughts from anyone about this meditation experience?"

"Loved it," Celeste says, "but I know I'm gonna need support to keep believing and do the work when I get home."

"Same!" Andi exclaims as several women say, "Me too!"

Biss says, "I'll provide video and audio recordings of The Four GoddessPower Activation Tools for you to use every day at home. Remember to always journal immediate after meditation."

Esmerelda's music begins to play.

"My beautiful, brilliant Goddesses," Biss says, "it's time for lunch."

# Lunchtime: Food is Fuel for Your Goddess Mission

Delicious aromas welcome you into the Atrium, where tables are nestled amidst trees, plants, the stream and flowers.

"Ladies," Esmerelda says, "please sit wherever you desire."

You join Andi, Zeusse, Celeste, Jade and Sunshine at a table.

"I hope they don't serve rabbit food," Andi says with a scowl.

Concierges appear with plates covered by silver pyramids. They set the plates in front of each woman, and ceremoniously lift the lids. The food is arranged like artwork, and the scents rising with the steam are delectable.

To your right, Zeusse has grilled salmon over quinoa with steamed broccoli, and flourless chocolate cake for dessert. To your left, Andi is ogling a plate of spaghetti with turkey meatballs and banana pudding for dessert. Across the table, Celeste is delighted at the sight of a Cornish hen surrounded by redskin potatoes and asparagus spears, with carrot cake for desert. Next to her, Sunshine looks euphoric over angel hair pasta with seafood and veggies plus a slice of cheesecake covered with fresh strawberries. Beside her, Jade is ogling a burrito with rice, beans and avocado slices with key lime pie for desert.

On your plate is your favorite healthy meal, and it's cooked exactly as you like it.

"No rabbit food here," Andi says with a smile.

"Vegan lasagna!" Marla shrieks at another table. "I am in heaven!"

## Monday, Day 2

"Goddess food," Biss says, smiling as she strolls around each table. "Here at the Power Pyramid, it's time to rethink food as fuel. Not just what we like for its taste and flavor. That's important. And that's why The Biss Tribe's Culinary Team is custom-designing each of your favorite meals for the entire week in ways that maximize the nutritional value."

Biss heads to a glass podium that's adorned with The Biss Tribe Logo. "Ladies, before you take a bite, let's close our eyes and give thanks to the infinite, divine powers for gifting us with this experience and this nourishment that fuels our minds, bodies and souls to activate our GoddessPower, so we can create luscious lives that illuminate the world. And so it is spoken, and so it is done."

The women repeat a deep chorus of: "And so it is spoken, and so it is done."

Four women join Biss at the podium. "Ladies, as you enjoy your meals, please savor the flavors in a spirit of gratitude for our extraordinary culinary team."

Biss beams at them. "These talented food artists and nutrition experts have been in their GoddessGenius Zones, working diligently since you arrived at the Inn, to customize your meals and snacks. Now, from left to right, please meet our head chef, **Dr. Annapurna**, named for the Hindu Goddess of food, cooking and nourishment."

Dr. Annapurna, like the other women, wears a white chef uniform adorned with The Biss Tribe's purple and leopard print logo with her name embroidered over it. With a round, happy face and big dark eyes, she has a long black braid draping over her left shoulder to her waist.

She smiles, steps forward and speaks with an elegant Indian accent: "My parents named me Geetha when I was born in India, but when we moved to America, I fell in love with the story of Goddess Annapurna back when I was playing with my EasyBake

## The GoddessPower Pyramid

Oven as a little girl. Then I went to culinary school and earned a PhD in nutrition science. And now I'm here to help you activate your GoddessPower by understanding how food can either help or hinder your mission."

Biss smiles, then extends an arm to the next woman. "As you enjoy your desserts, you can thank **Ixcacao**, named in honor of the Mayan Goddess of chocolate and cocoa."

Tall, thick and freckled with blue eyes and red hair, Ixcacao bows. "My GoddessVision, when I came through this program, was to bring sweetness to the palates of women like you, who are on a mission to become great. Think on that as you enjoy your desserts."

The next woman—who has mocha skin, short hair twists, and a slim physique, steps to the podium with Biss, who says, "Meet **Pomona**, named for the Roman Goddess of Orchards. She's our food operations director who sources fresh produce from the best local farms, and makes sure all the ingredients are fresh, organic and prepared to perfection."

Pomona holds up a red apple. "I am from Martinique," she says with a French accent. "My name comes from the French word, 'pomme,' for apple. And today's talk is about how an apple a day keeps the doctor away, and how food is fuel for the amazing lives you're creating."

Biss steps toward the fourth person. "Meet **Ukemochi**! She's named for the Japanese Shinto Goddess, and she ensures that you enjoy the highest quality seafood, meats, eggs, tofu and other proteins."

Ukemochi, whose straight black hair is tucked under a white hair net, says, "Welcome, my sisters. I am from a Blue Zone in Japan, where people often live past 100 years. I want you to know that the fruits, vegetables and herbs were grown in The Biss Tribe Farm and Orchard, located in Valley Village near the Inn. And the

## Monday, Day 2

seafood, poultry, meat and dairy products come from farms that are organic, non-GMO, free-range, grass-fed and committed to humane practices."

Ukemochi smiles. "I'm also a Biss Tribe success story. Here I learned how to get into my GoddessGenius Zone. And that is serving delicious and nutritious food for you. So seeing your expressions today while you enjoy your lunch, I'm thrilled to hear some of you moaning with delight."

Biss steps to the microphone. "My Goddesses, let's give our amazing Biss Tribe Culinary Team some applause!"

You and the women shoot to your feet for a standing ovation. The Culinary Team bows.

"Please be seated," Biss says. "Dr. Annapurna is going to talk about your power to make food as fuel or poison for your GoddessMissions."

"Thank you so much, Biss." Dr. Annapurna stands behind the podium. "Ladies, you may call me Dr. A. Your GoddessMission requires you to radically rethink what you put in your mouth."

Andi groans. "Oh here goes, a lecture about everything I love to eat that's bad."

Jade covers her ears. "If she mentions ice cream—"

"Sssshhhh!" Zeusse casts a warning look at them.

"What you eat and drink every day," Dr. A says, "can either provide premium fuel for your GoddessMission, or it can stall your mental and physical engines and even make them inoperable."

She makes eye contact with several women and asks, "How many of you make your daily food decisions based on whatever you're craving or what tastes good?"

"Guilty!" Marla says.

"That's me, all day long," Jade says, pointing to her plump belly. "And you can see, I'm wearing my afternoon favorites of candy bars, and my nighttime binges on beer, meat lover's pizza, chips

## The GoddessPower Pyramid

and ice cream. I just want to feel better and have more energy. But I'm lazy and eat bad."

Bianca raises her hand. "I'm skinny, but I eat garbage and know it's bad. I'm clueless about what to eat. Everything that goes into my mouth gets there through whim and emotion."

Celeste shakes her head. "I'm guilty of sampling my cakes and pies. And when I'm stressed, my cherry cobbler with ice cream is my valium."

Dr. A nods. "Your honesty is commendable. Now let's get you started on a new mindset that energizes your brain and body, and connects you with Spirit to amplify your GoddessVoice; she will guide your eating choices."

As you continue to savor your lunch, Zeusse whispers, "Damn, this is the best flourless chocolate cake I have *ever* had in my life. It's almost better than sex."

Dr. Annapurna says, "I'll keep this short and sweet, but serious. Dead serious. Your eating habits may be killing you, bite by bite, right now."

"She is such a Debbie Downer," Jade whispers. "I really don't want to hear this."

"Yeah, sweetheart," Zeusse says, "you do. That's why you're here."

Dr. A asks, "Do you know that processed foods, especially bacon and lunch meats, are known to cause cancer? Do you know that sugar actually feeds colds, viruses and cancerous tumors? And do you know that drinking any amount of alcohol greatly increases your risk for breast cancer?"

A collective moan rumbles through the women.

"Sorry, not sorry!" Dr. A says playfully. "I speak the truth. And if you want to elevate into an extraordinary life, you need to nourish yourself like a Goddess. That means first understanding nutrition,

## Monday, Day 2

and learning how to calibrate it to empower your mind, body and spirit."

Andi whispers, "Why do I feel like I need to have a funeral for favorite foods?"

"So they don't kill you first," Sunshine responds softly without looking away from Dr. Annapurna.

"Before you leave here," Dr. A says, "we will customize an eating plan for you to follow when you return home to build your empire. That will require extraordinary energy, and you'll need to optimize the fuel that you put into your body and brain. The high-frequency nature of the foods that we will prescribe will also enhance your ability to connect with Spirit as you use your four GoddessPower Activation Tools every day."

You and the women are silent except for soft groans of resistance rising from every table.

"You may recall," Dr. A says, "that a physical examination was required as part of your application process to come here. Our expert team of physicians and technicians have analyzed your specific biological profiles, and that analysis enables us to calibrate your nutritional plan for the best results for your health and vitality. This includes consuming herbs and macronutrients that can help reverse conditions such as diabetes and eczema."

"Damn, this is intense," Celeste whispers. "We're about to get Goddessified down to our blood and bones, literally."

"Of course this is entirely voluntary," Dr. A says. "We cannot force you to do anything. But something brought you here, and the women around the world who have been crowned in The Biss Tribe and are now doing extraordinary things in the world, are following every step of the guidance we provide here, including and perhaps especially, food."

A screen drops behind her, showing Sasha Maxwell in a sleek red convertible. "If you purchase a luxury car, you're going to fuel it with premium fuel. It's more expensive. But it will enhance your vehicle's performance and prolong its life. You can drive it faster, and it will be the smoothest ride. So think of your body the same way."

The screen behind her shows video of machines churning beige goop in giant vats, then dropping plops of the stuff on a conveyor belt, where the globs are covered in chocolate and drizzled with caramel, then dried and wrapped in colorful candy bar packaging.

"Did you know that manufactured foods are actually created in laboratories where scientists are working right now to create the most addictive combination of salt, sugar and fat?" she asks as video shows a machine dropping frosting between two cookies, then bite-sized yellow nuggets that get sprayed with fluorescent orange powder and sealed in small bags that say "cheese snacks."

"This combination is highly addictive and activates the same pleasure centers in your brain as opioids that include cocaine," Dr. A says as video shows machines making potato chips. "These foods lack fiber and therefore never fill you up, and their chemically-addictive nature keeps you eating until the package is empty, then craving more."

"That's me, all day long," Jade says loud enough for Dr. A to hear.

"You have the power to change that and feel better," Dr. A says. "Here's how."

The screen shows colorful video of fruits, vegetables, legumes, grains, nuts and seeds. The words "plant-based" and "whole foods" scroll across the enticing images.

"These four words are your guidelines for the GoddessPower Diet," she declares. "It's that simple."

"Huh?" Kiki says. "That's *too* simple."

"It's not simple to give up candy!" Marla complains.

## Monday, Day 2

"Yes, it's very simple after you make the decision to eat like a Goddess." Dr. Annapurna smiles as delicious-looking video images correspond with what she's saying:

"Begin your day with a Green Goddess Smoothie. Lunch can be a large salad with olive oil and herbed dressing, topped with a healthy protein such as salmon and perhaps half a baked sweet potato, with fruit for dessert. Dinner can be a vegetable stir fry with lean protein over quinoa or brown rice. You can snack on fruit, nuts, seeds and raw vegetables. Avocadoes are an extremely satisfying food that you can add to meals for flavor, texture and satiety. If you enjoy dairy, Greek yogurt is high in protein and provides probiotics for optimum gut health, which enhances overall mental and physical health."

The atrium is silent except for the gurgle of the stream.

"If you approach every time you eat," Dr. A says, "with the guidelines of whole foods and plant-based eating—"

Kiki raises her hand. "I'm sorry, what does that mean?"

"A plant-based diet means that the majority of what you consume comes from plants," Dr. Annapurna says. "This includes fruit, vegetables, nuts, seeds, beans, potatoes—all best prepared in their natural form, not processed, fried or covered in sugar and oil. Understand?"

Kiki nods. "Got it. Thank you."

Dr. A continues: "You'll realize that processed foods are not included, because they contain many chemicals, additives, preservatives and artificial colors—some of which are proven carcinogens, which means they cause cancer. Studies have shown that these manufactured foods can have a negative impact on your mental health and cognitive skills while causing obesity and wreaking havoc on your blood sugar, insulin levels and heart health, which can lead to deadly diseases such as diabetes, hypertension and cancer."

# The GoddessPower Pyramid

"That's not appetizing," Andi says.

On the screen, video shows a woman sleeping peacefully, then jogging on the beach, meditating, and leading a meeting of dozens of businesspeople in a sleek board room.

"Your GoddessLife," Dr. A says, "should inspire you to replace processed foods with plant-based eating, and you'll enjoy mental clarity and calm, your skin will glow, your energy level will spike, you will sleep better, your body will detox, the fiber will cleanse your digestive system, your libido will be more vibrant than ever, and you will have more clear meditations that amplify your GoddessVoice, which provides the guidance you need to use the five foundations to build your empire."

Sunshine whispers, "I don't know if I can give up pepperoni pizza."

"Or hot dogs!" Andi says sadly.

"Once you gain momentum and learn about the power of food as fuel," Dr. Annapurna says, "you will automatically shift into wanting better nutrition, because you'll feel and look so much better."

Dr. A gestures toward Esmerelda, who's sitting at a table with Biss and the culinary team. "Ladies, you probably noticed Esmerelda's radiant skin, high energy level, peaceful mood and mission-driven life here in The Biss Tribe. You'd be shocked to learn her age, because she's healthier than many women who are much younger."

Esmerelda dabs the corners of her mouth with a white linen napkin, then beams. "Beautiful sisters, I've been on the Goddess nutrition plan for decades, and I have extraordinary energy, I never get sick, all my numbers such as blood pressure and blood sugar are perfect, I sleep peacefully, and I have zero pain in my body. Zero! This, after I discovered the power of nutrition to heal

## Monday, Day 2

a debilitating and painful illness that once left me bedridden, back when few people were talking about the curative powers of food."

"I want to glow like her," Sunshine says.

"And stop hurting," Andi says. "My body aches and I hate it."

Esmerelda adds, "When you return for your Intensives here at the Power Pyramid and at the GoddessWarrior Fortress, we'll teach you the medicinal qualities of food and herbs to heal your body and mind. The ancient Greek doctor Hippocrates said, 'Let food be thy medicine, and medicine be thy food.' I encourage you to follow Dr. A's eating plan when you get it, and take the initiative to research foods that can help your particular ailments so you can implement those foods into your daily diet."

Jade looks sad as she raises her hand. "I don't think I can give up ice cream. I mean, I crave it. I *have* to eat ice cream every night. It calms me down and brings me the only pleasure in my life besides my music. Even though I know sugar is terrible for me and my doctor says I'm pre-diabetic and overweight. And I'm only 35! I know it's just killing me, spoon by spoon."

Dr. Annapurna nods. "I understand. We all have emotional attachments to comfort foods, but it *is* possible to release them with love and replace them with healthier options. So rather than thinking of giving up something, would you consider giving yourself the gift of control over your health with more energy and the desire to find pleasure in other ways?"

"Wow!" Jade says tearfully. "I never thought of that. I'm so desperate to change. That's why I'm here." Jade sobs; Zeusse extends her arm as Jade cries into her shoulder.

"Please also consider food as part of the big picture of your life," Dr. A says. "Every bite you take every day of your life has an incremental impact on your wellbeing, and it can take you forward with energy and longevity, or it can take you backward into illness and a shorter life."

## The GoddessPower Pyramid

"Truth!" Zeusse exclaims. "That's truth if I've ever heard it. Everybody in my family down South got sick from traditional Southern cooking, but it was a time when nobody knew better. Now we know better, so we can do better."

Dr. A smiles. "Beautifully said! And an excellent segue to the fact that you're enjoying desserts during the retreat. You can still enjoy your favorite treats in moderation, and you might even enjoy them more when you eat them less frequently. Changing your diet is not a punishment. It's a gift to yourself. And it's an investment in making your GoddessLife your reality."

Biss joins Dr. Annapurna at the podium and says, "Thank you, Dr. A! My Goddesses, you truly are what you eat," Biss says, making eye contact with you and each woman. "You are a Goddess! And your body is a sacred temple. It's time to provide it with the most nutritious offerings possible. Now let's cheer a show of gratitude for Dr. A and The Biss Tribe's Culinary Team!"

As you and the women applaud, some standing, the trees sway in the sunshine that's pouring through the glass pyramid.

"Now," Biss says, "it's time for an invigorating walk on the GoddessFitness trail with our Biss Tribe Trainer, Jodi."

## Rev Your Body with GoddessPower Fitness!

Trainer Jodi, who seems to have more energy than one body can hold, leads you and the women along a gorgeous, wooded path where the sign says, "Hygieia Trail, named for the Greek/Roman Goddess of Health." Bianca rides in her electric wheelchair with her Concierge at her side.

"Ladies!" Jodi exclaims as the sunshine gleams on her smooth, cosmetic-free face and suntanned muscles. "Come this way!"

Biss, who's walking beside Jodi and Esmerelda, says, "Jodi is a testament to fitness being the fountain of youth."

# Monday, Day 2

"I'm about to turn 50," Jodi says.

"OhmyGod," Marla exclaims. "You look better than a lot of our friends in their twenties who are so obsessed with their skin."

Jodi smiles. "Lifestyle, baby! And thank you."

She leads you into a clearing that offers an outdoor gym. Wearing spandex shorts and a tank top that says The Biss Tribe, she jumps up to a bar and does 10 pull-ups. Then, resting at the top, her arms straight and muscles flexing as her hips rest against the bar, she laughs. "Don't worry! You don't have to do this now. But when you come back in two months, be ready."

The gold-adorned ends of her shoulder-length corn-rows bounce as she jumps down. "Let's talk about how GoddessPower requires a strong body. You don't need to become an Olympic weightlifter. You don't have to commit to fitness at all. Just know that a stronger body gives you more stamina to build your empire, and possibly even live longer to enjoy it. All this is totally your choice. Cool?"

Cheers mix with sounds of protest.

"I couldn't do a pull-up to save my life!" Sunshine snips.

"I hate working out," Andi says.

"Maybe I start off strong," Celeste adds, "but I fall off after a few weeks."

"Those days are over!" Jodi says, bouncing with excitement. "The trick is to design a fitness program that you love."

Sammie whispers, "She's annoying. She's too happy and she has too much energy."

"Hey sweetheart," Zeusse snaps, "maybe she upsets you because deep down you *wish* you looked and felt like she does. I suggest you pour out that cup of Haterade and start drinking from her fountain of wellness, so you look *that* good when you hit her age."

Sammie rolls her eyes and crosses her arms.

## The Goddess Power Pyramid

Jodi looks directly at you and says, "If you love roller-skating, or hula-hooping, or swimming, or bike riding, or dancing or simply walking, then that's what we'll design for you. And no matter your physical ability, we have exercises to strengthen your muscles."

Biss and Esmerelda join Jodi at a rack of dumbbells that range from five pounds to 100 pounds each. Jodi picks up two 35s and does arm curls. Her biceps pop.

"Strength training," Jodi says, "is not just about having great arms and a toned body when you put on that little black dress or bathing suit. It's about your health."

She sets the weights down. "When you do simple exercises like this—while you're watching a movie or listening to a conference call—you build muscle. Muscle mass increases your metabolism. And if you tweak your diet at the same time, you lose weight and replace fat with toned muscles."

Jodi grabs a barbell, puts it over her shoulders, and does squats while talking. "Strength training will make your booty pop, and make your legs strong. Plus, strength training can increase your bone density and reduce your risk for osteoporosis. That's the condition where bones get brittle and break easily as women age."

While Jodi continues her demonstration, Biss steps forward and says, "Ladies, as you know, I lost 100 pounds many years ago. I learned how to lift weights. It toned my body to look better than ever, and improved my mental health. It also spikes my energy for writing, working and enjoying life."

You watch and listen as much to Biss and Jodi as to the women's murmured comments about how much they dread exercising.

Esmerelda bursts out laughing, and everyone turns to her. "Ladies, if you could see some of your expressions! Please know that strength training is not for everyone. I don't lift weights. Yoga

## Monday, Day 2

keeps me sculpted and strong. Here again, the secret to your success with your physical GoddessPower is a customized experience. Just like everything on this journey. You have the power to decide."

"I'm all in," Zeusse says, picking up weights and doing arm curls.

Delaney does the same, as does Celeste.

"Oh Lord help me!" Celeste exclaims. "If I commit but quit one more time—"

Sammie glares at Jodi. Andi runs a hand through her hair.

Biss looks perturbed. "My beautiful Goddesses, this is a pivotal moment here on Infinity Mountain. We're providing the tools to transform your GoddessVision into reality. The more tools you use, the faster, bigger and better you can create your best life. Our solutions work, but they *require* work. And it's your choice to apply them."

Celeste huffs and puts the weights on the rack. "Biss! Jodi! And all the powers of the universe," she says, wiping sweat from her forehead. "What kind of accountability can you provide for me to stick to a healthy eating and exercise plan when I go home? I have to sample Celeste's Sweets!" She shakes her head, gazing down at the spongy brown mat that extends throughout the outdoor gym. "I'm not disciplined by myself."

Biss steps to Celeste and takes her hand. "You'll get that accountability in our weekly Goddess RoundTable video call. We also have fitness trainers who were crowned in The Biss Tribe in places all across the country, so we can pair you with someone who can work out with you and guide your food plan as well."

"I can't go to the gym," Sammie says. "It's full of Man Candy. And I have to go celibate for a year. Plus, at the gym, I'm so focused on my hair, my makeup, my outfit, and getting the right photos and

## The GoddessPower Pyramid

videos, I hardly exercise. So I need a trainer—a woman!— who'll come to my condo and work me out and tell me what to eat."

"Me too!" Andi says. "Or there's no way."

"We can find someone in The Biss Tribe for you both," Esmerelda says. "In fact, one Biss Tribe member who called herself a junk food junkie and the queen of laziness, hired someone from her Biss Tribe class who was a nutritionist and chef, to *live* in her house, shop and prepare all of her meals while she founded her very successful, international travel agency for women who want to travel alone safely. You'll meet them both when they speak at the GoddessWarrior Fortress."

Delaney ties her silver curls back in a scrunchie that was around her wrist. "I'd like that as well, to work with someone privately. I recently read that whatever habits got you to where you are now, won't get you to where you want to go. And if you want to change your life, *you* have to change. Until now I've been exercise-averse, save for yoga. But now I'm ready to do more."

"Excellent," Biss says. "So I'll stop preaching and hammering on this topic. The choice is yours. It took me a long time to get real with myself. And truly apply all the things we're teaching, before my empire finally came out of my imagination, off my vision boards, off the motivational notes on my walls, and into my 3-D reality."

Sunshine looks hopeful and sad all at once.

"We have the power to help make the world an exponentially better place," Biss says. "But only if we do the hard work that starts with personal transformation to blast away what's blocking us."

The Concierges hand out cold bottled water. You and the women drink silently as the breeze rustles the trees.

Biss puts her arm around Jodi. "Jodi will be traveling with us the rest of the week, to lead exercise sessions at each Activation

Station. Thank you, Jodi, for your pep talk today! My Goddesses, let's show some gratitude to our Biss Tribe Trainer, Jodi!"

The women applaud and cheer.

"Now let's head back to the Meditarium," Biss says. "We're going to meditate and *PowerJournal.* And I want you to set the intention in your meditations to discover whether you are truly, truly committed to do this. If the answer is no, the bus will be waiting to take you back to the airport, so you don't waste any more of your time, or our time."

# A Simple GoddessPower Activation: Sitting with Om

Back in the Meditarium, you and all the women sit in your lotus pods.

"Ladies," Biss says, "I'm going to show you the simple meditation technique that helped me heal and transform in miraculous ways. I hope it does the same for you. I call it 'Sitting with Om.'"

Andi asks, "How is it different from what we did this morning?"

"It's simpler," Biss says. "This is how I first learned to meditate. At first, it was terrible. But I did it every night, diligently. And pretty soon, magic happened. So be gentle and patient with yourselves."

Esmerelda plays her singing bowls and soft lavender light glows from the recessed lights of the ceiling dome.

Biss sits in her pod facing you and all the women. "Sit with a straight spine and your legs crossed. If you can't cross your legs, keep them straight in front of you."

Everyone shifts into position.

"Next," Biss says, "touch the tips of your thumbs to the tips of your index fingers, like you're making the OK sign. Keep that while you rest the backs of your wrists on your knees. Close your eyes and focus on the end of your nose or the space between your eyebrows, your 'third eye.' Press the tip of your tongue to the roof of your mouth; that helps your nervous system get into meditation mode. Then simply inhale and repeat *Om* in an elongated way. As we chant this tone, savor the vibration through your body, washing over you like a sound bath to purify your energy. Repeat *Om*, over and over, until you feel deeply relaxed."

Andi sounds cynical: "Does this get the same results as the whole routine this morning?"

"It does," Biss says. "I didn't know anything about chakras or light cleanses or guided meditations when I started this. But it connected me with Spirit and made me psychic. Plus, it's faster. You can use this technique anytime you need to calm down and get clarity on anything."

Kiki says, "This sounds too easy."

"I think the hard part," Bianca says, "will be actually making yourself do it every day."

"One hundred percent," Zeusse says. "Nothing worth doing is easy."

"Exactly," Biss says. "Meditation opened the GoddessGateway for me to step into my GoddessPower Lifestyle. As *Om* vibrated through me, peace and pureness permeated my mind and body. I started getting downloads: new ideas for writing, instructions on what to do the next day, guidance about my life purpose and even psychic flashes. Want to hear an example?"

"Yes!" Sammie and several women exclaim.

"So," Biss says, "one Saturday morning, I was meditating on the sofa when my son and his dad called from their weekend trip to a huge amusement park. 'I lost my keys,' my ex-husband said from the hotel room. He sounded agitated and worried. His key ring held keys to his car, his house and his business. He had last seen

## Monday, Day 2

his keys when they arrived and parked the night before, and said that he had already retraced his steps, finding nothing."

Biss shakes her head. "This could have a bad outcome, right? Stolen car, invaded house, robbery. A cascade of worst-case scenarios."

She imitates holding a phone. "So I told him, 'Let me call you back.' I resumed meditation, simply sitting on the sofa and repeating *Om* with my eyes closed. Then I 'saw' in my mind's eye, his keys at the hotel reception desk. I called him and said, 'Go to the front desk. Ask if anyone turned in keys.' He hung up, then called a few minutes later. 'My keys were at the front desk,' he said, amazed and relieved. 'How did you know that?' he asked. I smiled and thought, I just *knew*."

"Wow," Celeste says. "That's GoddessPower!"

Biss laughs. "Right, and that can be your story, too. You just have to practice. Remember, always set an intention before you meditate, to ask Spirit for guidance on anything you need to know. Then be prepared to journal the answers as soon as the meditation concludes. Here we go."

## The GoddessPower Pyramid

*Dear Goddess Reader:*
*You can use this QR code to learn how to do this meditation technique.*

*GoddessPower Tools*

Biss explains:

### Sitting with Om Meditation

- Sit with a straight spine and your legs crossed on a blanket, pillow, or yoga mat to provide a barrier between yourself and the floor or the ground.

- Infuse your brain and body with oxygen through *Pranayama*, or Alternate Nostril Breathing. Press your left thumb to close your left nostril. Inhale so deeply through your open nostril that your diaphragm expands, as if you're filling your gut with air. Lift your thumb, and press your ring fingertip to close your right nostril. Exhale through your open nostril, until all the air is expelled. Repeat several times.

- Touch the tips of your thumbs to the tips of your index fingers, as if making the OK sign.

## Monday, Day 2

- Rest the backs of your wrists on your knees.

- Close your eyes and focus on the end of your nose or the space between your eyebrows, your "third eye."

- Press the tip of your tongue to the roof of your mouth—between your teeth and that hump in the middle.

- Repeat "Om." Say it in a drawn-out way, like "Oooooooooommmmmmmmm." This ancient chant creates a soundwave of pure Goddess energy that attunes you to your spiritual power. Think of *Om* as the password for direct, clear access to a divine wi-fi network.

- Enjoy the vibration through your body, washing over you like a sound bath to purify your aura. You can ask a question or set an intention to receive divine guidance during the meditation. Then be open to receive words, images, and ideas that flow in very fast.

- Repeat *Om* until you feel deeply relaxed and until all of your questions are answered. Conclude with a feeling of gratitude to Spirit for providing the divine guidance that you received.

Biss says, "You'll notice that we're only chanting one tone, *Om*. The sound vibration of this universal tone, *Om*, attunes you to your GoddessPower. Like I said, think of *Om* as the password for direct, clear access to your divine wi-fi network. So now let's say it together, in an elongated way. Enjoy the vibration of this sacred sound through your body, washing over you like a sound bath to purify your aura."

Biss sits in her pod with her legs crossed, spine straight and head straight.

"Now let's try it together. Inhale. Now say *Om* in an elongated way. Ready? Inhale. *Ooooooooooohhhhhhhhhmmmmmmmmm.*"

You and the women join the loud vibration.

"Wow that's amazing," Sunshine says, "it gives me chills."

"Like we could blow the roof off," Andi says.

"Amps me up!" Jade adds. "I'm gonna write a song called *Om*."

Biss nods. "Now close your eyes and let's chant *Om* four times. Really savor the sensations of this deep vibration through your entire being. Let's inhale. *Ooooooooooohhhhhhhhhmmmmmmmmm.*"

Biss leads the chant three more times, then says, "Now journal about any information that you saw, heard or felt during the meditation."

After a few minutes, Biss says, "How was it?"

"I can definitely do this every day," Zeusse says. "I got a lot more information, plus it mellows me out."

"This way is easier than what we did this morning," Jade adds. "I felt like I was connecting with a hidden part of myself that was silent until now, and now she won't stop telling me stuff. I think I can write a thousand songs this way."

## Getting Guidance from Your GoddessVoice

"Perfect segue," Biss says. "In meditation, you're hearing your GoddessVoice, spoken by your Supernatural Self, providing wisdom to guide you. Your GoddessVoice is attuned to Spirit, and you amplify it and hear it through meditation. The more you flex your meditation muscles, the more you'll be able to hear your GoddessVoice, even when you're not in meditation."

## Monday, Day 2

The definition streams across the Meditarium's ceiling dome and Biss reads it:

"Your GoddessVoice is the divine voice within you, speaking your authentic truth, unhindered by the chaos of the thinking mind. This voice of your female superpowers speaks the language of your intuition, which channels a supernatural frequency that helps you receive information from your heart and soul, Spirit, and the universal field of knowledge. Your Supernatural Self speaks to you through your GoddessVoice."

Jade raises a hand. "Is this like our inner voice?"

"Yes," Biss says. "Think of it as a soundboard where you have different audio channels all coming together from different input signals and merging them into one sound. Your GoddessVoice is all the information that Spirit is telling you, and it may be coming from different divine sources such as angels or ancestors, all merged into one message."

"That rocks!" Jade says.

"I've ignored my intuition so many times," Sunshine says, "and that always gets me into trouble."

"Now that you know better," Biss says, "you can do better. All of you. Our GoddessVoice speaks to us all day long, and it's very easy to ignore. It warns you about people, places and things, like, 'Don't date Jake' or 'Take the long way home.' But we all have free will to make our own decisions, and we often ignore divine guidance because we think we know better or are tempted by something that makes us ignore the warning. For example, if you go ahead and date Jake, and he turns out to be an abuser, or you take the short way home and get in a traffic jam, you face the consequences. However, when you listen and follow the guidance, you'll be protected and rewarded."

Marla and Sammie raise their hands at the same time, then laugh. "You go," Marla says.

"Biss, how you can tell what's your GoddessVoice and your own mind just making stuff up because that's what you want to hear?" Sammie asks.

"Great question," Biss says. "Your GoddessVoice gives you ideas faster than you can think. The information flashes into your thoughts at lightning speed, and you just *know* something, or you feel an impression, or a scene or image suddenly appears in your mind. Your GoddessVoice shares information suddenly and out of the blue, and it's often something that you might never have thought about before."

## Monday, Day 2

Zeusse raises her hand. "Biss, sometimes in my head, I get contradictions. I can't tell if it's my intuition or fear talking to me."

Sunshine nods, along with several other women.

"It's a noise-fest in my mind," Bianca says. "So loud! I shut it all out, because I don't know what to believe."

"Same!" Jade quips. "And that just leaves me anxious, trying to figure things out on my own, so I numb out on the couch with ice cream and Netflix."

Biss places her hand on her heart. "My meditation teacher taught me the tool of discernment. I was going through terrible anxiety after someone stole from me and I was terrified that something awful would happen as a result. I couldn't tell if my thoughts were lies coming from fear, or the truth coming from intuition."

"That's my problem," Zeusse says.

"Here's the solution," Biss says. "I called my meditation teacher, and they said, 'Use discernment. Ask your heart the question and listen for the answer. It will be clear and truthful.'"

Biss gazes at you and all the women. "Try this. Put your hand on your heart, and silently direct the question to your heart. Warning: be ready to hear the answer in a split-second, and don't ignore it if you don't like it. It will come faster than you can think. Ready?"

You and the women put your hands over your hearts.

"Now in your mind," Biss says, "ask your heart the question that's been giving you contradictory answers."

The Meditarium is silent.

"Holy shit!" Andi exclaims. "Holy shit!"

Marla shrieks, "Oh. My. God!"

Sammie's eyes widen and she keeps her hand on her heart. Tears drip from Delaney's eyes. Bianca sobs.

"I can't believe it!" Sunshine says.

"I don't like my answer," Celeste adds. "But it's what I need to hear."

Biss smiles. "Now you have a tool to get clarity when you need it most. Anybody want to share?"

Zeusse's hand shoots up. "I asked if one particular female would be good to join my team for the academy, and my heart told me, *She's a thief!*"

"Wow," Biss says.

"Something in my gut had been warning me about her," Zeusse says, "even though on paper, this chick is the bomb. But I'll go with the guidance, not the paper. Plus, that B wasn't anywhere in my meditation with the angel earlier."

## GoddessPower Activation Tool #4: Journaling

Biss holds up a *PowerJournal.*

"Now it's time for part two of the GoddessLife script exercises that we started yesterday at SeaGoddess Castle," Biss says, "that involved using your thinking mind to describe your GoddessVision. Today we'll ask Spirit to reveal ideas and details that may be bigger and bolder than you ever imagined. So please turn to the GoddessGateway worksheet that you began yesterday."

The domed screen swirls with colorful lights around the word GoddessPower.

"We're about to do the official *PowerJournal* technique," Biss says, "that you can do any time at home. This valuable exercise for you will show that sometimes we think small, when Spirit has a much bigger plan. You're about to see it and learn how you can take action."

Biss raises a hand. "How many of you as girls had a diary with the little lock on it?"

## Monday, Day 2

Most of the women's hands shoot up.

"Yes!" Biss exclaims, smiling. "That was the start of journaling, which I've been doing since I was a little girl. So when I started meditating, I journaled about my fantastical experiences with Spirit, so I could refer back to the guidance—especially when it was way more spectacular than I ever imagined. This process was so transformative, I created workbooks called *PowerJournal*® with my sister, Catherine Greenspan, and we published them through our company, Two Sisters Writing & Publishing®. Now we have different workbooks for different topics."

The screen shows the silhouette of a woman meditating.

"Now we're about to ask Spirit to answer four questions," Biss says, "using the 'Sitting with Om' technique. First, I'll read the question that sets your intention for the meditation. Then we'll chant *Om* four times while you ask Spirit to provide answers. Then you write nonstop to pour every detail onto the pages. Got it?"

The screen shows the director's slate, movie camera and theatre marquis.

"Remember, this exercise helps you flesh out the movie script that we created yesterday at SeaGoddess Castle," Biss says, "and to identify hidden blocks and provide action steps that take you through the GoddessGateway into your GoddessLife. So after this, you can go back to that GoddessGateway worksheet and fill in the action steps that you learn in meditation. Everybody understand?"

Andi runs a hand through her hair; purple light from the dome reflects on her rings. "That's a lot all at once!"

"Yeah, I'm slow," Kiki says with a giggle. "I need one thing at a time."

"I got you," Biss says. "OK my Goddesses, sit up straight, close your eyes, focus on the tip of your nose or your third eye, put the tip of your tongue at the roof of your mouth, and inhale, then exhale."

## The GoddessPower Pyramid

You and the women follow her instructions, then Biss reads the first question:

1. **Define who you are as Goddess, your Supernatural Self.** Who is she, the ultimate version of you? Ask Spirit to reveal her in ways you never imagined, as the wildest fantasy of yourself, courageously and confidently living your most uninhibited, powerful potential. How does she think, speak, behave, dress, live, love, work and play?

"Hold this question in your mind," Biss says, "and ask Spirit to answer it while we chant *Om* in an elongated way, four times." She leads everyone in chanting *Om* four times.

"Now write everything Spirit said and showed you," she says. "Every detail. Stop when Esmerelda sounds her gong in five minutes."

*Dear Goddess Reader:*
*Write your responses on the lines provided after each question.*

_____

_____

_____

_____

## Monday, Day 2

After five minutes, the gong sounds, and Biss reads the next question:

2. **What's blocking you from becoming the Goddess version of the current you?** Ask Spirit to reveal internal and exterior barriers that you are not aware of. And ask Spirit to tell you the specific **action steps** you need to take to blast past these blocks to enter the GoddessGateway to become your Supernatural Self for the rest of your life.

"Hold this question in your mind," Biss says, "and ask Spirit to answer it while we chant *Om* in an elongated way, four times." She leads everyone in chanting *Om* four times.

"Now write everything Spirit said and showed you," she says. "Every detail. Stop when Esmerelda sounds her gong."

_____

_____

_____

_____

After five minutes, the gong sounds, and Biss reads the next question:

3. **Define your GoddessLife.** Ask Spirit to show you a detailed scene from your GoddessLife that's bigger and better than you ever imagined. Ask Spirit to reveal what your heart and soul crave, and what hidden feelings, experiences, creations, accomplishments and legacy are waiting inside you to

## The GoddessPower Pyramid

come out into the world. Ask Spirit to provide details about what you're doing, seeing, feeling, tasting, touching, hearing and experiencing.

"Hold this question in your mind," Biss says, "and ask Spirit to answer it while we chant *Om* in an elongated way, four times." She leads everyone in chanting *Om* four times.

"Now write everything Spirit said and showed you," she says. "Every detail. Stop when Esmerelda sounds her gong in five minutes."

_____

_____

_____

_____

4. **What's blocking you from living your GoddessLife?** Ask Spirit to reveal what's stopping you from getting what you truly desire and deserve? Write a scene where you've obliterated any obstacles and are free to succeed on every level. Ask Spirit to tell you the specific **action steps** that will enable you to enter the GoddessGateway and live, love, work and play this way for the rest of your life.

"Hold this question in your mind," Biss says, "and ask Spirit to answer it while we chant *Om* in an elongated way, four times." She leads everyone in chanting *Om* four times.

## Monday, Day 2

"Now write everything Spirit said and showed you," she says. "Every detail. Stop when Esmerelda sounds her gong in five minutes."

_____

_____

_____

_____

After five minutes, the gong sounds. The ceiling dome lights brighten slightly, casting a golden glow over the Meditarium.

"Holy shit!" Andi exclaims as several women sniffle and sob.

"Holy moley is right," Sunshine cries. "I can't believe it!"

"My mind is officially blown," Zeusse says.

"I can't even talk right now," Sammie sobs.

"Oh I want to give everyone a hug," Biss says softly. "Please tell me more."

Andi has a shaky voice as she says, "One of my blocks comes from a past life when I was put in prison for being gay. I died there. That woman Nell showed up again. She said that horrible experience stayed stuck in me like a blueprint that I relived in this life, by putting myself in prison by marrying a man, and the life lesson has been to find the courage to break free and live as I want."

"Wow," Biss says. "What action steps were you given?"

Andi sighs. "Man! I have to come out to every single person I've ever been terrified to tell that I'm a lesbian. Within two weeks of leaving here. Holy shit."

"You can do it, Andi," Biss says. "That will free you beyond measure. All of you, when you take action on the things that you fear most, you'll elevate to a whole new way of thinking, and things that once scared you will have no power to block you."

"Bring it on, mama," Marla says with a squeaky voice. "I need that. I had a past life thing, too. That I was a victim of brutal 'honor killing' in a country where girls aren't even allowed to go to school. I had run away with a boy, my parents caught me, and the whole village shoved me in a pit and threw stones at me until I died. They killed me! Because I shamed my parents for not being a virgin."

Marla sobs. Sammie leaps out of her pod, and into Marla's to rock her while she cries.

"That's horrible, mama," Sammie says, stroking her head. The women are silent except for their own sniffles and sobs.

Biss speaks softly. "Marla, did Spirit provide action steps to heal this ancestral wound that's blocking you in this lifetime?"

Marla blows her nose. "Yeah. I have to do a meditation by myself to connect with the people who killed me, and tell them I forgive them so I can heal and get that trauma out of my soul."

"Beautiful," Biss says. "I suggest doing that meditation as soon as possible while here in the vortex of Infinity Mountain, which accelerates healing."

Still beside Marla, Sammie says, "Mine is quick. Spirit said I have to get all the affirmation I've been getting from guys, from within myself. I have to take myself on three dinner dates all alone at my favorite fancy restaurants in three different cities, and it won't work unless I'm actually happy doing it."

"That sounds mortifying," Kiki says. "Like, everyone will stare."

"Thanks, bitch!" Sammie snaps sarcastically.

"Actually," Biss says, "eating alone in a nice restaurant is extremely empowering. I recommend that each of you try that when you get home. Dress up, put on makeup if you wear it, go and enjoy your own company. A Goddess loves her own company and feels complete by herself."

# Monday, Day 2

"That's aspirational for me," Delaney says. "I agree with Kiki; I'd feel like everyone is staring at me. But incredibly, Spirit said for me to truly know self-love, I have to believe that I'm enough, all alone, even on a dinner date by myself. And that I have to take a vacation alone to Poland, where my family's lineage started. I've always wanted to go, but my husband has no interest. And I've been afraid to travel alone. Now Spirit says I must."

Delaney wipes her nose and dabs her eyes. "Biss, I'd like to connect with the Biss Tribe Goddess who started the travel agency for women to travel alone."

"I'll make that happen," Biss says.

Sunshine sobs. "If I can stop crying—" She takes in a long, deep breath. "Get it together, girl. When I asked about my blocks, Spirit showed me my mother, literally body-blocking me from going forward! She kept saying, 'My life was so hard, I want to protect you, my precious baby girl, from exposure in business and from the pain of marriage if it doesn't work out.' She was like a guard on a basketball court, her arms all up in the air around me, blocking me every time I tried to get past her. And I was crying, begging her to stop."

"Sunshine," Biss says, "did Spirit reveal how to stop your mother from blocking you?"

"I have to be in meditation and ask this angel, he was really big with a sword and shield, a protector," Sunshine says.

"Archangel Michael," Biss says.

"I have to ask him to tell my mother that he's protecting me," Sunshine says, "and that I'm safe to be in the spotlight with my company and to find love that won't hurt me."

"How do you feel about that?" Biss asks.

"I believe that I can do it," Sunshine says.

"Dang, Sunshine, that's me, too, one hundred percent," Zeusse says, casting a slight smile at Sunshine, then looking at Biss. "Spirit reminded me of a time I had forgotten about, when I was fifteen, at my grandparents's farm in Alabama. While I was growing up, I spent the school year with my dad in Harlem. He raised me while my mother was locked up. So while Pops worked, I spent the summers in Alabama with my grandparents. My grandfather was the mayor of the town and he had a lot of businesses at a time when it wasn't common for a Black man to build wealth. So he taught me things about being an entrepreneur. Well I helped my high school basketball team win the New York state championships, and the kids down South were always asking me to show them some moves."

Zeusse sighs. "So I decided to start my own summer basketball camp. I had 25 kids, boys and girls, age 13 to 18. Their parents signed them up and paid me, and it started off smooth. But on the second day, this guy, he was a bully to all the kids at church since we were little, and called me the worst names because I didn't dress like a girl and I've always been tall with a deep voice. Well, he didn't make the team at school down there, and he was so jealous that I was an all-star in high school and now I was making a business out of it on what he thought was his turf. So he shows up at my camp with his daddy's gun. We're all the court doing drills, and this mo-fo starts to shoot."

"OhmyGod," Marla says.

"Tell me nobody died!" Sammie exclaims.

Biss steps close to Zeusse's pod and gazes at her with a comforting expression.

"Can't believe I had forgotten all about this," Zeusse says. "Everybody ran. Nobody was hurt. But the kid turned the gun on himself and died. Everybody was too upset to continue the camp and I had to refund all their money. And I never did the camp again. I was so messed up, all I did was go to the gym and read

## Monday, Day 2

every book by my favorite Harlem Renaissance authors, especially Zora Neale Hurston, for the rest of the summer."

Zeusse is silent for a moment. "In my meditation, Spirit said that experience, the trauma... the failure... and the fear of people getting hurt in a basketball environment that I created, has blocked me from starting the academy."

Biss asks, "Did Spirit reveal how to remove this block?"

"Yeah," Zeusse says, "they—it was a bunch of people talking to me, including my grandparents and Mrs. Jones from Sunday School—they kept saying, 'That was then, this is now. Fear not. Do it now. You are safe.' Over and over. My action step is knowing that I'm safe to succeed in my own business this time. They told me what to write out to say to myself every morning and night, until I really believe it."

"Excellent, Zeusse, you can do it!" Biss says. "Thank you for sharing. All of you. Now let's get up and stretch!"

You step out of your pod as do the other women, and face Biss and Esmerelda.

"Raise your arms," Esmerelda says. "Streeetttttcchh to the left and inhale deeply, then exhale. Stretch up! And inhale. Exhale. Stretch to the right. Inhale. Exhale." Bianca does this while seated in her pod.

"I'm going to lead you through a series of yoga poses called a Sun Salutation," Esmerelda says. "Savor the sensations of all those muscles stretching. Breathe. Feel that luscious blood going into your brain. Close your eyes and become very aware of how your body feels."

When it's over, Biss says, "Thank you, Esmerelda. Who's got an oxygen buzz from that?!"

"I'm zen," Zeusse says. "Needed it bad."

## Get Into Your GoddessGenius Zone

As you and the women settle back into your pods, Biss points up to words streaming on the domed ceiling: "Get into your GoddessGenius Zone."

Andi raises a hand. "Genius? I'm sorry. That's a big word. Doesn't apply to me."

Sunshine nods. "I'm still trying to get used to calling myself a Goddess."

A murmur of agreement ripples through the room.

"I get it," Biss says. "Goddess and Genius are big, big words. Maybe so big, they don't even resonate with you. Yet. But consider this. If you're uncomfortable calling yourself a Goddess... and a Genius... think about why. Have you ever called yourself a fucking loser or an idiot? A stupid bitch? A dumb ass? Have other people ever called you vile names? Have you ever been verbally abused?"

Too many women in the room nod or say, "Yes."

Biss walks amidst the pods as she speaks. "Hateful self-talk and verbal assaults by others are totally unacceptable. But we let them replay over and over in our minds until they create tracks that become the mental road we travel and where our self-image calls home. Our self-esteem gets stuck in these muddy ruts. And just when we get close to escaping, a downpour of disappointment, despair or even depression, pushes us back into the muck."

Biss looks directly at you, then all the women, as she says, "You free yourself by changing how you think of yourself, and by knowing that you are a genius in at least one area of your life."

Andi shakes her head. "That sounds really grandiose. I have never thought of myself that way."

"Me either," Sammie says sadly.

Several women nod and say, "Same here."

## Monday, Day 2

Biss looks disturbed. "It's time to get grandiose, Goddesses! Repeat after me, 'I am a genius!'"

The women mumble it.

"Oh, hell no!" Biss exclaims. "Let's do that again. Say it like you believe it! Say, 'I am a genius!'"

The women say it a little louder.

"I feel like I'm lying," Jade says sadly.

"Me too," Sunshine whispers, looking down.

Biss shakes her head. "Okay, who here has ever called herself an idiot?"

Hands fly up.

"A fucking loser?" Biss asks.

More hands shoot up.

"After you leave here," Biss says, "you will never, ever speak to yourself like that. You will declare loud and proud that you are a GoddessGenius, and the world better look out!"

"Yes!" Celeste cheers. "I'm all over that."

"Count me in," Andi says.

"I'm ready to fake it 'til I make it," Jade says.

A chorus of "Me, too" ripples through the group.

"So let's try it again," Biss says. "Say, 'I am a genius!'"

The air vibrates with passion and conviction as you join the women in declaring, "I am a genius!"

"That feels good," Delaney says. "There's a first for everything."

Celeste laughs. "I'm going to declare that every day. Out loud for all to hear."

Biss glances up at the ceiling dome. "I made up this definition." She reads:

"Your supernatural source of unique and extraordinary talent and passion that elevates you into your creative genius zone. In this trance-like flow state, you joyously do what you love in ways that fulfill and prosper you—and may be a positive influence on others."

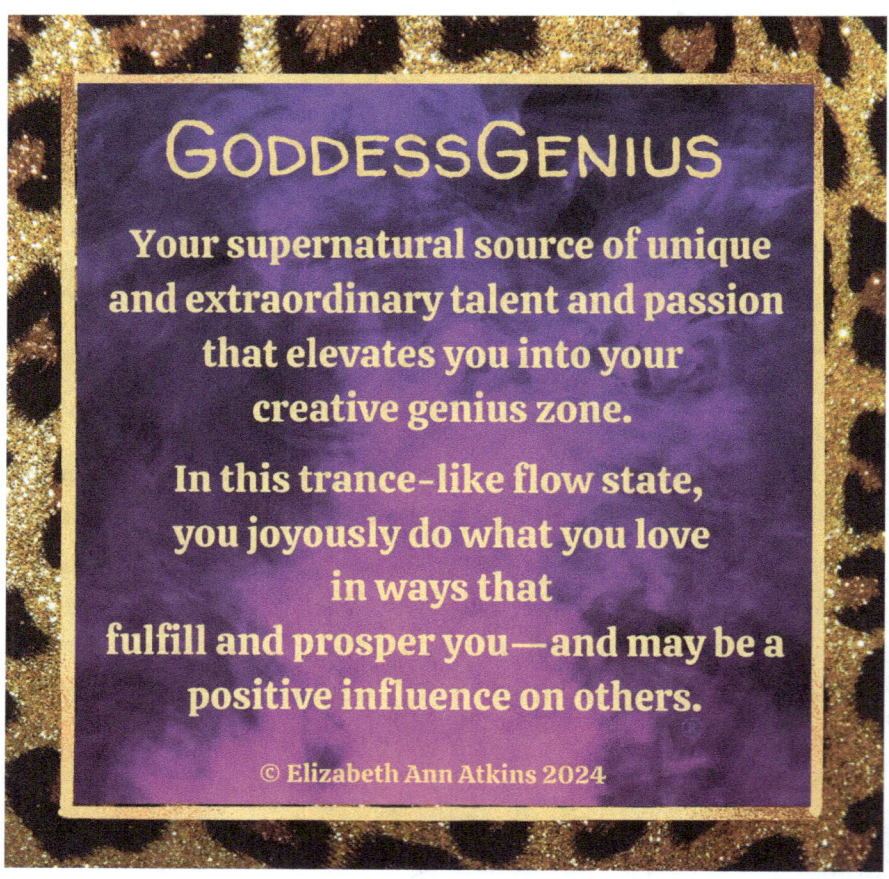

Biss looks around. "Somebody give me an example of your GoddessGenius."

Sunshine raises her hand. "I love cooking. Finding the perfect recipes, shopping for the best ingredients, laying them all on the counters, prepping whatever I need, using the best pots and pans and the perfect flame or oven temp, then concocting it all together to create a delicious symphony of flavors." She moves her hands in the air as if conducting.

## Monday, Day 2

"I love it so much," Sunshine says dreamily, "even if it's just for me. And when I share it with people I love, it's even better. That's why I want to include my own restaurant in The Turquoise Experience, serving my favorite recipes."

Biss high-fives Sunshine. "Rock that GoddessGenius Zone!"

Sunshine beams.

Biss looks around. "Everybody hear this? We're talking about the time and space where you're in total alignment with your fully activated Power, Pleasure, Prosperity, Protection and Peace.

"Right now," Biss says, "I want you to write in your *PowerJournal*. Describe your GoddessGenius Zone, an activity where you're in perfect flow, loving it, losing all track of time, wishing you could do this one thing forever, feeling overjoyed for the gift, talent and desire to do this activity. It fulfills you and may be something that you can monetize to prosper yourself and help others at the same time."

*Dear Goddess Reader:*
*Describe your GoddessGenius Zone.*

_____

_____

_____

_____

## Sounding the Alarms in Your GoddessPower Mission Control Center

Biss points to the ceiling, where the screen shows video of a woman in the cockpit of a glass airplane, flying through clouds, then blue sky and outer space.

"When you embark on your GoddessMission," Biss says, "you'll be flying a glass airplane. First, after you lay the five foundations of GoddessPower, you'll feel like you're flying. You might literally feel physical sensations like dizziness or a stomach flutter, like you're shooting up, out of your body into a fast-moving realm that feels infinite. It can be startling. But it's amazing. And you want to feel safe."

As you and the women look up at the screen, she adds, "So think of yourself as flying a glass airplane equipped with bullet-proof glass and an anti-radar shield. You command and control the airspace, flight plans and destinations, and how fast you navigate the wide open skies with the whole universe open to your exploration. This airplane can take you anywhere, anytime. It's fueled by the fire of your spirit."

On the screen, a green forcefield glows around the plane. "Your GoddessPower creates a forcefield of supernatural protection, but unfortunately, a long list of forces may try to shoot you down. The most threatening force is also the most difficult to stop. It's our self-sabotaging beliefs and behaviors—often rooted in fear of success, fear of failure, and fear of consequences from our families, employers, faith communities and society."

Suddenly a red flash over the screen tries to stop the airplane. The red light flashes on the women's faces as you all watch the video.

"People and circumstances will try to impose a 'no fly zone' on the new you and your dreams faster than you can say 'Air Traffic

## Monday, Day 2

Control,'" Biss says. "It's really twisted, but these outside forces may have done such a good job programming your flight patterns, that you may automatically comply with their travel restrictions."

Fighter jets appear on the screen, shooting at the glass airplane.

"That's why the second most threatening force to your Goddess launch is people who benefit from keeping you grounded," Biss says. "They may try to manipulate the systems that keep the plane flying, because they know the inner workings of your mind, your personality and your life. These are people who don't want to see you activate your GoddessPower or live your GoddessLife, because you will no longer conform to their agendas and/or comply with their controlling tactics."

Several women snicker.

Sunshine moans, "I've got 25 people just waiting for me to come home and tell me to get my head out of the f-ing clouds. They look at all my past failures and shoot down anything I try to do, telling me to give it up and just get a real job."

Andi adds, "My family will *hate* the real me. That's why I've kept her in the closet all these years. At my own expense. I'm so damn tired of hiding who I am. No more, man! It's time to fly."

Sammie shakes her head. "My parents love that I make so much money, but they still don't understand what it means to be an influencer."

Bianca raises her hand. "People are always telling me that I'm limited by my mobility challenges. Including people at my job. Even the few close friends I told about this retreat, they were like, 'Bianca, you can't.' Yes, I can!"

"Don't even get me started on *that,*" Celeste quips. "Even though I'm the CEO and visionary who turned our company around, the board of directors is always trying to squash my ideas. Let them eat cake! Like Marie Antoinette once said."

# The GoddessPower Pyramid

Biss shakes her head. "These are all people who think they know best for us, so they try to play Air Traffic Control to monitor and dictate where we fly. They'll tell us to restrict our travel to the zones they deem safe or acceptable. They'll tell us we can't handle the engine power we're intending to steer, nor can we navigate the unknowns of the uncharted territory we want to explore and conquer."

Sammie stands up, outside her pod, shoots her hands up in the air, tilts her head back, and closes her eyes. "I am so fucking *done* with letting anybody control me! Let's fly, bitches!"

Biss dashes over and gives her a double high-five, then laces their fingers together, over their heads, so they form a bridge.

"Everybody, get up!" Biss says. "Find a partner! This is officially our group's secret greeting."

As you and the women hop up and join hands over head, forming human bridges—archways—Biss says, "Look into each other's eyes. See the sparkle. The fire. The GoddessPower. Speak with your eyes. Love. Support. Empowerment. Sisterhood. And say the GoddessPower motto: 'You can do it, Goddess, because *you* have the power!'"

The room explodes with a wild cacophony of shrieks, laughter and joyous expressions as you and the women connect and exclaim the GoddessPower motto. Everybody makes their way past Bianca's pod to lock hands and eyes with her and say the motto.

"Now move to another person," Biss says, doing the same. "Until you've done this GoddessGreeting with every woman here. Each group that ascends Infinity Mountain in The Biss Tribe creates its signature gesture, and this is yours, officially for your class number 88."

## Monday, Day 2

After you and the women settle back into your lotus pods, Biss says, "Now, back to our flight."

On the screen, the glass airplane is dodging bullet- and bombbursts of red and yellow, shot from fighter jets amidst thick clouds with zero visibility.

"We cannot allow these forces to stop us from declaring that yes, we are going to board our proverbial Goddess plane and take a solo flight toward the infinite horizon, then land and stake our claim on the thrilling new territory of Power, Pleasure, Prosperity, Protection and Peace."

Jade claps and shouts, "Let's go!"

The screen shows video of a tower where people are frantically pushing buttons and monitoring screens.

"This may throw Air Traffic Control into a frenzied strategy to keep you grounded," Biss says. "Few people like change, especially if it upsets their kingdom. Know this and proceed with caution. Keep your personal safety a top priority when making drastic changes. Whether leaving a boyfriend or husband or partner, or outing an enemy on the national stage, backlash happens, and it can be deadly. So make a plan to proceed with the utmost safety for yourself and your children if necessary."

On the screen, the Goddess plane is free and clear of attackers and obstacles, soaring up into the infinity of blue sky.

"Goddesses, it's time to fly!" Bis shouts. "Say it with me."

You and all the women shout, "It's time to fly!"

# Dinner in the Vortex– The GoddessFeast in the Pyramid

The GoddessFeast is served in The Vortex, a ballroom beneath the pyramid. Cobalt blue beams of light spaced three feet apart shoot from the edges of the polished black onyx floor. The blue beams glow against the black granite walls and splash onto the high, dark purple ceiling where tiny dots of light sparkle like stars in outer space.

The dimensions of the room, and the colors, create a far-away feeling as you sit in ornate silver chairs at a serpentine-shaped table with 12 women on each side.

Golden light glows on their faces from candles set in frosted-glass lantern centerpieces nestled in white and blue lotus flowers bursting from long bowls displayed on palm fronds on the white linen tablecloth.

Biss and Esmerelda sit at the heads of the table. Sasha Maxwell is on Biss's left, and her camerawoman, Cinnamon, is to Biss's right.

You're seated beside Cinnamon and across from Zeusse. Sultry music plays as the women chatter.

Sasha tells Biss, "Girl, it's like I was just sitting here yesterday, and I blinked, and bam! My GoddessVision became my real life. I cannot *wait* to speak tonight."

Andi, sitting to your right, is staring at Biss and Sasha and tells them, "First, you look alike. It almost hurts my eyes to look at the two of you together. There's like this energetic fire blazing from each of you by yourselves. But together, man, it's an inferno."

Sasha flashes a huge smile that makes her even more radiant. "That's GoddessPower, baby!"

"Cinnamon," Andi says, "not to leave you out. You've got the glow, too. Love your name."

## Monday, Day 2

"Thank you," says Cinnamon, raising her forearm and touching her chin-length straight bob hairstyle. "It's my nickname. As a kid, my cousin said my hair and skin were that color."

"Still are," Andi says. "Stunning."

Sasha turns to Zeusse. "I am so in awe of you, girlfriend. I watched all your games and I was like, there goes a Goddess on the court. So to see you here, I know you'll build a phenomenal empire."

Zeusse holds a hand to her chest, bows her head toward Sasha, and smiles. "Coming from you, I'm honored. Thank you. We got a mutual admiration society goin' on here, because I watch your show every day. You spit some real truth on that mic. And you do it in a way I've never heard before. You keep it real and raw."

"Then let's do that when I interview *you* sometime," Sasha says.

Zeusse smiles even bigger. "I'm all in. Just let me know when."

"They call you the Queen of the Court," Sasha says, "so naturally you belong on *The QueenPower Show*. Tell us how you do what you do!"

Beaming, Zeusse says, "I'd be honored."

Sammie, who's beside Zeusse, looks pale. She's shaking. "I feel so freaking claustrophobic in this place. I hate being underground. What if there's like, an earthquake, and we all get crushed—"

Beside her, Marla chuckles. "Chill, bitch! This place is like a bunker." She glances at the security guards near the doors. "I'm sure the security crew will make sure we're safe."

The Concierges appear with plates covered by gleaming silver pyramids topped by lightning bolt-shaped handles.

"Oh girl," Sasha exclaims, "look at *them!*"

She gazes at the male, female and androgynous Concierges, whose beautiful physiques showcase luscious hues as they sport ancient Egyptian-style clothing of drapey gold satin. Swirling gold bands adorn their biceps and shoulder muscles. Rounded necklaces display colorful stones. Heavy black eyeliner makes their eyes alluring. And brown leather strings zig-zag up their toned calves from open-toed sandals.

Sasha's eyes devour the muscular man who places a plate in front of her and lifts the lid.

"Madame," he says, "lobster tails and scallops with your favorite peri peri dipping sauce. A mixed green salad. And fresh berries for dessert."

Sasha purrs, looking up at him with an intense stare. "Mmmm, delicious."

He smiles. "I'm at your service for the duration of your stay here at the GoddessPower Pyramid."

Lust burns in Sasha's green eyes as she gazes up at him. "I have a ravenous appetite, so I'll be calling on you."

"At your service, madame," he says before stepping away.

A beautiful woman serves Zeusse, whose eyes dance with delight, while Andi is mesmerized by her female Concierge.

"I can't wait to hear Sasha Maxwell speak," Celeste says. "I love the way she spins her topics on her show. Makes you think about relationships and love and women in a radical new way."

"My friend was a guest on the show," Jade says. "She's a therapist. They were talking about 'throuples;' that's three people in a committed relationship. She was also on talking about polyamory. I love when people explore relationship styles outside of traditional rules. I want that. Said the chick who has zero love life."

Several women laugh as your Concierge places your meal before you, raises the cover, and says, "May I get you anything else?"

You take in the sensory extravaganza: aromatic steam rising from one of your favorite meals arranged like artwork on your plate; the sexual energy emanating from your Concierge; and the

## Monday, Day 2

electrifying joy of each woman nearly swooning over the food and the people presenting it.

"Thank you," you say as Concierge fills your crystal flute with the celebratory beverage of your choice. Some women opt for champagne or cocktails, while others have sparkling water, iced tea, cider or kombucha.

"My Goddesses!" Biss exclaims, standing at the head of the tables and raising a champagne glass. She's wearing a royal blue satin halter dress that hugs her curves and has ostrich feather trim at the cleavage and around the bottom of the short skirt.

"Let's toast to another delicious indulgence here in The Biss Tribe! You're about to experience the phenomenal Sasha Maxwell tonight!"

Everyone raises her glass. Clinking crystal echoes through the room as the Concierges depart.

"Ladies, before you eat," Biss says, "let's close our eyes and give thanks to the infinite, divine powers for gifting us with this experience and this nourishment that fuels our minds, bodies and souls to activate our GoddessPower here at the Power Pyramid, so we can create luscious lives that illuminate the world. And so it is spoken, and so it is done."

You and the women repeat: "And so it is spoken, and so it is done."

"Now let the Goddesses feast!" Biss announces.

You sip, then savor the first bite, which you never want to swallow, because the flavors and textures are your favorites, prepared perfectly to your preferences.

"I'm having a food-gasm," says Zeusse across the table. "I mean, this lobster, salad and cornbread are off the chain."

No one responds, because they're also blissing out with every bite.

# The GoddessPower Pyramid

## GoddessFeast Speaker: The Sasha Maxwell Story

After Sasha completes her entrée, Biss stands. "My Goddesses! It's time to meet one of The Biss Tribe's most outstanding success stories! Sasha Maxwell!"

She beams down at Sasha, who's wearing a shimmery white leather dress that outlines her hourglass shape and exposes toned shoulders and arms. She smiles up at Biss.

"As I said yesterday," Biss says, "The Biss Tribe was the incubator where Sasha conceived the concept for her mission to empower women by serving as an example and talking loud and proud about it. So let me start by reading a recent review about her that was published in the national media:

"Sasha Maxwell is the sexy sauce that bubbles, steams and spices up your mind and heart when you combine intelligence, spirituality, woman-power, and provocative curiosity about love and life. She brings a unique ethnic flavor to contemporary media, thanks to her diverse background. *The QueenPower Show* is a must-watch, must-listen experience if you're seeking to view life through a new lens from angles you've never imagined. Sasha is a thought-shifter, and she'll add some sizzle to your day on every show. She may even inspire you to unleash your wild side to make your secret fantasies a reality."

The women applaud.

"Sasha?" Biss says.

Sasha stands, and Biss holds her hand.

You and the women continue eating while beholding Sasha's wild tumble of golden-brown corkscrew curls, green eyes, and pouty pink mouth.

"She's tall," Jade whispers.

## Monday, Day 2

"I think she's five-nine, *before* the four-inch heels," Celeste adds. "And she is *wearin'* that dress."

"*Day*-um," Zeusse says, scanning Sasha from head to toe. "That is one beautiful female."

"Ladies!" Biss exclaims. "Sasha Maxwell is in a class by herself. *The QueenPower Show with Sasha Maxwell* is one of the world's top podcasts, as millions of people around the world tune in every night to hear the hot topics that she explores with her guests. And these aren't just any hot topics. They're questions about relationships and life that Sasha gleans from her personal experiences in love and romance."

Biss beams at Sasha, who glows brighter.

"If you've read her best-selling book, *Eleven Men,* then you'll see how she chronicled her sexy quest to enjoy eleven men, and talk about her experiences on her show. Who's read the book?"

About two-thirds of the women raise their hands, including Celeste.

"That book was hot as blazes," Celeste whispers. "My married ass had to live vicariously through her sexcapades, and I loved every romp. So did my husband."

Biss says, "I couldn't be more proud to introduce our speaker tonight, Sasha Maxwell."

Sasha hugs Biss, then faces you and the women.

"Goddesses!" Sasha exclaims. "Listen! You're sitting on the launchpad to become the most bodacious, bad-ass bitch of your dreams, right here in The Biss Tribe!"

The women cheer.

"But are you *really* ready for that?" Sasha asks. "Are you scared? Or are you ready to rock the world?"

"Rock the world!" Jade shouts.

"Yes, girl!" Sasha says. "I love your spirit. Because the best fuel for you to rocket up out of your everyday reality and into a whole new galaxy of YouPower, is absolute and urgent *rejection* of your current mindset and circumstances. Like, no more! And as Biss says, 'I deserve better! I deserve the best!'"

Sasha looks at you and each woman in the eye. "If you can pause eating that delicious food for a hot minute, say it with me: 'I deserve better! I deserve the best!'"

You and the women repeat that in unison; your voices echo off the sleek black walls and floor as the sultry instrumental hip-hop music plays.

"I love it!" Sasha exclaims. "And here's the key: only *you* know what better and best are for you. It might be something so radical, so crazy, you've never said it out loud. Well, mine was, and now I'm doing it, and talking about it to folks around the world."

Delaney, who's on the other side of Andi, crosses her arms and huffs softly, but loud enough for you to hear. "I just know she's about to lambaste the institution of marriage. I'm so tired of people trying to shame me for enjoying a monogamous marriage with a man."

"No, no," Zeusse whispers. "Don't take it like that. I've heard her talk about this on her show. Sasha's got her groove, you've got yours, so do *you*. There is no right way. There's only *your* way."

"Agreed," Jade whispers.

Sasha notices them whispering. "Ladies? I'll be happy to take questions later."

Delaney, Zeusse and Jade give her their full attention.

Sasha continues: "Let's talk about trust for a minute. You have to trust yourself, first and foremost. And being here, tapping into your supernatural GoddessPower, that's how you get clear answers that you can trust. That boosts your confidence and courage to act on the guidance you receive. You take action, get good results, and keep it moving onward and upward until you're living your GoddessLife."

## Monday, Day 2

Sasha shakes her head. "Once you trust yourself, you have to trust your team, especially each other, to help you elevate. Now I know, if you've been burned by female friendships gone wrong, this one can be tough. But you cannot do this alone. Everybody hear me?"

"Yes," several women say loudly.

"You cannot do this alone," Sasha says. "You need your Biss Tribe sisters to push you, prod you, propel you! Everybody else may be tellin' you you've lost your damn mind when you start talkin' about crowns and empires and castles and reaching for the stars. So you need a team that's speaking your language and believing that you are limitless and unstoppable. And you need to trust your team when you call each other at three in the morning, exhausted and crying and upset and needing a pep talk. Trust! Got that?"

"Loud and clear," Andi says.

Sasha smiles. "Good. So I know Biss talked with you last night about being a Bad Ass. That's what you gotta be, and then some."

Marla raises a fist. "We're so ready!"

"Teach!" Celeste says.

"I'll start with my story," Sasha says. "Here goes." She makes eye contact with you and each woman while you enjoy your meal. Her sparkling cream-and-rhinestone stiletto sandals tap the shiny black floor as she walks around the table while speaking over a sultry bass beat.

> All you beautiful Goddesses, I am so thrilled and grateful to be here with you. You all have a mission. Well, my mission started with a declaration to myself:
> 
> *I will never suffer at the mercy of one penis again.*

By "suffer," I mean allowing one man to control *when* and *if* I can get the dick that I crave so much, every damn day.

Sadly, I had *thought* that my gorgeous, sexy, business mogul husband and I would indulge a lifetime of erotic decadence together, in the private, safe sanctuary of our marriage. That was how our love story started. And that's what he promised would be forever.

And for awhile, I had it All: successful husband, two smart kids, a beautiful home, a booming business of my own, and a future stamped *The Ultimate American Dream.*

But my X fucked it all up. He tried to recreate our first erotic interlude—and the sexcapades that we enjoyed from Miami to L.A.—with someone else. Early in our marriage!

Then, after years of me holding on for the sake of the kids, wishing and praying that he would change his ways, things only spiraled into an abysmal hellhole. His business got slammed by a bad investment with a rogue client, and that gave him a one-way ticket to lose his mind somewhere under his accountant's miniskirts, a cloud of ganga smoke, and a torrent of Hennessy splashing them both into delirium.

Booty, booze, and blunts made my man go MIA and forget all about his devoted life partner, the one he'd promised God that he'd spend forever with, you know, loving and cherishing.

*Whoosh!* That was the sound of him pulling the plug on my successful PR firm, Say It Write!

## Monday, Day 2

He burned so many bridges and ruined my reputation, so most of my clients left me, too. Because his buddies—corporate execs, doctors, lawyers, pro athletes—were my clients. It didn't matter that my skills had made public relations magic that rescued them from the ruins of scandal. They sided with my X, and I was done.

He also sabotaged my efforts to sign new clients by spreading malicious lies about me. A bogus lawsuit resulted and sucked me dry, despite my company's high seven-figure annual profits. Within months, I shut down my entrepreneurial dream and slipped into the nightmare of a $15-an-hour temp job on the midnight shift at a bank.

Well, I was so mad about how that pinprick had jacked up my life, going AWOL while I and our kids lived in my aunt's tiny apartment struggling to eat, I just had to speak about it.

So I do—live on the airwaves, thanks to the $50 million deal I landed for my live streaming video podcast, *The QueenPower Show*. This is my big, bold platform to talk loud and proud about the most raw relationship topics, sex questions, and women's empowerment secrets that the Internet has ever seen.

It wasn't long after my X triggered my demise, this unstoppable bad ass boss bitch named Sasha Maxwell rose from the ashes with a vengeance as a multimedia boss, *and* as an extremely bodacious woman.

You see, while I started to rock the mic on my show to make my professional life blaze, I also started setting off fireworks in my personal life.

## The GoddessPower Pyramid

Yawl know you wrote the vision for your professional GoddessLife, then the vision for your personal GoddessLife? Well, I may have written the most scandalous personal GoddessVision in the history of The Biss Tribe!

I wrote it, and I did it, then wrote a book about it. Sasha Maxwell embarked on a quest for erotic indulgence with *Eleven Men*. You may have read the book, or heard me talk on my show about each of them and the provocative questions that each of them raised about sex and relationships.

Well now I'm off on a whole new adventure, so stay tuned for new shows and another book chronicling more hot stuff that will blow your mind.

So why did I make that my vision? To have coast-to-coast sexcapades? To make up for all the hot, horny years when my voracious hunger as a monogamous, married woman went unsatisfied. Let me tell you, my success is such sweet revenge after the disrespect and humiliation that my X inflicted on me.

So now, let that mother fucker eat cake all by his damn self on our wedding anniversary, August 11th. That's the date that I embarked on my wild romps with *Eleven Men,* and I continue to do something wild on the 11th day of every month as I gather content for my show and books.

But first, ladies, let me be clear—this isn't even about my X.

This is about the unstoppable Goddess who awakened in the abyss of his neglect and negligence. In hindsight, I'm grateful for his wicked

## Monday, Day 2

wake-up call, my GoddessAwakening, because it transformed me into a global icon of women's empowerment, a multimedia sensation, and one lucky bitch who's unapologetically indulging her wildest desires.

All while sharing provocative details as I host red-hot dialogue every day on my show. I'll never have a shortage of content, because dating, relating, fucking and frolicking all inspire drama, and lots of questions. Questions that fascinate me. Like:

*Why does our first love have such a hold on our hearts and minds, even decades after things didn't work out?*

*Why do some people need a commitment for forever, before they can enjoy the present moment in a relationship?*

*What inspires people to have kinks, and how do they go about indulging them?*

*What are new ways to have relationships if society's hetero-monogamous template feels boring, broken, and wrong for you? And how do you find the courage to blaze your own trail in the bedroom and beyond?*

*And why does activating our GoddessPower make us have zero tolerance for anyone or anything that doesn't meet our new standards?*

Something inside me cracked wide open, right here in The Biss Tribe. It unleashed me to radically change. I felt like a rocket ship launching off Infinity Mountain into a whole new stratosphere of life. And believe me, I've been doing what Biss says, to "live bigger, better and bolder and manifest your wildest dreams."

For me, that means doing something about what I despise—and that is, society's oppressive conventions for how a woman should think, behave, live and love.

So let me take you back to how it all started:

With me, alone in bed at night, while my husband was on business trips and who knows where else. I was home with our two small kids, rocking my business by day, but at night feeling abandoned and betrayed. He rarely touched me, but I was so determined to re-ignite our fiery passion and mind-blowing sex, I spent years praying for a miracle.

I didn't understand how having it all could feel so empty inside, or how my husband could just abandon me, emotionally and physically, and think that was OK.

Even though my body was red-hot *all the time*, I never even kissed another man. Instead, I channeled my frustration into my very wild imagination.

I started plotting to get the sexual satisfaction that I craved—how I wanted it, when I wanted it, and from whom I wanted it. For years, I compiled a roster of dream lovers, knowing that someday, they would be mine, after my marriage ended. Little did I know that would happen when hubby went straight-up MIA and pulled the plug on my business, leaving no support for me and our kids.

We lost the house and everything. Living with my aunt was hell. And I hated the temp job.

That whole experience killed something in me: the polite, people-pleasing side of Sasha that people knew, loved, cheated on and took for granted.

## Monday, Day 2

But I wasn't about to suffer in silence. So I spoke my mind to any- and everyone who would listen.

Especially my mother and my sister and my friends and my co-workers. And one day, a sista from my church invited me to speak at a women's conference about what I was going through, and how faith was my Rock. When I got in that pulpit, girl, this spirit overcame me, and I'm tellin' you...

I lit up the place! I mean, every word was like fire shooting from my soul. And the ladies got hot!

"Preach it, girlfriend!" they shouted.

"Shout it, sista!"

"Tell it just like it is!"

And I did. For an hour.

About how my X had called me the worst names in the book, and my GoddessAwakening happened, just like Biss. I literally heard Spirit tell me during my most depressing times, "You are Goddess."

So I told these women how a supernatural peace and power overcame me, and I transformed from furious and worried, to calm and confident. In that moment, I became fiercely determined to bring my messages of women's empowerment to the world through a podcast, books, and events.

I told those women that, at the time, I didn't even own a microphone, but suddenly when this GoddessPower overcame me, I just knew that the Universe would bless me with all the resources I needed to launch *The QueenPower Show*.

I declared and commanded it in front of these women, claiming my dream and calling it into existence.

## The GoddessPower Pyramid

Even though I was newly divorced and had about $20 in my purse—desperately trying to dig out of a financial hellhole.

As I spoke in that church, I laid out the raw truth about love and marriage and children and society and sex and money and how that freakin' double standard tries to put us in our place, but is, let me tell you, failing miserably to do so with *moi*.

The ladies exploded! The standing ovation was so thunderous, the pastor peeked in at the uproar, then slinked right back out of the sanctuary, which caused even more hysteria.

Well, before I could leave the pulpit, dozens of women mobbed me, inviting me to speak all over town. And pretty soon, cell phones and emails were spreading the word about the empowering experience when Sasha Maxwell speaks. I got invitations to speak all over the country. For money.

Then I serendipitously met Biss at the gym in Detroit. We became instant besties, and I joined the next session of The Biss Tribe. Being here helped me focus my GoddessVision and create a clear path to where I am now.

As soon as I earned my crown here, and took action to manifest my GoddessVision, the Universe delivered all the resources I needed to launch *The QueenPower Show*. Because Biss believed in me so tough, she invited me to co-host a few episodes on topics that light us up.

So, if you don't already, please listen and watch as I explore the hottest topics about relationships, sex, and dating. If you're looking for new ways to

## Monday, Day 2

live and love, I'll show you ways to defy the hetero-monogamous conventions that confine us to oppressive rules that were created by men to maintain their power over women.

As someone who's been to hell and back, I share Biss's mission to help you enjoy some erotic indulgence in your life. You'll see what that's all about tomorrow at The Pleasure Tent.

The bottom line is that your power and pleasure start with loving yourself first. We all need that, especially if you're going through something right now.

I'm here to testify that *you don't have to look or feel like what you've been through.* It's easy to let struggles and disappointments make you look haggard, or get you addicted to taking drugs and drinking, or shove you into depression.

Not on my watch! Ladies, you have to love yourself—first and most. That wasn't my story for a long time. Got teased so much for being different. But as soon as I embraced being different as a gift, I became unstoppable and proud that God only created one Sasha Maxwell.

I'm what Brazilians call *mistura fina*: exquisite mixture. I'm a 100% premium, all-American blend: Mom's Black and Italian American mixed with Daddy's French Canadian, Native American, and English (he traced his family tree back to King Edward VIII). That pedigree might sound international and bourgeoisie, but I was born and bred in the meat-and-potatoes Midwest—Detroit!—to hard-working, good people who believed in sexual freedom, education, and colorblind love during the racial chaos of the sixties.

I love me!

And if you don't love you, I'm going to change that.

Unfortunately, in this man's world, sometimes the more you as a woman love yourself, the more others hate you. Especially men who don't want you to step into your power and run wild with your independence to be and do whatever and whomever the fuck you so desire.

I know this, because a lot of men hate Sasha Maxwell. They say my women's empowerment mission is evil. That I encourage women to leave their boyfriends and husbands. That I'm sparking a revolution in the way women think, act, live and love. They like to disrespect me by mispronouncing my name: the correct way is sensuous and beautiful—SAH-sha, with the a's sounding like when you breathe a sigh of relief and say, "Aaaahhhh." But these men, they call me SASH-uh, like a sash on a dress that rhymes with gash or slash or smash.

So let those motherfuckers accuse me of being a revolutionary.

And let them try their hardest to slut-shame me. I don't give one flying fuck what they say, because I'm not hearin' it, or havin' it. In case you're not aware, slut-shaming is when people try to shame a woman for being sexually liberated and independent. It's vicious and can destroy careers, reputations, and self-esteem. That's why the threat of it is so powerful and effective at keeping too many

## Monday, Day 2

women oppressed and afraid to even dream about their GoddessLife.

I'm here to say that we need to rise up against these rules that are designed to rob us of power and pleasure.

By being here, you're joining our GoddessPower revolution to live bigger, better and bolder, and manifest your heart's wildest desires.

I'm doing this, because the supernatural power that I activated in The Biss Tribe has transformed Sasha Maxwell into a messiah. A visionary. A prophet. Those men who call me a man-hater can't deal with the fact that I'm articulate, bold, brassy and sexy-as-Hell to boot. And they're terrified of their wives, girlfriends, and sisters discovering their GoddessPower to become as dynamic as me. Those men who've seen me on every national TV show and heard me all over the radio and on top podcasts promoting my show, *wish* they could even think about taming me.

But listen, ladies. They won't. I've been through too much to stop now. And the cool thing is, now I'm *paid*, living in a gorgeous penthouse, writing my children's college tuition checks, and thanking God for showing me this calling to help women like you.

I'm standing here as an example for you to see that anything is possible. You can start at ground zero like I did, build your empire, and exceed even your wildest dreams.

Like Biss always says, "You can do it, Goddess, because *you* have the power!"

The women shoot to their feet in an explosion of clapping and cheering. Biss hugs Sasha, and so does Esmerelda, as every woman gets out of her seat to surround them with hugs and cheers, as if they'd just won the Super Bowl.

## A Dance Party Celebration

Funky music booms through the ballroom. And you join the women in a fun, uninhibited joy fest of dancing and laughing and feeling a million miles away from everything on the shiny black floor under a ceiling sparkling with stars and walls glowing cobalt blue.

Biss, Sasha and Esmerelda dance to the center of the women.

"OK my Goddesses!" Biss says into a wireless microphone, grasping Sasha's hands and raising them up over their heads, fingers laced together. "Let's do our GoddessGreeting! Remember to say our motto!"

The music booms as you and the women grasp hands high above your heads, forming human archways. You all look into each other's eyes and shout, 'You can do it, Goddess, because *you* have the power!'"

The dancefloor becomes a wild, exuberant, ecstatic swirl of smiles and laughter and love as everyone connects, says the motto, and moves to the next woman. After everyone has done it with every person, Biss exclaims, "Now say it with me, 'I am Goddess! I rule my empire wearing a crown of confidence from a throne of power!'"

The women declare this while dancing to the sultry hip-hop beats.

Biss says, "Now say, 'I am infinite! And I have the power! I am Goddess!'"

As everyone shouts this, the electrifying excitement of 26 women ignites the air and sparkles back into you and each woman

Monday, Day 2

as courage and confidence that yes, you *can* carry this energy out into the world and make all your wildest dreams come true.

"Shout it one more time!" Biss yells, rousing the women to shout at the top of their lungs: "I am infinite! And I have the power! I am Goddess!"

# Continue Your Transformation on Infinity Mountain

*Dear Goddess Reader:*

*Tomorrow, you'll travel up Infinity Mountain to the next Activation Station. Here's the schedule:*

Sunday: The Biss Tribe Inn
Monday: The GoddessPower Pyramid
**Tuesday: The GoddessPleasure Tent**
Wednesday: The GoddessTreasure Cave
Thursday: The GoddessWarrior Fortress
Friday: The GoddessPeace Garden
Saturday: The GoddessPower Studios to record your personal podcast, followed by the Coronation at SeaGoddess Castle, then the GoddessFeast and evening cruise on SeaGoddess yacht.
Sunday: Fly home to begin building your empire.

Two months from now, you'll return to The Biss Tribe for bi-monthly GoddessLife Intensives that give you guidance and advanced trainings on each of the five foundations of Power, Pleasure, Prosperity, Protection and Peace.

## The GoddessPower Pyramid

These four-day Intensives conclude with a training and celebration to mark the one-year anniversary of your entrée into The Biss Tribe and GoddessLife.

You can do this, Goddess, because *you* have the power!

## Books in The Biss Tribe Series

Available at TwoSistersWriting.com.

1. The Biss Tribe: Where You Activate Your GoddessPower
2. The Biss Tribe: Where You Activate Your GoddessPleasure
3. The Biss Tribe: Where You Activate Your GoddessProsperity
4. The Biss Tribe: Where You Activate Your GoddessProtection
5. The Biss Tribe: Where You Activate Your GoddessPeace
6. The Biss Tribe: Where You Celebrate Your GoddessCoronation

Each book has an accompanying *PowerJournal.*

1. PowerJournal to Activate Your GoddessPower
2. PowerJournal to Activate Your GoddessPleasure
3. PowerJournal to Activate Your GoddessProsperity
4. PowerJournal to Activate Your GoddessProtection
5. PowerJournal to Activate Your GoddessPeace

*Monday, Day 2*

# Stay Connected and Inspired in the Goddess RoundTable Community

Don't stop your transformation and inspiration when you finish this book and wait for the next one.

You can get your daily dose of GoddessPower when you join my online community, The Goddess RoundTable, which also includes in-person events. As a member of The Goddess RoundTable, you'll:

- Enjoy a weekly, virtual energy cleanse, guided meditation and lively conversation about how to find your peace and power.

- Learn rituals and manifestation techniques that make magic happen in your life.

- Continue your ascent into your GoddessLife amongst a safe, supportive sisterhood of diverse women from across America and beyond.

- Get discounts on private, one-on-one GoddessPower Coaching where I help you create and sustain a daily self-care regimen that includes healthier eating, exercise that you love, a spiritual practice (if desired), mindset shifts and lifestyle improvements that help you put yourself first, and the accountability that you need to make your GoddessLife your new reality. I want to help you level up so dramatically that every day you declare, "I've never felt better!"

- Get discounts for my Goddess, Write Your Book! program to compose your novel, memoir or business book in my virtual book coaching program that births best-selling authors.

- Get discounts on my virtual and in-person retreats. Goddess RoundTable members get priority and exclusive entrée into my events and programs.

- Get automatically entered in my free give-away of a private, 45-minute coaching session ($300 value) to Activate Your GoddessPower. During this virtual experience, we'll: explore where you feel powerless; describe your GoddessVision and GoddessLife; do an energy cleanse and guided meditation to get guidance from Spirit on the action steps you need to take to step through your GoddessGateway; and discuss a daily action plan for you to use the four GoddessPower Activation Tools to manifest your dream life.

When you join The GoddessPower RoundTable, you commit to making the rest of your life, the best of your life. You can do it, Goddess, because *you* have the power!

Join us at TheGoddessPowerShow.com.

# Roster

## The Biss Tribe Class #88

**Marla Santos**—25, a social media influencer and co-founder of a skincare line with her best friend, Sammie Smithville.

**Appearance**: almond-shaped eyes, brown sugar-hued skin and a mane of straight black hair.

**Background**: grew up in Los Angeles in a large, Filipino-American family led by her father, a pastor.

**Lives**: in Miami, Florida, with Sammie.

**Why she's here**: To liberate herself from her parents's brainwashing that has guilted and shamed her to fear sex to the point that she's never had an orgasm, even by herself.

**Goal**: Expand her businesses to launch her skincare line, and get on the Forbes 30 Under 30 List, earning high seven figures.

**Sammie Smithville**—25, social media influencer and co-founder of a skincare line with her best friend, Marla Santos. Appearance: Long, pin-straight blonde hair, blue eyes, vanilla skin and glossy pink Betty Boop lips.

**Background**: Grew up in Savannah, Georgia, in a wealthy family.

**Lives**: In Miami, Florida, with Marla.

## The Goddess Power Pyramid

**Why she's here**: To free herself from a destructive cycle of dating disappointments and man addiction.

**Goal**: Expand her businesses to launch her skincare line, and get on the Forbes 30 Under 30 List, earning high seven figures.

Kiki Khalil—24, a friend of Marla and Sammie.
**Appearance**: Glassy, almond-hued skin, plump lips, thick black lashes, platinum-tipped brunette hair, and a slim, petite build.

**Background**: Grew up in an Arab American family in Dearborn, Michigan.

**Lives**: In Miami, Florida, with her brother and his wife.

**Why she's here**: To find herself.

**Goal**: Figure out her life purpose.

Zeusse—30, retired WNBA champion.
**Appearance**: 6'4" tall with an athletic build; cosmetic-free skin that's as rich and smooth as coffee beans; long, skinny dreadlocks; and wide-set eyes that convey wisdom and an "old soul" energy.

**Background**: Grew up with her father in Harlem, New York, and summered on her grandparents's farm in Alabama.

**Lives**: In a brownstone in Harlem.

**Why she's here**: To find the same courage and confidence that she has on the basketball court, in the business world.

**Goal**: To strategize how to open and sustain a global franchise of girls basketball academies.

## Monday, Day 2

**Jade Rogers**—35, office worker and guitarist in a girl band, The Star Chix.

**Appearance**: Tattoos of green vines sprouting blue flowers and Greek goddess busts adorn her thin, milky-white arms. Blue eyeliner accentuates her hazel eyes and round, slightly plump face. She has pink hair.

**Background**: Grew up in an affluent White family in suburban Chicago, Illinois.

**Lives**: In a loft downtown Chicago.

**Why she's here**: To free herself from her parents's belief that she can't make a career of being a music artist.

**Goal**: To leave her corporate job and travel the world with her girl band.

**Sunshine Bylilly**—44, a struggling life coach and self-described narcissist magnet.

**Appearance**: Wears her dark hair in a high ponytail that showcases her caramel complexion and large, dark eyes highlighted by perfect black-winged liner and thick, natural lashes. She wears a sterling silver hummingbird pendant on her turquoise-beaded, choker-style necklace.

**Background**: Raised by her grandmother in the Navajo Nation in Santa Fe, New Mexico.

**Lives**: In a house she inherited from her grandmother in Santa Fe.

**Why she's here**: To find her self-worth and belief in herself.

# The Goddess Power Pyramid

**Goal**: To create a life coaching center called The Turquoise Experience that hires Indigenous women entrepreneurs while earning a seven-figure income. Also wants to find a loving, devoted husband.

**Bianca Hernandez**—47, a therapist at a mental health clinic specializing in girls and young women with anxiety. Uses a wheelchair after a car accident and has ADHD.

**Appearance**: Her turquoise hair matches her braces and the birds and flowers in her large tattoo of Mexican painter Frida Kahlo. With clear, peaches-and-cream skin and a silver scar on her cheek, she sparkles with rhinestones that she applies to her clothing, and in her crystal bracelets and a tiny Mexican flag pendant necklace.

**Background**: Raised in San Diego, California, by parents who own a restaurant.

**Lives**: In a condo in San Diego.

**Why she's here**: To find peace of mind and to focus on finishing what she starts.

**Goal**: To open a nonprofit called Amy's Oasis, a girls's enrichment center, to honor a patient who chose suicide after she didn't get into Harvard like her parents wanted.

**Celeste Williams**—54, CEO of a prominent company who's burned out by a demanding career while being a wife, mother of two sons, active in her faith community and caretaker of two parents with dementia.

# Monday, Day 2

**Appearance**: Close-cropped, peroxide-blonde waves and a bronze complexion that glows like sunshine beaming through a jar of molasses. Her light brown eyes sparkle despite puffy under-eye bags obscured by concealer. Her blingy clothes and diamond wedding ring suggest affluence.

**Background**: Raised in Detroit, Michigan.

**Lives**: In a beautiful home in an affluent Detroit suburb.

**Why she's here**: To learn how to make self-care a top priority after stress caused an agonizing eczema outbreak.

**Goal**: To leave her corporate CEO position and open a bakery and café, Celeste's Sweet Shop.

Andi Sullivan—61, coming out as gay on a mission to follow her dreams after a life dictated by her family.

**Appearance**: Thick with a masculine build and clothing style, she has an oval, cosmetic-free face distinguished by thick brows, gray eyes and freckled beige skin with tiny lines extending from the outer corners of her eyes when she smiles. Her chestnut-brown hair is shaved bald on one side and falls in a straight chop toward her chin on the other. She wears multiple silver hoop earrings and rings.

**Background**: Grew up Worchester, Massachusetts, in a large Irish American family that founded a successful chain of hardware stores. She lived her parents's expectations to marry a man, have kids, and work in the family business.

**Lives**: In her own house in her hometown.

**Why she's here**: To leave the family business and to find the courage to live on her own terms.

**Goal**: To open her beachfront art studio and to find a wife.

**Delaney Cohen**—74, an Ivy League university professor who is in a long-term marriage.

**Appearance**: She resembles the actress Meryl Streep but with curly, silver shoulder-length hair parted on one side and tucked behind an ear. She wears simple silver jewelry and dresses with an artsy, flowy-linen vibe.

**Background**: Grew up on New York's Upper East Side, in a Jewish family with a disapproving mother.

**Lives**: On a country estate near Princeton, New Jersey, with her husband.

**Why she's here**: To find inner peace and self-love so that she feels that despite her many accomplishments, she is enough just as she is.

**Goal**: To explore new possibilities for the next 25 years as she strives to live to a healthy 100 years old and beyond.

## The Biss Tribe Team

**Biss**—Founder of The Biss Tribe, where she leads life-changing retreats and teaches all the tools that have enabled her to transform from the inside out and create her dream life. A best-selling author and multimedia journalist.

## Monday, Day 2

**Appearance**: Curly yellow hair, suntanned French vanilla skin, green eyes, athletic curves. She wears colorful clothing, crystal jewelry and lots of sparkle.

**Background**: Grew up in Michigan in a loving, multiracial family.

**Lives**: In The Biss Tribe Inn, at SeaGoddess Castle and in other residences.

**Why she's here**: To follow her GoddessMission.

**Goal**: To continue her divine life assignment to activate the infinite power in women everywhere and thus make the world a better place.

Esmerelda—Age unknown. Goddess leader, yogi, singer and sound bowl artist.

**Appearance**: With trim, toned muscles, her skin is so dewy and smooth, it reminds you of melted milk chocolate. Her blue eyes glow brightly from the luminescent contours of her face. Snow-white swirls of hair cascade down her back. It's impossible to tell her age or her ethnicity, and she radiates mesmerizing authority and warmth.

**Background**: Grew up in New Orleans, Louisiana.

**Lives**: In The Biss Tribe Inn and at SeaGoddess Castle.

**Why she's here**: She transformed in The Biss Tribe and never left.

**Goal**: Helping women experience healing and success.

## The Goddess Power Pyramid

**Panther**—Executive Assistant and DJ. Tall with jet-black-hair and a sparkling nose ring.

**Vee**—The bus driver and an assistant. Her emerald-green hair matches the colorful mermaids tattooed on her arms.

**Concierges**—The personal assistants each assigned to a Biss Tribe retreat-goer.

## The Culinary Team—

**Dr. Annapurna**, named for the Hindu Goddess of food, cooking and nourishment, is the head chef and helps you create a healthy eating plan.

**Ixcacao**, named in honor of the Mayan Goddess of chocolate and cocoa, creates amazing desserts.

**Pomona**, named for the Roman Goddess of Orchards, is the food operations director.

**Ukemochi**, named for the Japanese Shinto Goddess, ensures that you enjoy the highest quality seafood, meats, eggs, tofu and other proteins.

**Fitness Trainer Jodi**—The Biss Tribe's physical fitness expert who creates a customized exercise routine for you.

# About the Author

## Elizabeth Ann Atkins

Elizabeth's renegade spirit to blaze her own trails in life and love springs from her parents's scandalous union after her father—a Roman Catholic Priest who was French, English and Native American—left the church to marry a Black woman 25 years younger during the turbulent 1960s.

Their defiance of racial and religious conventions—all in the name of love—inspired Elizabeth as a multiracial woman to write herself into American literature with novels *White Chocolate, Dark Secret,* and *Twilight* with Billy Dee Williams, all published by the Tor/Forge imprint at St. Martin's Press.

Then, after a fairytale wedding and a nightmare divorce, Elizabeth's disillusionment with dating and traditional relationships inspired her to write an erotic trilogy, *Husbands, Incorporated*, about a company that provides legal, fantasy marriages that give women immense power and pleasure. The series is written under Elizabeth's pen name of Sasha Maxwell. Sasha's next book is *Eleven Men.*

To amplify messages of peace and empowerment, Elizabeth and her sister, author Catherine M. Greenspan, co-founded Two Sisters Writing & Publishing® in 2016, first publishing their own fiction and non-fiction books that celebrate colorblind love and self-identity.

They have since published more than 50 books, mostly against-the-odds success stories by diverse authors from across America. Their authors include former Detroit Mayor Dennis Archer, the former president of the American Red Cross, judges, lawyers, physicians, surgeons, healers, executives and motivational speakers.

Two Sisters published their mother's book, *The Triumph of Rosemary: a Memoir* by Judge Marylin E. Atkins, which was developed into a screenplay with the goal of creating a Hollywood feature film.

Most recently, Elizabeth co-authored *Healing Religious Hurts: Stories & Tips to Find Love and Peace* and *Joyously Free: Stories & Tips to Live Your Truth as LGBTQ+ People, Parents and Allies* by Elizabeth Ann Atkins and Joanie Lindenmeyer.

**Learn more and order books at TwoSistersWriting.com.**
*The Biss Tribe: Where You Activate Your Goddess Power* by Elizabeth Ann Atkins is the first in a series of books that aim to awaken and empower women everywhere.

The books echo themes that Elizabeth writes and speaks about at TheGoddessPowerShow.com, which links to her podcast, *The Goddess Power Show with Elizabeth Ann Atkins*®. The show's mission is to explore sometimes taboo topics and inspire people to live bigger, better and bolder and manifest their hearts's wildest desires.

You can watch episodes on the YouTube channel for *The Goddess Power Show*. And you can listen to episodes on Apple Podcasts, Spotify, iHeart radio, and wherever you listen to podcasts. TheGoddessPowerShow.com provides links to all of the above, as well as the blog.

## About the Author

Elizabeth also co-hosts an Emmy-nominated TV show about mental health. *MI Healthy Mind* airs every Sunday on networks across Michigan and two episodes that Elizabeth hosted—interviewing a human trafficking survivor and people who became "wounded healers" by using their pain to help others—were nominated for Emmy Awards. Please visit MIHealthyMind.com and watch nine years's worth of episodes on YouTube.

Elizabeth's education laid the foundation for her career as a best-selling author, award-winning print journalist, Emmy-nominated TV show host, speaker, podcaster and publisher.

She earned a Bachelor of Arts degree as an English Literature major at the University of Michigan, where she began her journalism career as a reporter and editor at the campus newspaper, *The Michigan Daily.*

Then she earned a Master of Science degree from the Columbia University Graduate School of Journalism in New York City, where she focused on broadcast news and international reporting. During that time, she had a part-time job as a copy clerk at *The New York Times,* which published a portion of her master's thesis about mixed-race people.

**Elizabeth is an inspiring speaker.**
On diversity, she rouses ovations by performing her autobiographical poem, "White Chocolate," then invites audiences to explore their perceptions about race and identity. They walk away with a new understanding to never judge a book by its cover.

Elizabeth has spoken at Columbia University, the University of Michigan, GM's World Diversity Day, Gannett, Beaumont Health, 100 Black Men, the NAACP, national conferences, and many other venues.

As a wellness speaker, Elizabeth shares her long struggle with food and fat, and the depression and suicidal ideation that it triggered, and how she triumphed over that with faith and fitness. She talks about how she lost 100 pounds after childbirth (without drugs or surgery) and celebrated her transformation on *The Oprah Winfrey Show*.

Now a certified fitness trainer through ISSA, Elizabeth coaches others on how to achieve a mindset shift as the first step to transforming one's body and life. Learn more on the Wellness page at TheGoddessPowerShow.com.

Deeply spiritual, Elizabeth shares her experiences, perspectives, and tools for high-vibe living in her best-selling memoir, *God's Answer Is Know: Lessons From a Spiritual Life*. She shares how meditation has helped her heal and awaken her most authentic self and serve as a spiritual teacher for others.

As an Intuitive Practitioner certified by Lori Lipten's Sacred Balance Academy in Bloomfield Hills, Michigan, Elizabeth teaches meditation and energy clearing.

In *The Biss Tribe* books, Elizabeth shares the tools that she uses every day to look and feel her best, connect with Spirit, manifest blessings, and achieve a creative flow state in her creative genius zone. This includes a technique that combines meditation with journaling, which inspired Elizabeth and Catherine to create the *PowerJournal*® series of workbooks for self-discovery.

Elizabeth's GoddessMission was born during terrible moments of verbal abuse after a relationship. Spirit infused her with the peace and power of God energy to cultivate strength to persevere through difficulties, which ultimately resulted in miraculous healing and harmony.

As America's Book Coach, Elizabeth guides aspiring writers along the sometimes-treacherous terrain of writing, publishing, and promoting a book. Learn more about her "6 Months to Best-Selling Book Success" group coaching program at TwoSistersWriting.com.

## About the Author

Elizabeth has taught writing at Wayne State University, Oakland University, Wayne County Community College District, and at national conferences.

As an actress, she plays a major role in the feature-length film, *Anything Is Possible*, nominated for "Best Foreign Film" by the Nollywood and African Film Critics Association. It's now streaming on Amazon Prime and Peacock.

Elizabeth also plays a 1950s journalist in the international shipwreck drama, *The Andrea Doria: Are The Passengers Saved?* The award-winning film is in Italian with English subtitles.

Elizabeth composed an original screenplay, *Redemption*, a gritty drama about a Detroit gangster and a writer.

Elizabeth has been a guest on *Oprah, Montel, NPR, Good Morning America Sunday, The CBS Evening News, Black Entertainment Television (BET), The NBC Nightly News, The Today Show, Tyra* and many national and local TV programs.

Her work has been published in *The New York Times, The San Diego Tribune, Essence, Ebony, HOUR Detroit, BLAC Detroit,* and many publications. Her *Detroit News* articles on race were nominated for the Pulitzer Prize, and she wrote a biography for the Presidential Medal of Freedom tribute for Rosa Parks.

Elizabeth runs, cycles, lifts weights, does yoga, journals, travels, reveres nature, and meditates to cultivate a joyous and peaceful mind, body and spirit.

Elizabeth's life mission to cultivate human harmony through the written and spoken word, and through daily interactions with people, was born when she was one day old and her father baptized her in the hospital room, asking God to make her a "Princess of Peace." As a one-year-old, she helped unite a divided family, opening the door for loving unity for generations.

## Welcome to The Biss Tribe

Now through a multimedia platform and The Biss Tribe series of books, Elizabeth continues her mission to help create a better world.

You can contact her at TheGoddessPowerShow.com and at TwoSistersWriting.com.

*Goddess Website*

*Website*

Please subscribe to the YouTube channels for Two Sisters Writing & Publishing® and The Goddess Power Show with Elizabeth Ann Atkins®.

## About the Author

You can also follow Elizabeth on Instagram:
@elizabethannatkins
@thegoddesspowershowpodcast.
And on TikTok:
@thegoddesspowershow.

www.ingramcontent.com/pod-product-compliance
Lightning Source LLC
Chambersburg PA
CBHW070721240426
**43673CB00003B/98**